THE DECARBONIZATION IMPERATIVE

The
DECARBONIZATION
IMPERATIVE

TRANSFORMING THE GLOBAL
ECONOMY BY 2050

Michael Lenox and Rebecca Duff

STANFORD BUSINESS BOOKS
An Imprint of Stanford University Press
Stanford, California

STANFORD UNIVERSITY PRESS
Stanford, California

Special discounts for bulk quantities of Stanford Business Books are available to corporations, professional associations, and other organizations. For details and discount information, contact the special sales department of Stanford University Press. Tel: (650) 725-0820, Fax: (650) 725-3457

Printed in the United States of America on acid-free, archival-quality paper

Library of Congress Cataloging-in-Publication Data
Names: Lenox, Michael, author. | Duff, Rebecca (Senior research associate), author.
Title: The decarbonization imperative : transforming the global economy by 2050 / Michael Lenox and Rebecca Duff.
Description: Stanford, California : Stanford Business Books, an imprint of Stanford University Press, 2021. | Includes bibliographical references and index.
Identifiers: LCCN 2021007428 (print) | LCCN 2021007429 (ebook) | ISBN 9781503614789 (cloth) | ISBN 9781503629622 (epub)
Subjects: LCSH: Greenhouse gas mitigation—Economic aspects. | Carbon dioxide mitigation—Economic aspects. | Climate change mitigation—Economic aspects. | Green technology—Economic aspects. | Technological innovations—Environmental aspects.
Classification: LCC HC79.A4 L46 2021 (print) | LCC HC79.A4 (ebook) | DDC 363.738/746—dc23
LC record available at https://lccn.loc.gov/2021007428
LC ebook record available at https://lccn.loc.gov/2021007429

Cover design: Christian Storm

Text design: Kevin Barrett Kane

Typeset at Stanford University Press in 10/14 Minion Pro

In honor of my mother, **Lynn Lenox**,
who fostered my interest in trying
to solve complex puzzles

In honor of my children, **Charlie and Grace Ann Duff**,
who inspire me to work toward a better,
more sustainable future

CONTENTS

FIGURES

PREFACE

Climate change is the challenge of our lifetimes. If we fail to act, and act soon, we risk leaving our children a world in which humanity's ability to flourish will be severely tested. The simple premise of this book is to take a detailed look at what needs to happen for us to mitigate the worst impacts of climate change by radically reducing our carbon footprint. Its central assumption is that addressing our global warming challenge will require substantial innovation across a wide number of industrial sectors that promises to disrupt existing technologies and business models and usher in cleaner industries that do not emit greenhouse gases.

This book serves as a complement to Lenox's 2018 book *Can Business Save the Earth? Innovating Our Way to Sustainability*, also from Stanford University Press. In that book, Lenox and his coauthor, Ronnie Chatterji, discuss the importance of the innovation system in generating disruptive sustainable technologies. Structured around the core economic players in the innovation process—innovators themselves, managers, financiers, and customers—the book highlights the broader institutional envelope that surrounds the innovation system and the role played by private intermediaries and public interveners in driving the rate and direction of innovative activity.

In this book, we take a deep dive into the challenge of climate change and the need to effectively reduce net greenhouse gas emissions to zero by 2050. Using a sector-based approach, we analyze emerging clean technologies in five large sectors: energy, transportation, industrials, buildings, and agriculture. We assess the likelihood of technology disruptions leading to a decarbonized future in each sector and, more important, provide suggestions on various public and private levers that could be pulled to catalyze innovation and disruption to meet our 2050 goal. We end by providing a practical and comprehensive technology policy to get the world to net-zero emissions. We note that there are numerous reports and books available that explore each of these sectors more deeply. Our intent is to provide a broad view of technology disruption across all of them and help readers to better understand the scope and scale of collective work that will be needed to decarbonize the global economy by 2050. For those interested in detailed simulations of the "path to 2050," one of our favorites is the En-ROADS Climate Solutions Simulator. Our goal in this book is not to replicate these detailed simulation models, but rather to leverage our understanding of technology disruptions to gauge the likelihood of shifting markets toward sustainable technologies and to posit levers to encourage such changes. In doing so, we hope to illuminate the mechanisms that help accelerate disruptive change, mechanisms that are often obscured in a complex simulation.

Climate change is a global issue, and carbon emissions know no boundaries. To decarbonize by 2050, actions taken by developing countries to curb their emissions while growing their own economies will be crucial. Throughout each chapter we identify and discuss briefly those countries with the most influence to change the emissions trajectory within that sector over the next thirty years. While the primary focus of this book is on the United States economy, we believe that the technologies explored, and the opportunities and levers needed to accelerate their adoption, are transferable to other country economies if given the right market conditions.

In pursuing this project, we have benefited greatly from conversations and engagements with our academic colleagues, students, business leaders, policy makers, and leaders of nongovernmental organizations. The genesis of this book was a series of research reports that we developed as part of the University of Virginia Batten Institute's Business Innovation and Climate Change Initiative. In addition, under the auspices of the initiative, we hosted two events that brought together leaders from all walks of life to discuss the issues raised in this book: the 2018 Jefferson Innovation Summit to catalyze innovation and entrepreneurship to tackle climate change and the 2020 ClimateCAP MBA Summit on climate, capital, and business. We thank all the participants for their contributions.

In addition, we wish to recognize our various coauthors and collaborators who have shaped our thinking on sustainability over the years: MIT professor emeritus John Ehrenfeld, Ronnie Chatterji at Duke, Andrew King at Boston University, Chuck Eesley at Stanford, Jen Nash at Harvard, and Jeff York at Colorado, among many others. We also wish to recognize the support and influence of the community of scholars that make up the Alliance for Research in Corporate Sustainability. Lenox also benefited from feedback received at academic seminars on this work at MIT, Cornell, and the University of Virginia.

We wish to recognize the support of our colleagues and students at the University of Virginia's Darden School of Business. They have greatly influenced our thinking and provided inspiration for our efforts. The Batten Institute at UVA provided financial support for this project for which we are most grateful. More important, the Institute provided significant support in terms of both time and talent as the home to the Business Innovation and Climate Change Initiative. A special thanks goes to Erika Herz from the Batten Institute, who was a passionate advocate for our work and primary contributor to the initiative.

This book would not have been possible without the expert research assistance provided by Isabel Brodsky. The figures and tables in the book were created by Leigh Ayers. Thank you for your contributions. They have greatly enhanced the end product. Thanks as well go to Steve Catalano and the entire team at Stanford University Press. In addition, we thank our external reviewers. We greatly appreciate all of your suggestions and feedback. The book is much improved due to your feedback and guidance.

Last, but certainly not least, we wish to thank our families. The latter stages of writing of this book took place during the global pandemic of 2020. We have done our best in the book to reflect the changing world as a result of the pandemic. We greatly appreciate the patience and understanding of our family members as we tried to balance writing with the demands of home life during quarantine. Your love and support kept us moving forward to complete the project.

CHAPTER 1

THE PATH TO 2050

IMAGINE IT IS THE YEAR 2050. You travel to work in your electric vehicle. At home, the car is powered by a solar panel on your house which is connected to a smart grid that trades electricity so that you have electricity on cloudy days and you power others when you have excess. The home itself is made of and filled with low-carbon materials: mini-mill-produced steel, green cement, sustainable timber, and green plastics. The food on your table comes from sustainable farming that minimizes the need for nitrogen-based fertilizers and includes protein from sources other than beef.

Fanciful? Perhaps. Necessary? Absolutely. Because if we are going to avoid the worst effects of climate change, we are going to need to effectively "decarbonize" the global economy by 2050. Think about this for a second. This doesn't mean a modest, or even a drastic, improvement in fuel efficiency standards for automobiles. It means 100 percent of the cars on the road being battery-powered electric vehicles or some other non-carbon-emitting powertrain. It doesn't mean a substantial increase in renewable solar and wind energy. It means 100 percent of our global electricity needs being met by renewables and other zero-carbon-emitting sources such as nuclear power. It means global electrification and material substitution in the industrials sector, eliminating scope 1 emissions—emissions in production—across steel, cement, petrochemicals, the backbone of the global economy. It means electrifying all residential and commercial buildings. It means sustainable farming and preservation of carbon sinks while still feeding a growing global population.

This is the challenge of our age. This book is about how we might realistically get there.

THE LOOMING CRISIS

Every day the evidence accumulates. Hurricanes. Floods. Droughts. Extreme weather not observed in anyone's memory. The five hottest years ever recorded have occurred since 2015.[1] By 2020, global average temperature had increased 0.5 degree Celsius compared to the 1986–2005 average.[2] Sea levels have risen by five to eight inches on average globally since 1900.[3] While these changes are seemingly minor in scale to some, scientists warn that they portend more significant disruptions by the end of the century if action is not taken.

The consensus is near universal among climate scientists. Since the beginning of the industrial age, human activity—in particular, the burning of fossil fuels—has increased the concentration of carbon dioxide and other greenhouse gases in the atmosphere. Prior to the last century, the parts per million of carbon dioxide in the atmosphere varied between 180 and 280 ppm, never exceeding 300 ppm. In 2013, carbon dioxide concentration passed 400 ppm and continues to grow unabated.[4] This increased concentration precipitates the greenhouse effect, by which these gases trap solar radiation coming to earth from the sun, leading to global warming and changing the climate in regions throughout the world.

The implications are dire. Warming threatens to increase desertification in some regions and multiply the number of days of life-threatening heat waves around the globe. Warmer air holds more moisture, raising the risk of extreme weather events such as hurricanes and floods. Warming leads to thermal expansion of the ocean and the melting of landlocked water on glaciers and the vast ice sheets of Antarctica and Greenland which together leads to rising sea levels. Warming increases the risks of diseases and pests that threaten trees, crops, and human health.

The direst impacts to our quality of life are likely to be economic and sociopolitical. Imagine the disruption to supply chains and the flow of goods as extreme weather interferes with manufacturing operations, shipping lanes, and trade routes. Imagine the destabilizing impacts on governments of a refugee crisis created by the displacement of millions due to rising sea levels. Imagine the wars that might erupt as precious commodities such as potable water become scarcer in certain parts of the world. Imagine the rise of nationalist governments that try to protect their own in a world of rising climate crisis.

These outcomes are not that hard to imagine. Some have argued that the emergence of the Arab Spring and consequent civil war in Syria began when bread and other food prices skyrocketed in the face of increased droughts in the region that limited the supply of grain. The war led to a refugee crisis that spread to Europe in the summer of 2016, resulting in a battle over immigration policy and leading to the rise of several nationalist political movements that threatened well-established democratic institutions. There is a reason why the US military views climate change as one of the greatest geopolitical risks of the foreseeable future.[5]

THE CRITICALITY OF 2050

To help mitigate the worst impacts of climate change, scientists have argued that we should try to limit global warming to 1.5 degrees Celsius. To do so will not be easy. From 1750, at the dawn of the Industrial Revolution, to 2014, we emitted approximately 545 gigatons of carbon equivalents into the atmosphere.[6] In 2019 alone, we produced 9.5 gigatons of CO_2 globally.[7] Despite global efforts to reduce greenhouse gas emissions in the past decade, emissions continue to rise. While there are a number of natural processes that absorb carbon dioxide and offset our emissions, including oceanic and terrestrial sinks, the average net release of greenhouse gases over the last ten years was 4.9 gigatons of carbon (GtC) per year.[8]

Clearly, our annual carbon emissions far outstrip the earth's natural capacity for absorbing those emissions. As a result, we continue to spend our "carbon budget"—the amount of emissions before significant warming is unavoidable. The best estimates suggest that we must hold CO_2 concentrations below 430 ppm to limit warming to 1.5 degrees Celsius.[9] The International Panel on Climate Change (IPCC), the United Nations body for assessing the science related to climate change, estimated in 2018 that we had a remaining carbon budget of 118 GtC to have a 66 percent chance to keep concentrations below that target.[10] Once that budget is spent, we will have to reduce annual global net emissions to zero from that point forward.

Net-zero emissions could be achieved either by reducing our greenhouse gas emissions or by increasing carbon sinks to absorb emitted carbon dioxide (or some combination of both). This book follows the lead of others and refers to the process of achieving net-zero emissions of greenhouse gases as "decarbonization." Given our remaining carbon budget and the rate we are spending it, it is hard to avoid having to decarbonize the global economy by some point in the not too distant future.

On our current trajectory, with greenhouse gas emissions increasing roughly 0.5 percent per year, we will spend our carbon budget by the year 2040 if not sooner. Global economic downturns, such as the pandemic-induced downturn in 2020, only give us a temporary reprieve from emissions, pushing out the date only a year or two. Assuming that efforts are made to change our current trajectory, the budget can be stretched out further. In 2018, the Center for Climate and Energy Solutions (C2ES), in partnership with the RAND Corporation and the Joint Global Change Research Institute, released a report looking at scenarios to get us to decarbonization by 2050. The IPCC has targeted 2050 for decarbonization as well.

Figure 1.1 shows what a path to 2050 may look like. Starting in 2021, we will need to begin significantly reducing global emissions. The longer we delay significant emissions reductions, the sooner our "net zero" date arrives. If annual emissions continue to increase over the next few years, our day of reckoning may come as soon as 2035. What is clear is that we need to significantly change the trajectory of global emissions and to do so quickly. The next decade is absolutely critical.

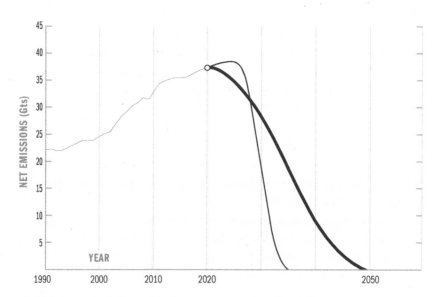

FIGURE 1.1   The Path to 2050
Source: Data from Our World in Data, GitHub

Some argue that the time to mitigate climate change has passed. Decarbonizing the global economy by 2050 is darn near impossible. We will never achieve the Paris Accord target to limit global warming to 2 degrees Celsius, let alone 1.5 degrees. We must own up to this fact and focus on adaptation not mitigation. We must prepare for sea level rise that will swamp many existing cities. In some cases, this will require massive infrastructure investments in sea walls to try to hold the ocean at bay. In many cases, this will lead to evacuating and abandoning cities and regions deemed too difficult, or expensive, to save.

Yet while adaptation will most certainly be necessary, mitigation is still imperative. For if we fail to eliminate greenhouse gas emissions, increasing concentrations in the atmosphere will only accelerate and intensify the impacts of climate change. While there remains much uncertainty about the impacts on climate as greenhouse gas concentrations increase, climate scientists believe that the impacts are likely to be nonlinear with concentrations. This means the impacts could be orders of magnitude greater than under the 2 degrees Celsius scenario. Consider in the extreme, if all glacial ice and ice sheets melted, sea levels would rise by over two hundred feet, swamping millions of acres of land and displacing much of the world's population.

While decarbonizing the global economy by 2050 is daunting, it remains necessary.

THE INNOVATION IMPERATIVE

Let's consider the concept of decarbonizing the economy by 2050. What exactly does that mean? Figure 1.2 shows annual greenhouse gas emissions broken down by sector. Roughly a quarter of all emissions comes from the production of energy, specifically electricity and heat. Another 10 percent comes from other energy sources. Transportation, including automobiles, trucks, airplanes, and ships, accounts for another seventh or so. Surprising to some, agriculture represents roughly a quarter of all emissions, driven mainly by the use of nitrogen fertilizers and the release of methane in beef production. Industrials, such as the production of steel and cement, account for another fifth of emissions. Finally, roughly 6 percent of emissions come from the built environment, such as the use of natural gas for heating and cooking within buildings.

Decarbonization basically entails driving each of these sectors to net-zero emissions.[11] We adopt as a fundamental assumption that decarbonization cannot be achieved without massive innovation and improvement in zero-emission, or clean, technology across these sectors. The five sectors identified in Figure 1.2—transportation, energy, industrials, agriculture, and buildings—will each

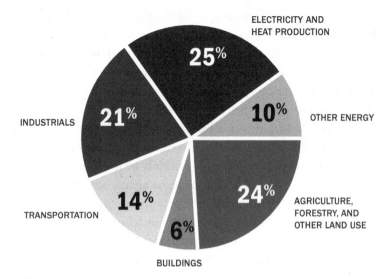

FIGURE 1.2   Annual Global Greenhouse Gas Emissions by Sector
Source: IPCC, Contribution of Working Group III to the Fifth Assessment Report of the Intergovernmental Panel on Climate

have to be fundamentally disrupted to be decarbonized. We use the term *disrupted* in the economic sense, meaning that existing technologies and business models are replaced by innovative new products and services that, typically, fundamentally reshape the existing competitive order.

Some argue that the world currently has all the clean technology necessary to achieve a decarbonized future. All that is needed is the will to adopt it. We beg to differ. Markets are where technology and innovations find their value expressed. The failure to adopt clean technology may reflect a market failure from a societal perspective, but it typically reflects a market reality that the clean technology is not as desirable as alternative technologies on existing dimensions of merit. Innovations that reduce costs and create value can make clean technologies desirable in the marketplace.

Arguably, the quickest path to adoption of clean technologies is if these technologies are preferable on the current dimensions of merit. Consider renewable energy. In an increasing number of applications and regions, photovoltaic solar cells are on par with, if not lower cost than, alternatives such as natural gas. In these cases, the market is responding quickly, building new solar-generating capacity even in the absence of any government intervention to create an external price signal such as clean energy subsidies or carbon taxes. Renewable energy is simply the cheapest, and thus preferred, way of generating electricity, at least in some applications.

Another interesting transition is occurring in automobiles. The rise of battery-powered electric vehicles pioneered by Tesla and others is raising the potential for a massive technology disruption in the auto sector. While subsidies for the purchase of electric vehicles in the United States and elsewhere have certainly played an important role in their adoption, for many purchasers, it is the other attributes of electric vehicles—superior acceleration, precise handling, regenerative breaking, and increased reliability, not to mention cool styling and advanced digital controls—that are driving their growth. In markets, consumers desire those products that give them the greatest net value conditioned on budget constraints, that is, the largest spread from desirability to the price paid. For an increasing number of auto customers, electric vehicles are superior even in the absence of a subsidy.

To be clear, we are not arguing for a laissez-faire approach to new clean technologies, for an extreme form of free-market capitalism. We believe that markets function within a broader set of institutional structures that establish the rules of the game and determine how they function. The success of renewable energy and the rise of electric vehicles would not be possible without any number of institutional interventions in the markets, from subsidizing of public R&D at universities to the underwriting of risk in entrepreneurial start-ups to infrastructure investments necessary for clean technology to demand incentives such as subsidies and taxes to drive the desire to innovate.

No doubt, decarbonization will not occur without substantial and substantive interventions in the policy arena from both public and private entities. Throughout this book, we will be highlighting how such interventions may help shape markets, drive innovation, and ultimately lead to the widespread adoption of clean technologies. We will explore interventions, or levers, such as subsidizing R&D in clean technology, providing fertile grounds for innovators and entrepreneurs to bring clean technologies to market, and, of course, sending demand signals by putting a price on carbon.

We believe that an endeavor as audacious as decarbonizing the global economy will require pulling many of the available levers. If we assume that it is highly unlikely—even with interventions—that industry will shift to sustainable technologies, then we may need to incentivize adoption of carbon dioxide removal (CDR) and carbon capture, utilization, and storage (CCUS) if we are to address our climate challenge. Arguably, CDR and CCUS will never be market solutions per se as they will always be costlier than *not* doing CDR and CCUS. Therefore, we will need government to incentivize their adoption and, unlike subsidies for electrical vehicles or renewable energy, these market interventions will never be able to be removed as there is no technology cost curve that will drive market adoption independently. Similarly, some have called for geoengineered solutions, such as seeding the stratosphere with aerosols, to help create a global cooling effect. Beyond the obvious concern for unintended consequences of such interventions, the effort would have to be borne by some government or global consortium willing to assume the costs. Given this, we consider these as last-resort levers and focus on technology replacement and the likelihood of cleaner alternatives that cost the same as or less than traditional carbon-intensive ones or create more consumer value, thus leading to mass adoption of the new technology.

THE ECONOMICS OF DISRUPTION

Central to our analysis is an understanding of the dynamics of markets and how disruption typically takes place in such markets. There are some common patterns observed as new technologies disrupt existing markets. Earlier on, it is often the case that the new technology is inferior to existing technologies on any number of dimensions. Perhaps the technology does not provide any additional functionality compared to current technology. Or perhaps it is simply too expensive. Many clean technologies have languished in this early emergent phase of development, holding great promise but not quite becoming market viable.

Research and development in this early phase may seem like throwing good money after bad. Experiments fail. Paths down one technology trajectory prove fruitless and require a new approach. Sometimes this experimental phase can be quite brief. More often than not, it can seem interminable. Many of the technologies we take for granted today had long gestation periods. Smartphones were a concept going back to at least the early 1990s (much earlier if we consider portrayals in science fiction). Apple was an early pioneer with the Newton, a smart device that did not have phone capabilities. Released in 1994, the Newton was an abject failure. A product before its time.

In the cleantech space, hydrogen fuel cells have been explored for over a half century. In fits and starts over decades, scientists and innovators have been trying to advance this power source that promises cheap and clean energy. Great progress has been made, but the technology is still not quite ready for primetime. Cost and efficiency, not to mention the need to create a viable hydrogen supply chain, have hampered efforts to bring the technology to the mass market. Yet efforts persist and a hydrogen future may still be realized. Toyota, which has been a big proponent of hydrogen-fuel-cell-powered automobiles, recently debuted the second generation of its Mirai line of fuel cell vehicles.

Obviously, if a technology is to disrupt the market, eventually it must find traction. More often than not, the first viable market for a new technology is in some niche application. For example, the earliest adopters of digital cameras were photojournalists who could justify the high price tag and bulking equipment of early models. In the cleantech space, the earliest adoption of solar panels was for powering satellites in the 1960s. Solar panels found initial traction in consumer markets in a number of small niches including solar-powered calculators and as a power source for marine use.

Eventually, a disruptive technology—to be disruptive, by definition—finds broader adoption and begins to replace the existing technology in the marketplace. We typically observe a broadening of the consumer base and exponential growth in sales. During this growth period, we often see an "annealing" process during which the new technology coalesces into a dominant design. *Annealing* is a material science term referring to the hardening of a material as it cools. In this context, it refers to the competition within a new technology between alternative possible manifestations of that technology that eventually results in a dominant design—a particular technological trajectory that comes to dominate the market.

Consider the rise of the automobile industry, over a hundred years ago. When the automobile first appeared, numerous competing powertrains were being advanced. Of course, there was the gasoline-powered internal combustion engine (ICE). Some manufacturers experimented with kerosene engines. The Stanley Steamer was a fanciful steam-powered automobile in the early days of the industry. Many entrants pushed battery-powered electric vehicles. In fact, as late as 1930, over 30 percent of delivery vehicles in New York City were powered by electric batteries. Eventually, a dominant design emerged in the form of the gasoline-powered ICE. Why the ICE came to dominate is up for debate. What is interesting is the return to exploring the electric vehicle "technology trajectory" nearly a century later.

Of course, not every technology reaches this growth phase. In fact, few do. History is littered with interesting inventions that never found commercial viability; promising technologies that are still waiting for that upward kink in the sales curve. Of course, it is difficult to know which technologies will succeed and which ones will fail during the early stages of development. What is clear is that once market dynamics are put in motion, disruption can occur quickly. For example, the New England whaling industry, an important source of energy for the good part of a half century, especially for applications such as lighting, had a rather swift death in the 1860s as the discovery of oil in western Pennsylvania and the invention of kerosene from oil created a massive technology disruption.

As a new disruptive technology begins to accelerate, a number of interesting patterns are observed. First, it is often entrepreneurial ventures that pioneer the new technology. Entrepreneurs arguably are freer to explore novel, even crazy, ideas. They do not have the demands from capital markets to deliver quarterly earnings as do publicly traded firms. As the adoption of the new technology accelerates, others begin to enter the market—both newer ventures and established firms. Some of these established firms may currently compete in the existing market while others may be diversifying from adjacent sectors. A "gold rush" may ensue with tens, if not hundreds, of businesses offering the new technology.

Second, pioneering firms often lose money at first on the new technology. There are a number of reasons for this. For one, there is still often uncertainty on the specific design. Firms need to spend heavily on research and development to advance the technology. Continual effort is needed to move down the learning curve, improving the technology and reducing its cost of production. Another reason is that, in many cases, pioneers simply do not have the scale—the volume of sales—to offset the fixed costs of production. This can especially be the case when firms need to build manufacturing and distribution capabilities. Amazon posted losses for over a decade as it built out the logistical infrastructure to dominate e-commerce. This profit challenge can be compounded by the speed of acceptance on the demand side, which may slow the pace of sales of the new technology.

Third, as the technology improves and competition intensifies, a shakeout often occurs. A shakeout refers to the exit of players in the new market either by shutting down of operations, bankruptcy, or acquisition. Shakeouts can be quite pronounced, with hundreds of relatively new entrants exiting in a short period of time. Modern examples are all around us. The early days of the smartphone market saw the entry of new ventures such as Blackberry, established cellular phone providers like Nokia and Motorola, and diversifiers such as Microsoft and Sony. After the smoke cleared, Apple and Samsung emerged as the main survivors, with many, many others exiting the market.

Fourth, as the shakeout plays out, we typically see the industry begin to mature. Growth in the new technology may be quite pronounced, but eventually will slow as the market becomes saturated and the new technology comes to dominate. The rate of innovation of the technology also begins to slow and the marginal impact of every dollar spent on R&D declines. The old technology begins to fade—though it may persist for quite some time, often being relegated to niche markets a fraction of their previous size. For example, there is still a small, enthusiast market for film despite the ubiquity of digital cameras. Competition, in general, becomes more muted and tends to shift from the underlying product or service to production and operations efficiencies. This period may sow the seeds of a new disruption as intrepid innovators begin looking for radical new ways to do it better, cheaper, faster.

OUR ANALYSIS

To help unpack the potential path to 2050, we leverage the economics of disruption to look for patterns to gauge the likelihood of a transition to clean technology in the major emitting sectors of the global economy. Are we seeing incumbent players and entrepreneurs offering clean technology alternatives? Is the number of entrants in clean technology accelerating? Is sales growth following the classic s-shaped diffusion curve? Is there a standards battle brewing between different visions of the technology? Is a dominant design starting to emerge? Is a shakeout imminent?

Figure 1.3 summarizes the basic patterns observed in the life cycle of a (successful) new technology. The technology curve captures the improvements being made to the underlying technology. The revenue curve captures the cumulative sales of the technology as it comes to dominate the market. The competition curve captures the density of firms competing in the industry, highlighting the boom-and-bust nature of shakeouts.

It is important to recognize that these patterns are stylized. While they are common and persistent, no two industries evolve in exactly the same fashion. The individual actions of inventors, entrepreneurs, CEOs, and investors can have a significant influence on how a specific technology plays out. Equally important are the influence of numerous private and public intermediaries who help set the rules of competition and influence how competitive dynamics play out: legislators, policy makers, regulators, activists, university researchers, unions, trade associations, and so on. While much of the fate of a technology seems driven by luck or happenstance—a brilliant discovery in the lab or an unforeseen event to awaken demand—we take great solace in the fact that the actions of individuals and institutions can and do matter.

We organize the book around an analysis of each of the major greenhouse-gas-emitting sectors. In Chapter 2, we tackle energy, with a specific focus on the

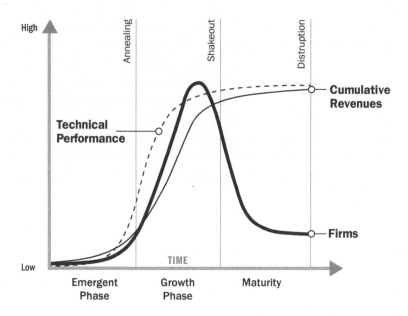

FIGURE 1.3   The Industry Life Cycle

production of electricity. In Chapter 3, we turn our attention to the transportation sector and automobiles. In Chapter 4, we examine industrials, focusing on the three largest emitting industries—steel, cement, and petrochemicals. In Chapter 5, we tackle buildings, both commercial and residential. And last, in Chapter 6, we take on agriculture and the myriad of sources of greenhouse gases emitted in the production of food.

In each chapter, we will focus on "scope 1" emissions—emissions directly from the production of goods or services in the sector. "Scope 2" emissions, those emitted during the production of electricity to support operations, often by an electric utility, are addressed in Chapter 2 during our discussion of the energy sector. Similarly, emissions in the value chain ("scope 3"), say from transporting food to the marketplace, are handled where the emissions occur, in the transportation sector not the agriculture sector, for example. In a world with interconnecting global supply chains, a focus on scope 1 emissions gives us the clearest understanding of how to drive net-zero emissions.

In each sector, we discuss the current patterns observed, the clean technologies that may potentially disrupt the sector, the barriers to their advancement, and the levers that may be pulled to accelerate their adoption. Are there currently viable clean technologies available in the market? What does their technology trajectory look like, especially compared to existing solutions? Do we see accelerated entry by entrepreneurs and diversifying incumbents? By examining the rate of innovation, the entry of competition, and adoption patterns, we can begin to assess the potential for a disruption.

To be clear, we are only interested in disruptive changes. Reductions of emissions by 20 percent or to 1990 levels, while helpful, are wholly insufficient. Anything less than complete decarbonization, that is, net-zero emissions, will put us on a path to fly past the 1.5 degrees target. The time for intermediate solutions has passed. Timing is absolutely critical. We take some comfort in knowing that change can happen fast. Just as kerosene quickly displaced whale oil, kerosene use was disrupted by electrification and the light bulb. Evidence suggests that the diffusion of new technologies is happening quicker than ever. Smartphones took less than a decade to reach near total penetration in many markets. Many technology forecasts miss the impact of exponential growth. In a few years, a nascent technology can become dominant.

Not that such dominance is guaranteed. A fundamental premise of this book is that the likelihood and speed of disruption are driven by the broader institutional envelope that surrounds the marketplace.[12] Public interventions by governments and regulators and private intermediaries such as universities and nongovernmental organizations all have a role to play. In each chapter, we provide the "upshot"—our current assessment of whether a sustainable disruption is likely in the sector, as well as a list of levers that may help accelerate decarbonization. We conclude the book with a chapter in which we advance a comprehensive clean technology policy strategy with a special focus on policy interventions that can help achieve decarbonization by 2050.

This book is an examination of how the trajectory of new clean technologies is currently playing out and, more important, an exploration of what interventions can help accelerate the displacement of current technologies with clean alternatives. The path to 2050 will not be an easy one. Decarbonizing the global economy is an audacious and fraught endeavor. We will likely have to pull most, if not all, of the available levers to us to make such a transition possible. Even then, we may still fall short. But try we must. For climate change threatens our ability to flourish as a global society.

CHAPTER 2

THE ENERGY SECTOR

TYPICALLY, when people think of the climate crisis, their attention immediately turns to the energy sector and fossil fuels. The burning of fossil fuels for electricity and heat represents 25 percent of global greenhouse gas (GHG) emissions.[1] Fuel extraction, refining, and processing are responsible for another 10 percent of global GHG emissions.[2] Oil, natural gas, and coal are critical feedstocks for everything from transportation to petrochemicals to industrial processes such as steel production. Electricity generation touches every major sector, from buildings to industrials to agriculture and, increasingly, transportation as vehicles electrify.

For our purposes, we begin our analysis with a focus on electricity generation. The use of gasoline and other fuels for transportation will be covered in Chapter 3. On-site consumption of fossil fuels in industrial processes will be covered in Chapter 4. Burning of natural gas and oil for residential and commercial heating and cooking will be addressed in Chapter 5. As we reduce the use of the fossil fuels in these applications, global production of fossil fuels will decline as demand diminishes, reducing carbon emissions from the extraction, refining, and processing of oil, natural gas, and coal.

So what is the potential of eliminating the use of fossil fuels in electricity generation? The global mix of electricity sources has long been diversified and has evolved over time (see Figure 2.1). In 2014, global electricity production was 40 percent coal, 22 percent natural gas, 16 percent hydroelectric, 11 percent nuclear, 6 percent renewables (mainly solar and wind), and 3 percent oil.[3] By 2019, coal had largely fallen out of favor in the United States and Europe, in large part due to lower prices for natural gas due to shale fracking. In the US, coal made up only 24 percent of electrical generation while cleaner-burning natural gas use had grown to 38 percent—greatly reducing the carbon footprint of the US electricity sector. However, overall coal continues to represent more than one-third (37 percent in 2020) of electricity production, driven mainly by increased generation in China, the largest electricity producer in the world.[4]

HYDRO AND NUCLEAR:
THE ORIGINAL DECARBONIZED ENERGY

The story for decarbonized sources of energy is equally mixed. Hydroelectricity was arguably the original renewable energy source. Using water to power machinery dates back thousands of years to the Greeks, who used it to grind flour. Hydroelectricity emerged in the 1800s just as electricity was becoming recognized as a major power source. The Niagara Falls plant, built in 1895, served as the first hydroelectric power plant in the United States.[5] In 1933, President Franklin D. Roosevelt's New Deal ushered in the so-called "big dam period" in the US, exemplified by the Hoover Dam.[6] By 1940, 40 percent of the nation's electricity was being generated by hydropower.[7] A similar story unfolded globally as other countries invested in large hydropower projects. The largest such project was the Three Gorges Dam, built in the Hubei Province of China. Completed in 2012, the dam is the world's largest power station, with an installed capacity of 22,500 megawatts.[8] Hydropower represents about 17 percent of China's electricity generation.[9]

While hydropower continues to play a significant role in global electricity generation, several challenges threaten its growth, including high construction costs and concerns regarding impact on local ecosystems. While hydropower is recognized as a clean energy source, environmentalists began as early as the 1970s to raise concerns about the wildlife and environmental impacts on local rivers of manipulating water sources. In the United States, federal standards that were changed to protect water resources included new dam licensing requirements that required extensive environmental studies, delaying permitting processes and adding significant costs to projects. As a result of these actions, and the fact that the sites with the most hydro potential had been developed, growth in US hydropower capacity began to

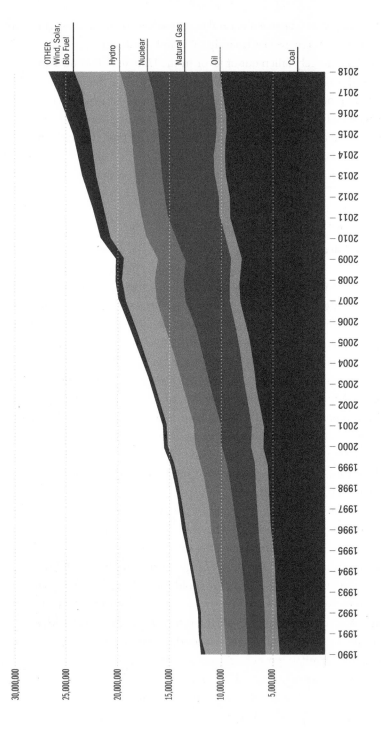

FIGURE 2.1 Global Energy Mix, 1990–2018 (GWh)

Source: "Electricity Generation by Source, World 1990–2017,"
https://www.iea.org/data-and-statistics?country=WORLD&fuel=Energy%20supply&indicator=Total%20primary%20energy%20supply%20(TPES)%20by%20source

slow and the technology started to lose share of overall electrical generation, representing only 6.5 percent by 2018.[10] Similar trends have been observed in other developed economies. Ironically, climate change is accelerating these trends, as it threatens the efficacy of hydropower in many parts of the world. Regional droughts can cause plant effectiveness to fluctuate within plus or minus 10 percent year to year.[11]

A similar story unfolded for nuclear energy. Nuclear technology was to usher in a future of cheap, clean electricity. In the span of twenty years during the 1970s and 1980s, nuclear energy grew to almost 18 percent of total electricity generated worldwide.[12] Then high-profile accidents in the United States at Three-Mile Island and the former Soviet Union at Chernobyl coupled with the challenges of disposing radioactive waste led to increased scrutiny and regulation of nuclear power. By the 1990s, more nuclear plants were being retired than built, and the share of generation remained flat for the next twenty years.[13] In 2011, a record number of plants were shut down following the Fukushima accident, including sixteen reactors in Japan alone. Nuclear hasn't kept pace with overall electricity generation growth, and by 2016 it had fallen to 10.5 percent of worldwide generation.[14]

In 2018, twelve countries produced 25 percent or more of their electricity from nuclear reactors. By 2020, there were 440 commercial nuclear energy reactors in operation around the world.[15] Yet the share of global energy production by nuclear has remained flat at 10 percent.[16] Plans are in the works to expand the nuclear fleet. About 50 reactors are under construction and scheduled for grid connection between 2020 and 2025,[17] and more than 100 power reactors are on order or planned, with Asia leading the way.[18] However, this growth is being partially offset by retirements in other countries. In France, where 75 percent of electricity is supplied from nuclear reactors, the country's 2018 energy plan reduces the share of nuclear to 50 percent by 2035, with plans to retire fourteen older reactors. The United States has the largest fleet of reactors in the world. However, with a median age of nearly forty years, many reactors in the US face closure.[19] Only one nuclear reactor has been constructed in the United States in the last twenty years. With the help of efficiency upgrades to current units, nuclear has maintained a 20 percent share in US energy production despite the decreasing fleet. Overall, nuclear plants around the world are a depreciating capital stock. The cost to build new reactors is simply too high, and the timeline to build too long, to compete with other energy sources without subsidies.

With hydro and nuclear largely stagnant, attention has shifted to the potential for wind and solar power to be the disruptors to put an end to electricity generated by fossil fuels. Solar and wind represent the fastest-growing generation sources worldwide, driving renewables share of global generating capacity to one-third in 2018 and accounting for two-thirds of installed new power generation.[20] With the exception of 2013 and 2018, solar and wind together have added more generating capacity to the US grid than natural gas each year since 2012 (Figure 2.2). According to EIA, solar and wind will lead renewables in surpassing nuclear and coal generation by 2021 and natural gas by 2045.[21]

Of course, the building out of new capacity is only part of the story. One of the challenges with wind and solar replacing traditional baseload

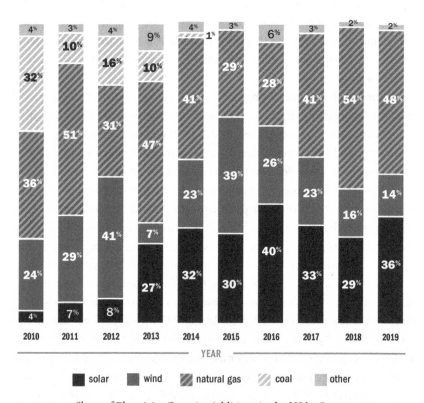

FIGURE 2.2   Share of Electricity Capacity Additions in the US by Source, 2010–2019

Source: SEIA, 2020, seia.org, via Statista,
statista.com/statistics/525735/share-of-us-electricity-capacity-additions-by-resource

energy sources is that they have low "capacity factors," defined as the ratio between what a plant is capable of producing at maximum output versus actual generation over a specified time period. Baseload power plants like nuclear and coal can operate continuously and have higher capacity factors compared to wind and solar, which operate intermittently. Natural gas plants can be ramped up or down to address peak periods and also offer higher capacity factors.

Given this, making a claim that solar and wind will serve as direct replacements for fossil-fuel power plants is misleading without also mentioning the need for supporting technologies that help to dispatch capacity more equally on any given day. Later in the chapter, we touch on energy storage and grid modernization, which can be deployed to support a wind and solar expansion. To be clear, we do believe that there is a place for other zero-carbon energy generators such as nuclear and hydroelectric power in a new decarbonized grid. However, our interests lie in the story of the disruptive innovation currently taking place around wind and solar that will change the way in which people generate, distribute, and pay for electricity in the future.

WIND: A MILLENNIUM-OLD TECHNOLOGY COMES OF AGE

In the United States, the use of wind energy to provide localized electricity dates back to the 1800s. However, it was not until 1941 that utility-scale wind power was demonstrated when a 1.25 MW turbine was installed on top of a mountain called "Grandpa's Knob" in Vermont and then connected to the electric grid.[22] Aside from smaller and more specialized applications, mass commercialization of wind energy wouldn't be seen in the US for another thirty years when, in 1974, Congress created the Energy Research and Development Administration (ERDA) with the purpose of expanding federal energy research and development, including the demonstration of new energy technologies.[23] Wind energy wasn't a new technology but required significant capital investment to prove the concept on a larger scale. Under ERDA support, the first prototype large-scale wind facility was constructed in Ohio in partnership with NASA to test components and collect performance data.

The door opened for commercialization in 1978 with the passing of the Energy Tax Act and Public Utility Regulatory Policy Act (PURPA). The Energy Tax Act provided a 30 percent investment tax credit for residential consumers for solar and wind energy equipment and a 10 percent investment tax credit for businesses for solar, wind, and geothermal installations.[24] PURPA provided an opportunity to smaller, non-utility generators to enter the market through requirements that utilities buy electricity from a "qualified facility" at avoided cost, or what it would have cost for the utility to generate the electricity. A qualified facility is a FERC-approved electric generating facility that either (1) generates less than 80 MW from renewable, biomass, waste, or geothermal sources or (2) produces electricity and another useful form of thermal energy (cogeneration facility). The Act would diversify electricity supply and allow renewables to compete with fossil fuels.[25]

Tax incentives were critical in the early days of wind energy deployment. Despite President Ronald Regan cutting federal funding of wind energy projects by 90 percent in the 1980s, a "wind rush" was under way in California, created by the California Public Utility Commission's first thirty-year Standard Offer Contracts requiring utilities to make long-term purchase agreements for alternative energy.[26] In 1986, however, US federal incentives expired, leading most American wind turbine manufacturers to go out of business and halting further expansion of wind power.

Hope in wind energy was restored when, in 1992, President Bush signed the Energy Policy Act that provided production tax credits to renewables, including $0.015/kWh for wind generation. Government research ramped up in the 1990s, primarily through the National Wind Technology Center, which was built with the goal of reducing the cost of energy for wind to compete with other energy sources.[27] Favorable state mandates and renewed Federal tax credits helped to increase US wind generation capacity to 2,500 MW by 1999.[28] Entering into the twenty-first century, these incentives helped to put wind on the forefront of the renewable movement. Several extensions of the tax credits have helped the overall growth of wind. In 2015, Congress passed a multiyear extension of the tax credits through 2019 and later extended these credits through 2020. By 2016, wind energy had grown to provide more than 5 percent of electricity to US customers.[29] With more than 107 GW installed by 2020,[30] wind had surpassed hydroelectric as the number one source of renewable capacity in the US.[31]

Interestingly, incentives, while helpful particularly in some parts of the country, may no longer be needed for growth in wind energy to continue. According to the Lazard Levelized Cost of Energy (LCOE) Analysis, onshore wind LCOE ranges from $28 to $54/MWh without government subsidies. In comparison, the LCOE for gas combined cycle is $44 to $68/MWh.[32] LCOE takes into account the costs of capital, fixed operations and maintenance (O&M),

variable O&M, and fuel. The LCOE Analysis provides a longer-term view of asset ownership, as the costs to construct a fossil-fuel plant may appear to be more favorable at the onset but not be cost-effective over the lifetime of that asset, which is critical for utility planning. The Lazard analysis shows that since 2009 onshore wind LCOE has decreased 70 percent, due largely to technology improvements and declines in system component pricing.[33]

It's worth noting that the Lazard LCOE Analysis does not consider the costs associated with the infrastructure needed to support the integration of variable renewable energy sources onto the grid. Electricity demand fluctuates throughout the day, which historically has required a vast network of baseload and peaking power plants controlled by utilities to deliver reliable electricity. Coal and nuclear are examples of baseload power plants, which provide a constant source of energy to meet the minimum demand. Peaking (or more typically combined cycle gas) power plants can be dispatched as needed to meet demand above baseload. Wind is a variable energy source that generates electricity only when the wind blows. It is neither baseload nor dispatchable without a way to store and efficiently distribute the energy. Energy storage and grid modernization will be critical to the continued growth of wind.

In general, what makes wind such an attractive option is the fact that fuel costs are zero and not at the mercy of the variable pricing that fossil fuels face. As manufacturing and installation prices come down, choosing wind is a matter of simple economics, especially as lower installation prices and increasing wind turbine efficiencies have led to declining levelized Power Purchase Agreement (PPA) prices for wind projects (that is, from $0.07/kWh in 2009 to $0.02/kWh in 2019).[34] A Power Purchase Agreement is a contract between an electricity generator and a buyer, under which the developer (owner or operator) designs, builds, and operates the renewable asset, selling the electricity to the buyer either at a flat or fixed escalator rate. These rates are locked in for ten to twenty-five years and are typically less than projected utility prices. The buyer might be a utility or corporate entity. There is an increase in corporate PPAs as large corporations such as Google, Facebook, Microsoft, and Amazon look for ways to shrink their carbon footprint. According to Bloomberg New Energy Finance, corporate entities have purchased 50 GW of clean energy since 2008.[35] PPAs allow renewable projects to be financed while also providing end users long-term price stability with potential for future savings.

While natural gas competes with wind today, longer-term projections suggest that gas prices will rise over time while wind PPA prices locked in today will remain competitive. As a result, there has been substantial growth in wind power generation across the United States, especially where climate and/or policy environments are favorable to wind. In 2019, Texas led the country with regard to cumulative installed wind capacity while Iowa held the largest share of in-state generation at 42 percent.[36] By 2020, fourteen states reported a share of wind energy generation greater than 10 percent, with most of those located in the middle of the country, where wind assets are greatest.[37]

Over the last ten years, wind power has represented 27 percent of capacity added to the US electric grid.[38] By 2020, wind energy represented 7 percent of total US electricity generation.[39] Similarly, wind power has been growing worldwide. Globally, there was more than 651 GW of wind energy capacity installed in 2019; installed capacity has doubled since 2013.[40] This capacity is capable of meeting 6 percent of the world's electricity demand.[41] The Asia-Pacific region is investing heavily in wind development, with wind capturing 51 percent of total new capacity installed in 2019.[42] In terms of cumulative installations, the United States holds the second spot. Collectively, China, the United States, Germany, India, and Spain represent 72 percent of total global wind installations.[43]

Continued growth in wind will be fueled by continued improvements in efficiency and cost as well as flexibility in siting. It is important to note that compared to solar, wind technology is nearing maturity, with turbines already extracting close to the theoretical maximum energy conveyed (just under 60 percent).[44] What this means is that for each dollar of R&D investment, the return on that investment with regard to performance improvement is lower. Capacity factor, or the power generated compared to rated power (in percentage), is the standard measure of wind turbine efficiency. Increases in nameplate capacity (that is, rated capacity at full load), hub height, and rotor diameters over the last decade have led to an increase in average capacity factor from 25 percent in 1999 to more than 40 percent today.[45] New-generation turbine designs continue to focus on these three areas with an emphasis on turbine height, which has significantly increased over the years.[46] Developers are also upgrading older wind sites with taller turbines and longer blades, extending the life of existing wind farms and improving operating efficiency.

Other technology improvements seek to address operations and management. For example, direct-drive turbines eliminate the gearbox (which drives blade rotation), a source of additional weight and component failures.[47] Incorporation of remote electronic controls could optimize wind production using data to adjust blade pitch as wind conditions change. Siting turbines in areas with optimum wind speed is key, and turbines are being built in cold climate areas where wind resources are favorable and populations low. However, turbines employed in cold climate areas require higher maintenance due to the need for de-icing capabilities and potential for lower yield that might be caused by blade icing. This is another area of research and investment.

Interesting efforts are also under way to design a radically different turbine. One start-up company in Spain, Vortex Bladeless, designed a turbine that captures wind energy without blades, using instead vorticity to oscillate the structure and turning kinetic energy into electricity. An added benefit of this design is reduced material costs, as the turbine doesn't need gears or bearings to work. However, the design will likely be limited in the total amount of power it can produce, particularly at higher altitudes.[48] Other proposed designs eliminate the tower completely. Google in partnership with Makani Power tested a kite-type device attached to the ground that orbits similar to the blade tip of a horizontal axis wind turbine. Altaeros Energies designed a buoyant airborne turbine that suspends a traditional horizontal axis wind turbine from a helium filled shell. In 2019, Google dropped the Makani project, citing a risky road to commercial viability, while Altaeros shifted their focus away from energy to a communications solution. Other companies are moving forward with airborne wind energy designs but have yet to bring one to market.[49]

Another area of exploration has been small, or distributed, wind (less than 100 kW). However, lack of education coupled with low turbine efficiencies (on average, capacity factor of 17 percent) and high installation costs (LCOE of $240/MWh) have challenged widespread adoption.[50] Installed cost of small wind increased between 2009 and 2014 and remained flat through 2017. In comparison, residential solar photovoltaic (PV), which is seen as a direct competitor, has steadily decreased and was about 40 percent cheaper than small wind in 2017.[51] With the number of installations declining each year and manufacturers leaving the industry, small wind seemed to be a dying breed. However, more recently, the idea of small wind has been revived, largely due to its microgrid potential. In August 2020, the US Department of Energy (DOE) announced the funding of eight distributed wind projects that seek to improve technology performance and evaluate the storage potential of small wind.[52] In addition, some small wind manufacturers are reporting improvements in cost with new-generation turbines. For example, Bergey Windpower's new Excel 15 turbine design boasts a LCOE of $78/MWh, down from $214/MWh for its previous generation turbine.[53] The next few years will determine the fate of small wind; though if it takes off, the opportunities will likely be limited to rural and remote locations.

Typical for an emergent industry, there has been significant turnover in wind turbine manufacturers in the United States over the past ten-plus years, but two companies—Danish manufacturer Vestas and General Electric (GE)—have consistently held the majority market share of wind installations. Competition heated up between 2007 and 2012 as the number of players increased from four to twelve manufacturers. However, due to more recent consolidations[54] and companies exiting the market, typical of a market shakeout, the number of manufacturers has returned to the 2007 level.[55] As of 2019, Vestas led the competition for turbine supply worldwide, followed by Siemens Gamesa, Goldwind, and GE.[56] These four manufacturers represented 55 percent total commissioned wind projects in 2019. GE is currently the only US-based turbine manufacturer competing on a global scale.

With increased competition among manufacturers, we have seen declining turbine costs. As presented in DOE's "2016 Wind Technologies Market Report," wind turbine prices in the United States were at $1,600/kW in 2008 due to several reasons, including "a decline in the value of the U.S. dollar relative to the Euro; increased materials, energy, and labor input prices; a general increase in turbine manufacturer profitability due in part to strong demand growth; and increased costs for turbine warranty provisions."[57] By 2018 product prices had fallen within the $700 to $900/kW range.[58] This decline in turbine cost has led to declining installation costs. The 2019 US national-capacity-weighted CAPEX (wind turbine, installation, and other development costs) is estimated to be $1,496/kW compared to $2,508/kW ten years earlier.[59]

With the costs for onshore wind now competitive with other energy sources, R&D investment has largely shifted to the opportunity of offshore wind. Just ten years ago, despite commercialization already happening in other parts of the world, offshore wind was considered a new application in the United States. Following in the footsteps of turbines onshore, DOE set out to help commercialize offshore wind. In 2011, the agency released "A National Offshore Wind Strategy: Creating an Offshore Wind Industry in the United States" with the goal of reducing the cost of offshore wind energy through technology development and reducing deployment timelines. Challenges cited in that report included the high cost of energy, technical installation and interconnection challenges, and permitting challenges due to lack of data and experience. Lack of data also drives up the financing costs for offshore projects, another roadblock to commercial deployment.[60] The strategy outlined the actions needed to reach a national capacity of 54 GW of offshore wind power and reduce capital costs by almost 50 percent, from \$4,259/kW in 2011 to \$2,600/kW by 2030.[61]

Since releasing the 2011 strategy, DOE has supported research and several demonstration projects in US waters, generating the experience and data needed to prove the technology and help address challenges in siting, permitting, and grid interconnection. According to DOE's "Wind Office Technologies Office Projects Map," ninety-five offshore wind projects led by private companies, nonprofits, national laboratories, academic institutions, and state and local governments were receiving financial support from DOE in 2020. In addition to demonstration projects, the focus of research ranges from technology development and modeling to environmental impacts and siting and grid integration.[62]

In 2017, DOE along with the New York State Energy Research Authority funded a nonprofit consortium for five years to work with private companies to identify priorities for funding offshore wind R&D. The state governments of Virginia, Maryland, and Massachusetts have also contributed funding. The mission of the National Offshore Wind R&D Consortium is to help address technological challenges and lower the risk and cost of offshore wind in the United States.[63] The three focus areas identified for technical research are plant development (fixed and floating platforms); resource and physical site characterization; and installation, O&M, and supply chain (including regulation and grid integration).[64]

Competition for offshore wind project development is heating up. The first commercial offshore wind facility, the 30 MW Deepwater Wind, was commissioned off Block Island, Rhode Island, in December 2016. The Deepwater Wind site remains the sole offshore project in US waters. The current pipeline of projects presented by the DOE National Renewable Energy Laboratory's (NREL's) offshore wind database shows that in 2019, 2,697 MW was added to the total US offshore wind capacity potential, which grew to 28,521 MW.[65] Most of this capacity (61 percent) is at the "site control" stage, in which the developer obtains control over the site through a lease or other contract. It will take several years for these projects to come online. Thirteen permitted projects representing more than 6 MW of wind generation are scheduled to be operational between 2023 and 2025.[66] One of the most promising projects is Vineyard Wind, which is in development just south of Martha's Vineyard and once complete will be the first utility-scale offshore wind plant and will power over four hundred thousand homes across Massachusetts.[67]

In the United States, offshore wind is somewhat challenged by the general perception that the view of turbines from the coastline will have a negative impact on beachgoers. Whether this perception is real or perceived, it is a consideration that threatens to delay offshore projects. The further out wind turbines are placed, the less of a concern the view may be according to at least one study.[68] However, installing turbines in deeper waters poses challenges to fixed-bottom platforms.

Floating wind turbines make it possible to harness stronger, more consistent winds further off the coast and in deeper seas where fixed bottom platforms are not technically feasible. In the United States, floating turbines could open additional wind resources off coasts of major energy markets where depths less than 60 meters are limited. DOE estimates that 58 percent of wind resources available to the US coastline comes from deep water.[69] In California, 95 percent of the coastline's available 112 GW of offshore wind resource is in waters deeper than 60 meters.[70] Floating wind is in the early stage of commercialization, with investments focused on R&D and demonstration projects. In 2020, there was one floating wind turbine project off the coast of Maine—the 12 MW Aqua Ventus—with plans to put the plant into operation in 2023. According to NREL, there are six more projects in the early planning phase.[71]

Investments in technology advancements, declining project costs, and growing interest by utilities and companies to purchase offshore wind suggest that it is following in the footsteps of the onshore market. How much energy could be tapped through offshore wind facilities? As much as 2,000 GW of capacity, or 7,200 TWh of generation annually, which is almost twice the nation's current electricity use.[72] However, there are several challenges ahead to realizing this potential that are unique to offshore wind. One of those challenges is creating the port infrastructure needed to provide capacity for all stages of construction, including project lay-down areas and assembly.[73] Another is grid connection and access, for which a new, multistate offshore grid or connection point could be established to facilitate the onshoring of wind power.[74] Since these projects fall in the jurisdiction of the Bureau of Ocean Energy Management, there are also leasing, permitting, and regulatory (federal, state, local) challenges. Addressing these issues will help to accelerate adoption of offshore wind in the United States.

Although the US market is only emerging, offshore wind is a proven technology that has been used in Europe for decades. The first offshore wind farm was constructed in Denmark in 1991. By 2019, the global installed capacity for offshore wind had reached nearly 30 GW. The potential of global offshore wind is significant, more than 420,000 TWh of power generation annually, which is more than eighteen times worldwide electricity demand.[75] Europe has been a global leader in both technology development and commercialization, and favorable policies have paved the way for the EU leadership in cumulative offshore wind capacity. However, China has emerged more recently as the leader in new capacity additions in 2018 and 2019. Industry analysts see the Asia-Pacific region as a driver of significant global growth through 2030. The Global Wind Energy Council (GWEC) predicts that 234 GW of offshore wind capacity will come online by 2030.[76]

Floating wind projects are quickly increasing in number worldwide, particularly in European and Chinese waters. The first floating wind plant was installed off the coast of Scotland—the Hywind Offshore Wind Farm—and became operational in 2017. Yet by 2019, 84 MW of capacity had been installed off the coasts of Europe and China and more than 3,000 MW of new capacity was planned in twelve countries with target commercial operation dates of 2025 or sooner.[77] Benefiting from economies of scale as well as technology development on the fixed-bottom side, the global cost of floating wind is quickly declining. In 2019, the LCOE ranged between $100 and $175/MWh. By 2032, industry analysts estimate that the LCOE will drop to $60/MWh, approaching today's LCOE for onshore wind plants and directly competing with fossil-fueled plants.[78]

GWEC projects that more than 200 GW of new wind capacity will be added worldwide through 2030.[79] The International Renewable Energy Agency (IRENA) estimates that wind energy (onshore and offshore) could represent as much as 35 percent of generation by 2050 if countries remain committed to goals set forth in the Paris agreement.[80] In the United States, DOE suggests that wind energy has the potential to provide 20 percent of electricity generation by 2030 and 35 percent by 2050, if costs continue to decline.[81] Efforts under way to improve technology efficiency as well as greater accessibility to wind resources will continue to drive down the cost of wind energy. New onshore wind power plants are already cheaper to build and operate than natural gas in the United States and in many parts of the world. Investments being made into offshore technologies and early projects that provide experience in siting, permitting, and grid integration will help to drive down the costs of offshore wind, accelerating the timeline for commercialization and helping to boost the global wind energy share of electricity generation. Wind will continue to serve as a leading generator of renewable electricity, particularly in regions where siting is most favorable.

SOLAR: FROM EMERGING TECHNOLOGY TO DISRUPTOR

Solar holds possibly the most disruptive potential for the electric utility sector. Solar technology research dates back to the 1800s, but the biggest breakthrough came in 1954 when US-based Bell Laboratories scientists Daryl Chapin, Calvin Fuller, and Gerald Pearson developed the first photovoltaic solar cell capable of powering equipment. The first-generation silicon solar cell came with a conversion (sunlight to electricity) efficiency of 4 percent. Bell Laboratories would improve on this efficiency, claiming 11 percent in lab conditions.

Over the next fifteen years, R&D efforts by Hoffman Electronics resulted in improvements in solar cell efficiency up to 14 percent. NASA served as a very important first customer and funder of the technology. During the 1960s, arrays were installed on several satellites, including Vanguard I, Explorer III, Vanguard II, Explorer VI and Explorer VII. NASA also installed solar arrays on the first Orbiting Astronomical Observatory, launched in 1966.[82] Yet solar photovoltaic (PV) technologies were still too costly for commercialization.

The door opened for solar commercialization in 1970, when Dr. Elliot Bergman introduced a lower-cost solar cell, using low-grade silicon and cheaper housings, which came at a price of $20 per watt (compared to $100 per watt).[83] Through the National Energy Act, solar would receive its first feed-in tariff before the end of the decade.[84] The discovery of thin film solar cells provided yet another breakthrough in technology in 1980. Thin film offered flexibility and versatility in applications, along with the improvement of solar cell efficiency to 32 percent. Ten years later, the first photovoltaic system was connected to the electric grid in Kerman, California, by Pacific Gas & Electric. Solar had gone from demonstration project to commercially viable technology.

Yet investors were still hesitant to invest in solar at the utility scale. The 2009 Recovery Act under President Obama provided early investment funding needed for solar companies to get off the ground. DOE issued $4.6 billion in guaranteed loans to build the first five utility-scale solar plants in the United States. The first to receive a DOE-guaranteed loan of more than $500 million, Solyndra, promised solar modules more expensive than polysilicon but less expensive to install. With polysilicon prices rising the company appeared to be a good investment. Yet due to the decline of polysilicon prices created largely by entry of cheaper Asian solar cells and modules, higher than anticipated installation costs, and poor management of the company overall in 2011, the company filed for bankruptcy. Such entrepreneurial failures are not unheard of, but using taxpayer money to cover these losses politicized the failure and led to condemnation of the entire clean energy sector, threatening to derail clean energy initiatives. Yet despite Solyndra and a few other defaults, the DOE loan program portfolio, which includes wind and other alternative energy investments, began to show profits of $30 million by 2014. The estimated loss ratio on DOE's loan program portfolio was 2 percent of total commitments, which is better than most venture capital firms.[85] Even though the Solyndra scandal received a lot of negative attention in the media overall, the program was a success in helping to catalyze innovation and scale commercialization.

That same year, DOE's SunShot Initiative was launched, which set forth an aggressive mission: to reduce solar costs by 75 percent by 2020 for residential, commercial, and utility-scale solar. To reach this goal, DOE invested in the development of innovative, early-stage technologies aimed at lowering costs and improving reliability and efficiency on the grid. By 2016 there were twenty-eight utility-scale solar plants (larger than 100 MW) in the United States and the cost to build utility-scale plants had fallen by nearly 60 percent since 2008.[86] In 2017, three years ahead of schedule, DOE met the utility-scale-grade solar LCOE target of $0.06/kWh. Residential and commercial solar prices dropped from $0.52/kWh to $0.16/kWh and $0.40/kWh to $0.11/kWh, respectively.[87] DOE has since set new 2030 goals that focus on driving down the cost of utility-scale solar by another 50 percent and cut the cost of concentrated solar power to $0.05/kWh for baseload plants to help address concerns about grid integration and storage.[88]

Over the last decade, solar has seen an average annual growth rate of 49 percent, and cumulative capacity grew to more than 85 GW by 2019.[89] In 2016, solar surpassed all other energy sources for additions of new generating capacity for the first time and has ranked first or second since.[90] In 2019, solar represented 40 percent of all new capacity added in the United States.[91] Globally, there has been a similar growth curve for solar installations. According to data provided by the World Energy Council, solar capacity in 2008 was 14.5 GW, with 71 percent attributed to Europe. By the end of 2015, total capacity had reached 227 GW, with leadership shifting to Asia.[92] Today, solar is leading renewables in new capacity growth worldwide. In 2019, renewables added 72 percent of net new capacity, with solar PV representing 55 percent of that capacity.[93]

Utility-scale solar is now competitive with fossil fuels. According to the Lazard LCOE Analysis, utility-scale solar LCOE ranges from $32 to $44/MWh. In comparison, the LCOE for a gas combined cycle plant is $44 to $68/MWh.[94] Since 2009, utility-scale LCOE has decreased by 89 percent, even without subsidies, due largely to declines in system component pricing.[95] Lazard estimates the capital cost of a solar PV-crystalline utility-scale plant to overlap the LCOE for a gas combined cycle plant.[96] As a result of lower installation prices and increasing panel efficiencies, levelized PPA prices for utility-scale PV fell by $20 to $30/MWh each year between 2006 and 2012 and continued to decline. [97] In 2019, most PPAs in the United States fell below $40/MWh, with some projects priced as low as $20/MWh.[98] In comparison, in 2011, PPA prices were well over $100/MWh.[99]

Cost-competitive modules coming out of China were behind these price drops, putting large-scale US solar PV manufacturing out of business. China's rise to the top started in the 1990s when Germany, overwhelmed by demand spurred by government incentives to promote rooftop solar, provided the capital, technology, and expertise to China to meet this demand. Supported by government investment in expanding solar manufacturing and low-cost solar materials, China created a worldwide glut, which it addressed through its own feed-in tariff program generating high demand domestically. China became the world leader in solar module manufacturing, essentially setting the price worldwide and making it difficult for US manufacturers to compete.[100]

In 2017, US-based solar manufacturers Suniva and Solar World Americas requested an investigation into the undercutting of silicon PV solar cell and module prices by Chinese manufacturers. The Section 201 case brought to the International Trade Commission requested a $.25 per watt tariff on cells and $.32 per watt tariff on modules plus a $.74 per watt import minimum. In November, the commission recommended a tariff of 35 percent to the Trump administration. In January 2018, the administration approved a 30 percent tariff, which would gradually decline to 15 percent by year four. Each year, the first 2.5 GW of imported cells will be excluded from the tariff. A tariff on imported solar cells and modules will increase capital costs and possibly halt projects awaiting financing, slowing construction and eliminating solar jobs in the United States. Impacts of the US tariff are expected to slow development in the short term, affecting utility-scale projects more than rooftop applications, but won't derail the growth of solar according to industry sources. Rapidly increasing global demand, largely due to supportive government regulation and incentives, will continue to push volume, decreasing price and making solar the most cost-effective solution for new capacity.

Industry rankings of the top ten global solar module manufacturers since 2010 reveal two things: (1) Asia, with China leading, is dominating the market, and (2) competition has been fierce, but consolidation could be on the horizon

(Figure 2.3). Between 2010 and 2015, the leaderboard changed every year, with some top manufacturers claiming bankruptcy.[101] However, the top five manufacturer rankings have not changed much since 2015, and the share of global shipments represented by the top ten companies is growing.[102] In 2018, the share of shipments was estimated at 63 percent and is projected to be more than 70 percent in 2020.[103] Asia has continued to dominate; in 2019, eight out of the top ten manufacturers were based in China.[104] Analysts predict that the top ten companies will continue to hold their positions in ranking and China will continue to dominate solar manufacturing, at least for the near future. Potential disruption could come from shifts in technology as the industry looks to go from commodity to higher-quality-performance products.

The predicted long-term growth of solar has not escaped the major oil and gas companies. In the last five years, traditional fossil-fuel players have started to invest in renewables, largely through acquisitions.[105] In December 2017, BP announced purchase of a 43 percent share in Lightsource Renewable Energy, Europe's biggest solar developer.[106] Two years later, Lightsource had expanded its business from five to thirteen countries.[107] In 2016, Royal Dutch Shell announced a $1 billion per year investment in clean energy through 2020.[108] Still others, like US-based ExxonMobil, are focusing on achieving GHG reductions through focused investment in CCUS technologies. While these clean energy announcements are getting headlines, the investment in capital projects by these large companies outside of their core fossil-fuel business is still less than 1 percent of total investments.[109]

Today, crystalline silicon (c-Si) is the most commonly used solar cell in commercialized solar panels. In 2020, c-Si cells represented 95 percent of global production.[110] There are two types of c-Si solar cell technologies available commercially: mono- and multi-c-Si. Mono-c-Si cells are cut from a single source of silicon, resulting in a slightly higher efficiency and cost compared to multi-c-Si cells, which are a blend of multiple silicon sources. High volumes and low-price multi-c-Si cells have created a commodity market for PV modules. This has helped to drive down prices. Cell efficiencies (that is, the portion of sun energy that is converted into electricity) in the laboratory have improved from 14 percent in 1960 to 26 percent and 22 percent in 2019 for mono- and multi-c-Si cells, respectively.[111] With the theoretical efficiency level for silicon cells at 32 percent, further improvements are likely.[112]

The challenge with solar cells is finding materials that are low cost, abundant, reliable, and tunable (with the ability to adjust frequency to maximize

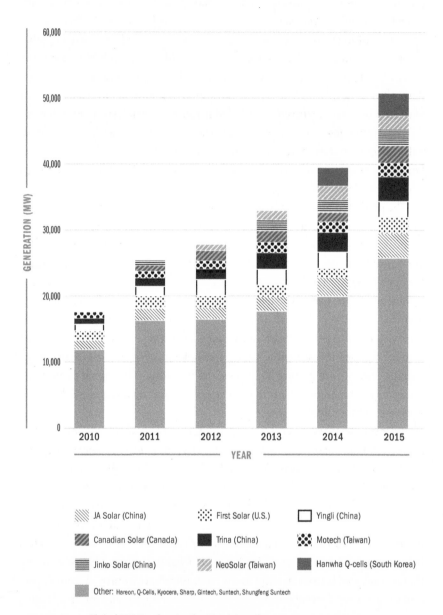

FIGURE 2.3 Global PV Production by Top Manufacturers, 2000–2015

Source: Paula Mints, "2015 Top Ten PV Cell Manufacturers," Renewable Energy World, April 8, 2016

absorption), and that yield high efficiencies. There are no solar cells commercially available yet that offer all these characteristics, but this is where researchers are focused. While the currently popular c-Si benefits from maturity, reliability, efficiency, and abundance of raw material (silicon) there are challenges in low defect-tolerance, which requires high levels of purity in manufacturing.

Efforts are under way to explore other solar cell technologies that will surpass the performance of c-Si cells. Multijunction III-V solar cells use multiple bandgaps that can be tuned to absorb specific regions of the solar spectrum and have demonstrated efficiencies in the laboratory of 45 percent and higher. However, they are costly and difficult to manufacturer, and have so far been reserved for space exploration.[113] Thin film solar cells such as cadmium telluride (CdTe) and copper indium gallium diselenide are reaching laboratory efficiencies close to silicon and are less costly and easier to manufacturer. For CdTe cells specifically, efficiency has jumped from 9 percent to 19 percent in just ten years.[114] Scientists are continuing to look for ways to boost efficiencies, and industry analysts predict future growth for this technology. In 2019, thin film solar cells represented about 5 percent of global production, with CdTe leading the way.[115]

The most encouraging development in thin film R&D came in 2020, when NREL revealed research that suggests the theoretical efficiency of perovskite thin film cells could match that of natural gas plants. Perovskite cells are made up of layers of materials that are printed, coated, or vacuum-deposited on a substrate. Like CdTe, efficiency improvements over the last ten years have been impressive; from 3 percent in 2009 to 24 percent in 2019.[116] However, DOE's Oak Ridge National Laboratory in 2020 revealed a proposed design that could reach an efficiency of 66 percent by reducing energy loss due to heat in current cell designs.[117] The efficiency of a natural gas plant is 60 percent. This super-efficient perovskite cell is far from commercialization, but if scientists are successful in producing a high-performance, low-cost solar cell it could mean the end to fossil-fuel electricity generation.

In addition to solar cell efficiency, energy production of a solar system also depends on mounting of the panels. Fixed panels, while the least expensive to install, are not able to be adjusted to respond to the angle of the sun, which changes depending on season and time of day. Adjustable panels provide flexibility to adjust the angle throughout the year, producing as much as 25 percent more energy compared to fixed arrays. Tracking panels automatically adjust to maximize the energy produced following the sun's movement and producing 30 percent more energy, but they come with a high cost.[118]

Market analysts are predicting significant growth in tracker installations, in the United States and globally. According to Wood Mackenzie, the global tracker market will experience a 45 percent increase in installations between 2020 and 2025.[119] More recent product introductions focus on designs that hold up in more challenging conditions (terrain and weather). These products will undoubtedly give a boost to the solar industry as flat parcel availability begins to challenge further expansion. As solar module prices decline and tracker volume grows, costs are falling. According to NREL, the cost for a utility-scale one-axis tracking system fell 80 percent between 2010 and 2018; from $5.52/watt to $1.13/watt (LCOE).[120]

Another opportunity is the continued development of solar installations on residential and commercial properties. Residential solar is benefiting from dropping solar module costs (Figure 2.4). In 2010, residential solar installations averaged $40,000; today, they cost roughly $20,000.[121] Further, with emerging community solar developments, residential solar is reaching customers who wouldn't otherwise have access to clean, affordable energy. Forward-thinking companies like Tesla are looking to incorporate solar into roofing products. Today, the cost of a Tesla solar roof is significantly higher than installing traditional solar panels but when packaged with the offer of on-site battery storage and an electric vehicle it offers homeowners the unique opportunity to be less dependent on the grid.

In the United States, solar is poised for significant growth, even with the stepping down of tax credits. Wood Mackenzie estimates that between 2021 and 2025, more than 100 GW of solar will be installed in the United States, which is 42 percent more than the previous five years.[122] Overall, the renewable share of electricity generation is projected to grow from 18 percent in 2018 to 38 percent by 2050; while wind's share of this growth slows over time, solar is projected to grow from 13 percent to 46 percent.[123] Globally, solar is the fastest-growing renewable energy source and is expected to continue leading renewable energy growth in the future. By 2024, renewables are projected to increase 50 percent by 2024, with solar PV representing 60 percent of this growth.[124] By 2050, renewables will represent nearly 50 percent of global electricity generation, again with solar in the lead.[125]

In several climate-favorable regions, utility-scale solar is at grid parity with other energy sources without financial incentives. While a dominant technology

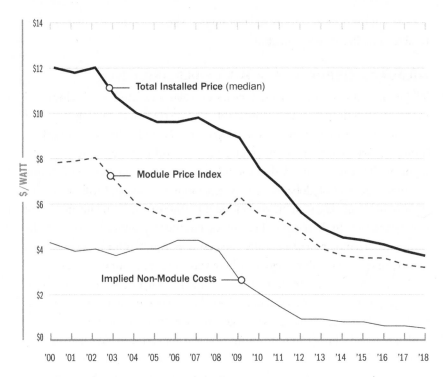

FIGURE 2.4   Installed Price of Residential Solar Panels, 2000–2018

Source: LBNL, "Tracking the Sun: Pricing and Design Trends for Distributed Photovoltaic Systems in the United States," October 2019

has emerged in multi-c-Si cells, there continues to be a focused effort on increasing cell efficiency and lowering manufacturing costs that will play out in the years to come. These technology improvements coupled with increasing volumes will continue to drive down solar panel costs and help to accelerate adoption. There are reasons to be optimistic that solar will be the lowest-cost source of electricity in most instances in the near future. However, though the future is bright for solar, as with wind, the challenge of intermittency presents a significant barrier to widespread adoption.

While the price of solar cells and installations continues to come down, a true apples-to-apples comparison needs to address the massive requirements for energy storage that are required to make solar preferable at wide scale. Given intermittency, there needs to be substantial investment in storage to meet the variable demands for electricity over the course of the day that do not necessarily, or likely, line up with the production of electricity by solar. Without concurrent innovations in storage technology, such as batteries, solar will not be able to realize its full potential.

WILDCARD DISRUPTORS: A MIX OF OLD AND NEW

While most attention justifiably focuses on solar and wind, researchers and innovators continue to pursue other potential disruptive technologies. Other low-carbon technologies such as wave, geothermal, and biomass energy show promise, particularly in specific regions of the world conducive to the technologies. These renewables have experienced slow growth to date, representing less than 3 percent of global electricity generation in 2019, and will likely continue to be small players in the generation mix. There is an abundant amount of energy available in these natural resources, but the technologies have yet to be commercialized on a massive scale. The best opportunities for these technologies are likely serving those regions where wind and solar siting is unfavorable.

Interestingly, there are efforts to revive and grow hydroelectric production by emphasizing "small-scale" dams. More than 90 percent of existing dams in the United States aren't being used to generate electricity and could generate 12 GW of new hydropower by retrofitting.[126] When compared to large hydropower plants, small-scale plants are less disruptive to the environment and less costly to build. Most small hydropower plants use a run-of-river approach, where water is diverted to pass through turbines and then returned downstream. In Canada, where large hydropower already provides 60 percent of electricity, run-of-river has found a niche in remote areas, where diesel generators have historically provided electricity. In some applications, run-of-river is close to competing with the cost/kWh of large hydropower plants.[127] After building five of the ten largest plants in the world, China is also looking to small hydropower, citing challenges in siting new prospects and competition from cheaper renewables.[128] Small hydropower is not a new concept to China; one-third of its hydropower generation is classified as small, or less than 50 MW.[129] More recently, the China National Energy Administration has imposed bans on some small hydropower projects due to environmental concerns.[130]

On the nuclear energy front, small modular reactors (SMRs) show promise. SMRs are defined by the World Nuclear Association as "nuclear reactors generally 300MWe equivalent or less, designed with modular technology using module factory fabrication, pursuing economies of series production and short construction times."[131] To compare, larger nuclear reactors scale up to 1,600 MWe. SMRs offer significantly lower capital costs, shorter construction times, and greater flexibility for future expansion, providing utilities the ability to quickly scale and supporting the overall trend toward a more decentralized grid.[132] These smaller reactors would also make it easier to protect the materials and the surrounding community in case of an accident and could be assembled at the factory. As of 2020, there were five SMRs in operation worldwide and seventeen under construction or near deployment, with the United States, China, and Canada dedicating significant funding to further developing the technology.[133]

The ultimate disruptive technology is nuclear fusion. Fusion research dates back to the 1970s and utilizes hydrogen isotopes deuterium and tritium to offer four times the energy of traditional uranium fission.[134] With regard to electricity generation, fusion is challenged by the need to heat the fuel to high temperatures and confine it long enough to allow not only for the initial ignition to happen but also for sustained reactions needed to take place to produce energy. Another challenge is that fusion has a lower energy density than fission (that is, gas versus solid fuel) and therefore fusion plants would need to be bigger to meet the same generation as uranium fission plants. For an industry already facing the challenge of new construction being cost-prohibitive, this will be a barrier to commercialization.

THE UPSHOT: DECARBONIZED ELECTRICITY IS POSSIBLE, BUT WILL REQUIRE INVESTMENT

Decarbonization in electricity generation will require a major disruption in current generation practices. While such a disruption may seem unlikely, it would not be the first major disruption for the electric utility industry. The first was in 1910, when coal surpassed traditional biofuels as the primary feedstock for global energy production, serving as a leader for close to a hundred years. Things began to change in 2000 when improvements in fracking shifted the pendulum away from coal to natural gas.[135] Most exciting, these shifts happen relatively quickly once the economics align. In the simplest terms, electric utilities will shift to whatever technology generates electricity at the lowest cost.

For these reasons, we believe renewables, led by wind and solar, will likely grow to dominate the electric utility sector in the coming years. Hydropower and nuclear energy will play supporting roles but face challenges as facilities age. Small-scale generation solutions in hydro and nuclear hold promise but are still far from widespread commercialization. Natural gas will continue to be a vital part of the new-generation mix but will find it difficult to compete longer term with renewables as capital and installation costs come down for wind and solar, even under a low-price gas scenario. Low natural gas pricing is putting coal out of business. Coal will not be able to compete with natural gas or renewables in the emerging clean energy economy.

Wind and solar technologies are quickly moving up the technology S-curve.[136] Wind is more mature and is cost-effective in comparison with fossil fuels today when considering capital, installation, and operation costs over the lifetime of the asset. Yet there is still room to improve. R&D efforts continue, aimed at improving turbine efficiencies and expanding wind into less optimal climates. Offshore wind offers significant capacity not yet tapped by the United States, and in Europe, prices are starting to compete with onshore wind. Exciting new offshore designs are emerging that could open up shorelines once commercialized.

Solar competes with wind in terms of market development. Today, c-Si dominates the solar cell market, but new more efficient technologies that begin to challenge fossil fuels on price and performance are on the horizon. There has been continued turnover in competition, as rankings in the top ten manufacturers shift and China comes to dominate the manufacturing market. Today, solar is cost competitive in favorable climates. As efficiencies improve and costs decline, solar will become the cheaper option in residential, commercial, and utility-scale applications. Analysts predict that solar will lead renewables into the clean energy future. Yet solar can't do it alone and needs the partnership of wind and storage technologies to grow.

Natural gas will continue to have an impact on renewable sources, with low prices forcing coal plants to retire, and will serve as a direct competitor to renewables for new capacity. Many countries, including the United States, see natural gas as a clean alternative to coal and as a key component of their future generation portfolios. Ironically, with lower demand for coal, the price of coal may drop and become more competitive with natural gas. Critical are the drivers of future natural gas prices. Innovations, such as occurred in the fracking of shale gas, could potentially increase supply and lower gas prices further. On the other hand, wars and embargos can limit supply and raise global oil and gas prices. For these reasons, the US Department of Defense is investing in renewables to build resilience to global disruptions.

With countries such as China and India still building coal plants to keep up with rising demand in consumption and natural gas capacity continuing to grow due to low pricing, decarbonization will take time. Globally, coal still represents the largest share of the generation market—37 percent in 2020[137]—driven largely by China. In 2016, the country announced plans to scale back new coal power plant construction, citing concerns around air pollution; however, since then, construction of new coal plants has continued in earnest. In India, coal power plants generate 72 percent of electricity.[138] While the rest of the world retired 1.8 GW of coal generation from 2018 to 2019, China added 42.9 GW of new coal generation capacity.[139] In India, coal represented 44 percent of new capacity additions in 2019.[140]

Yet the trajectory of renewables, specifically solar and wind, suggests they could become the dominant low-cost technology in the near future, giving us hope for a decarbonized electrical sector. We are already seeing the shift happen in the United States and Europe. Even in China and India, low-cost renewables are challenging coal for market share. According to EIA estimates, wind and solar will represent 42 percent and 50 percent of generation by 2050 in China and India, respectively.[141] The challenge in these markets, however, lies in the fact that renewables alone won't be able to meet projected demand so coal with continue to play a significant role, albeit a smaller share of the mix.

Overall, wind and solar are growing at a rapid pace but will hit a market penetration ceiling if issues around intermittency and distributed generation are not addressed. Intermittency requires means for storing renewable energy when it exceeds demand and then deploying the electrons onto the grid during times when supply is limited, such as cloudy days. Battery storage technologies are following a trajectory similar to that of solar in both performance and cost improvements, and in some cases are already directly competing with natural gas plants for peak generation. Lithium-ion (Li-ion) batteries have emerged as an early leader, benefiting greatly from R&D efforts in the automobile industry. However, the technology faces cost barriers and potential technical limits with regard to scaling as well as material supply and waste disposal concerns. As with automobiles, there could be an opportunity for hydrogen and fuel cells in this sector, but these technologies are still nascent.

Yet even with cost-effective storage, the grid itself needs to be nimble and flexible to handle distributed generation and storage on a massive scale. A modern grid is needed but what defines "modernization" is still being debated. Grid edge technologies are being introduced to enable two-way communication and to process potentially billions of energy transactions. Standardization of communications on the grid and between smart products is critical to ensuring a shared "language." Data analytics and artificial intelligence hold promise for enhancing grid reliability and functioning. Blockchain and currency tracking technologies may allow customers to more effectively trade "green electrons." A national grid that connects regional grids could further facilitate access and energy trading. While the cost for renewable "fuel" is essentially zero, transmission and distribution costs can be substantial and cost prohibitive without a more connected and modernized grid. While the future of wind and solar looks bright, grid modernization could be perhaps the biggest roadblock to their speedy adoption.

Fortunately, disruption is not only happening with generation technologies but also in the way electricity is distributed. In the United States and abroad, commitments to reducing carbon footprints being made by large and influential companies are driving demand for wind and solar. Major technology companies, such as Facebook and Amazon, are requiring that renewable energy be part of bids presented for perspective new construction locations.[142] Companies are joining together under the Renewable Energy Buyers Alliance to create a large pool of demand and connecting this demand to renewable energy sources. More progressive electric utilities are moving ahead with plans to expand renewable capacities and invest in grid solutions in response to increasing corporate and consumer demand. Micro and remote grids are forming around the world, bypassing the need for utilities completely. Utilities that fail to shift their business models to a service-based approach may be left out.

At the end of the day, the ability to scale renewables will depend heavily on an electric grid that can handle two-way communication and vast amounts of distributed resources and data, all while ensuring the lights stay on. Intermittency is a serious issue—the sun doesn't always shine and the wind doesn't always blow. To complete a clean energy transition will require substantial changes to electrical infrastructure that facilitate transmission and storage in a highly distributed network. The time it takes to build out such a new energy grid will determine how quickly the electric utility industry can decarbonize.

HOW CAN WE DECARBONIZE ENERGY BY 2050?

So how can we accelerate a global transformation to a clean energy future? Many countries are moving forward with ambitious clean energy plans, and renewables are benefiting from these plans. Demand for renewables in China is driving the growing global market and is expected to continue doing so. Between 2019 and 2024, IEA projects that China will represent 40 percent of total renewable energy capacity expansion over that time period.[143] China, Europe, and the United States will represent roughly 70 percent of renewables growth in 2020 and 2021.[144] In the US, federal government investment in R&D and tax credits have helped to accelerate commercialization of wind and solar technologies. Today, even without subsidies, these technologies are cost competitive with fossil fuels in many applications. Incentives are helpful in the short run but are likely to be phased out over time as wind, solar, and storage are expected to be cost competitive without them. In the US, in lieu of federal government standards, state renewable portfolio standards have created a demand for renewables nationwide. Many states have goals of 25 percent or greater renewables generation share within the next ten years. Federal government incentives help accelerate these dynamics, but increasingly are becoming less critical to the success of renewables.

That being said, federal actions aimed at subsidizing fossil fuels could slow down progress. In 2017, former DOE Secretary Rick Perry, citing resilience, asked FERC to issue a rule that power plants that keep a ninety-day supply of fuel on site receive subsidies. FERC denied that request and instead opted to work with independent system operators (ISOs) and regional transmission organizations (RTOs) on identifying needs for ensuring a reliable and resilient electric grid moving forward. ISOs and RTOs coordinate, monitor, and control the operation of the electric grid. Solar tariffs, positioned as a method to save US solar manufacturing, will have little impact on US global competitiveness and will cause delays in new construction as the price of imported solar panels rises. Ironically, tariffs may destroy more US jobs than they create, as most US jobs in renewables are in the construction and installation of solar projects. For renewables, federal government intervention may be more of a hindrance than an accelerant under proposed tariff rules.

Ultimately, the speed in which we can decarbonize the electric utility industry will depend on several factors. Central is how to continue to accelerate the adoption of renewable solar and wind. Other clean energy sources, namely nuclear and hydroelectric power, will continue to play a role in decarbonization but require further innovation to expand further and directly compete for new capacity. In the following, we highlight eight broad policy initiatives that may accelerate adoption of wind and solar: pricing carbon, raising the price of natural gas, regulating utilities, extending tax incentives, investing in storage, modernizing the grid, securing abundant supply, and innovating renewables.

Price Carbon

By far the most common response from environmental economists and policy makers is to put a price on greenhouse gas emissions. Creating a market in which companies buy and sell greenhouse gas emission permits and credits or, alternatively, simply taxing emissions, would facilitate greater adoption of renewables by raising the price of alternatives. This pay-to-pollute approach encourages electric utilities to explore new, clean technologies and favors renewable energy sources by offsetting capital investments.

One approach to price carbon is what is called "cap and trade" in which a cap on overall emissions is set and then generators trade permits to emit up to that cap. There are two such programs currently operating in the United States, along the East Coast and in California. The Regional Greenhouse Gas Initiative (RGGI) is jointly operated by Connecticut, Delaware, Maine, Maryland, Massachusetts, New Hampshire, New York, Rhode Island, Vermont, and Virginia. Started in 2009, RGGI covers CO_2 emissions from fossil-fuel power plants 25 MW or larger. A cap is established covering the RGGI region, and covered plants must obtain an allowance for each ton of CO_2 emitted annually. Plants comply by purchasing allowances at auction in the form of purchasing allowances from other generators in the region that have excess, or financially supporting offset projects.[145] Since the launch of RGGI, CO_2 emissions from RGGI power plants have fallen 47 percent, according to a report published in 2019 by the Acadia Center.[146] At the end of 2017, the RGGI states committed to another 30 percent reduction in CO_2 emissions beyond its initial 2020 cap, through 2030.[147]

California's cap-and-trade system is broader in scope, covering power plants, industrial facilities, and fuel distributors that emit twenty-five thousand metric tons or more of CO_2-equivalent. In addition to selling at auction, California also provides some allowances for free, though that will phase out over time. The program has received some criticism over the years regarding its performance. However, it's difficult to dispute the more than $600 million per auction that the state has generated in the last two years for a host of climate projects, including electric vehicle rebates, land preservation, and high-speed rail.[148] California's EPA has suggested potential changes to the program to make it more resilient to economic stress in response to a less than stellar May 2020 auction that brought in just $25 million.[149]

Similar carbon trading schemes have been launched by forty countries or jurisdictions around the world, including Europe, South Korea, Canada, Mexico, Argentina, Australia, and Japan. The EU trading program was the first to market with a carbon pricing program and has benefited from time, learning from early mistakes. Initially after its launch in 2005, prices soared between 2006 and 2008 only to then plunge 90 percent following the global recession. Since 2009, a surplus of allowances has grown and the government responded by postponing the auction of nine hundred million allowances until 2019–2020.[150] In January 2019, a market stability reserve was created to address the surplus but also to improve the system's resilience to market shocks, adjusting allowance supply as needed to keep the balance. After a decade of low pricing and concern about the program's future, carbon prices in the EU for the first time surpassed $20/ton. With exception of the early part of 2020, the price has stayed above $20 and by March 2021 was approaching $40/ton.[151] This is encouraging but it is still well below the price needed to achieve the Paris climate goals.

The World Bank estimates that carbon pricing needs to be between $40 and $80/ton by 2020 and between $50 and $100/ton by 2030 to achieve the Paris goals.[152] In 2020, more than half of the emissions covered by various trading programs reported prices of $10/ton or less.[153] Overall, prices varied widely from $1/ton to $119/ton. The addition of a Chinese cap-and-trade market could have a significant impact on climate change. Plans are under way to launch a national cap-and-trade program after running pilot programs in several provinces across the country. The emissions trading scheme will initially cover coal and gas power plants, with allowances determined by generation output. Once established, the Chinese trading program will be the largest in the world and cover 25 to 30 percent of global emissions alone (according to the World Bank, just over 20 percent of global emissions are currently covered by carbon taxes or trading schemes).

National cap-and-trade legislation has been proposed in the United States several times without success. In 2020, a bill submitted by Sen. Chris Van Hollen (D-MD) and Rep. Don Beyer (D-VA-8), the Healthy Climate and Family Securities Act, proposes a cap-and-dividend approach under which the revenue generated at auction would be returned to US citizens, equally. To date, cap-and-trade bills have failed to get the bipartisan support needed to pass, even with the redistribution of revenue to the taxpayer, which was thought to make them more attractive.

Another approach to pricing carbon is to apply a carbon tax to GHG emissions, with companies charged a dollar amount for every ton of emissions produced. A carbon tax would provide greater certainty to investors through price stability that a cap and trade market cannot offer, given fluctuating pricing. The revenue collected through a carbon tax could be used by the federal government to further invest in clean technologies and supporting infrastructure, or it could be returned to taxpayers through a dividend check. While a cap and trade program allows for a clear setting of a national emissions reduction goal, a carbon tax provides less certainty. Over time, the tax amount may need to be raised to accelerate a reduction if not on track to meet predetermined climate goals.

According to the World Bank, thirty national governments have implemented, or plan to implement, a carbon tax.[154] In the United States, a national carbon tax has yet to be passed, although more recently there have been signs of bipartisan interest. There have been nine carbon tax bills introduced, most notably (1) the Climate Action Rebate Act of 2019 (CAR Act) by Sen. Chris Coons (D-DE) and Sen. Dianne Feinstein (D-CA) in the Senate, and by Rep. Jimmy Panetta (D-CA) in the House, (2) the Stemming Warming and Augmenting Pay Act (SWAP Act) by Rep. Francis Rooney (R-FL) and Rep. Dan Lipinski (D-IL) in the House, and (3) the Raise Wages, Cut Carbon Act of 2019 (RWCC Act) also introduced by Rooney and Lipinski.[155] All three of the bills impose an upstream tax that would increase over time and return the revenue to taxpayers, either through a monthly dividend or reduction in payroll taxes, providing greater benefits to those in lower income brackets. The bills also set carbon dioxide reduction goals, with the CAR Act proposing the most ambitious goal of 100 percent reduction by 2050.[156] However, like cap and trade, the likelihood of a carbon tax garnering bipartisan support under current US political conditions is slim, and it may come down to state action to move the needle.

Raise the Price of Natural Gas

The economic favorability of renewables such as wind and solar depends on their price relative to the next best alternative. Today, that alternative is natural gas. If natural gas prices rise, renewables become more attractive. If natural gas prices fall, renewables will find a more challenging marketplace. This is exactly what played out with coal. Low natural gas prices created a market in which coal plants just can't compete. In many cases, coal plants are retiring ahead of schedule, citing poor economics. This trend will continue under a low-cost natural gas scenario. However, raising natural gas prices will make gas-fired power plants less competitive with renewables, which are seeing rapidly declining construction costs and offer zero fuel costs. The same gas plants being constructed today could be retired early as natural gas prices increase over time.

To illustrate these dynamics, consider the oil embargo of 1973 that created shortages of oil and natural gas and caused prices to spike. The nation needed immediate access to new energy sources and coal was in the best position to supply those needs, with both deep reserves and the ability to scale production quickly. Over the next few years, coal's share of US electricity generation jumped from 46 percent to 56 percent.[157] In fact, of the coal capacity available today in the US, 36 percent of it was added during this decade.[158] This increased demand led to coal prices doubling between 1973 and 1975, and prices would stay high until the early 1980s.[159]

Meanwhile, natural gas reserves in the United States and abroad were drying up and so were company profits. Companies like Exxon and Chevron attempted to tap into shale gas but failed. Then in 1998, Mitchell Energy, which had been applying fracking techniques for years, provided a breakthrough with a new "slick water" fracturing technology that would prove to be profitable, opening up the Texas Barnett shale formation. By 2000, shale production had begun to ramp up, and new entrants made a play in the shale market. A flood of new companies entered shale gas production, and as a result, shale gas increased from 4 percent in 2005 of natural gas production share to 24 percent in 2012.[160] With increased supply, natural prices began to respond, falling below the price of coal in 2009 and staying there. By 2015, natural gas had surpassed coal as the leading energy source in the US.[161]

In a wholesale electricity market, low natural gas prices often set the price of electricity. In these markets, pricing is determined through an auction process designed to match supply with demand, starting with the least expensive resource. ISOs sort the generator bids from lowest to highest (that is, a supply stack), dispatching generation sources available until the demand is met with available capacity. Once demand is met, the marginal resource available in the supply stack to satisfy the next increment of energy demanded sets the price. The price for the marginal resource is given to all of the resources in the supply stack. Given their low cost to operate, wind and solar are dispatched first but often cannot meet the total demand; typically, natural gas is the next lowest cost resource and makes up the difference. If the natural gas plant is only partially dispatched then it sets the price. Natural gas plants provide grid operators the flexibility to ramp output up and down as needed to bridge the gap between renewables and total demand. Energy storage and demand response (increasing or decreasing customer loads throughout the day on the basis of renewable inputs) are promising replacements for natural gas plants. However, the cost to incorporate energy storage on the electric grid is higher than that to build a new natural gas power plant.

So how can policy makers raise the price of natural gas? One answer would be to put a price on the carbon emissions coming out of such plants as discussed above, but arguably anything that raises the price of natural gas will have a similar impact. One solution would be to more aggressively regulate the fracking of natural gas. Fracking not only creates greenhouse gas emissions but has localized impacts on waterways and pollution. Regulating the production of natural gas by reducing these harmful impacts on the local environment ultimately raises production costs and the price of natural gas. Of course, any rise in natural gas prices could end up also benefiting coal and keeping it in the US energy mix longer. However, with states mandating clean energy portfolios and utilities and major corporations already making the shift to renewables, it's hard to envision a significant shift back to coal.

Regulate Utilities

Beyond manipulating the price of alternatives, government can simply directly regulate the generation of electricity. The electric utility sector has long been affected by various government interventions to promote one technology or another. Government support for new technologies can come in several forms. For renewables, tighter environmental regulations on traditional energy sources, utility restructuring and deregulation, and tax incentives aimed at increasing market adoption of alternative energy sources have served as primary drivers.

Since the Clean Air Act of the 1970s, emission and safety standards have put pressure on coal plants now struggling to compete with natural gas and renewables. For example, EIA cites the 2015 EPA Mercury and Air Toxic Standards as the reason why 30 percent of coal plants retired in April of that year.[162] Coal's fate seemed to be sealed on August 3, 2015, when the EPA finalized the Clean Power Plan. For the first time, CO_2 emission performance rates were established for fossil-fuel electric steam-generating units and natural gas combined cycle units. While states had flexibility in the means in which to meet new standards, EIA estimated that switching from coal to natural gas-fired generation would be the "predominant compliance strategy."[163] In 2016, the Supreme Court issued an eighteen-month hold on the plan, which ended up being repealed by the Trump administration and replaced with the Affordable Clean Energy rule in June 2019. Critics claim that the new rule will result in an increase in GHG emissions and slow the transition to a low-carbon economy. In January 2021, the court decided that the Affordable Clean Energy rule was legally flawed and threw it out. While this was good news to environmentalists, it also meant that the Biden administration will have to start from square one to develop a new one.

States have long served as leaders in creating opportunities for wind and solar development through renewable portfolio standards (RPSs). RPSs require investor-owned utilities, and in some cases municipal utilities and cooperative utilities, to produce a targeted percentage of electricity from renewable sources. Currently, thirty states plus Washington, DC, have mandated renewable portfolio standards, or similar policies.[164] Most states use a percentage of retail sales metric and require between 10 and 45 percent renewable share; however, fourteen states have requirements of 50 percent or greater.[165] Over the past decade, RPSs have had a big impact on the growth of utility-scale renewables. According to Lawrence Berkeley National Laboratory, 45 percent of the renewable growth since 2000 has been required through RPS states.[166]

Several states have also adopted broader 100 percent clean electricity goals. At the end of 2019, thirteen states had committed to 100 percent clean electricity targets through either mandates or goals. Most of these states define clean electricity as renewables plus zero-energy sources, which includes nuclear energy. Target dates range between 2045 and 2050, with the exception of Washington, DC, which has a 2032 target date.

State action is encouraging but it does create a patchwork of requirements across the United States. A national clean energy standard would force otherwise lagging states to act to accelerate the clean energy shift and provide some consistency. There is interest on Capitol Hill for such a standard. In 2019, the Clean Energy Standard Act was introduced, which includes a goal of 100 percent clean energy by 2050. The Act is still in the first stage of the legislative process. In January 2020, the House Committee on Energy & Commerce released a legislative framework of the draft Climate Leadership and Environmental Action for our Nation's (CLEAN) Future Act that also includes a goal of 100 percent clean electricity. Unfortunately, a national clean energy standard has yet to receive bipartisan support. There does seem to be a recognition from some Republicans of the need to do something on climate; however, legislative action proposed to date falls short of setting such standards.

Deregulation has provided consumers with the power to choose where they get their energy from, and renewables have benefited from this market restructuring. The Energy Policy Act of 1992, intended to be an amendment to PURPA, created a new class of generators: exempt wholesale generators (EWGs). The Act allowed EWGs to engage in interstate wholesale electricity transitions without SEC oversight and removed restrictions on the price charged for wholesale.[167] The Act paved the way for deregulation of utilities in the United States, and by 1999, states such as California and Texas were starting to deregulate energy services. In regulated states, the generation, transmission, and distribution are owned by the utilities. Deregulation separates the energy supply from transmission and distribution, allowing consumers to choose from multiple energy providers. Deregulation has provided for the entry of independent power producers, including companies specializing in renewable energy. By 2020, thirty states were partially (electric, gas, or some combination of both) deregulated.[168] No state is 100 percent deregulated, though Texas is close at 85 percent consumer choice.[169]

Extend Tax Incentives

There is no question that tax incentives for renewables have supported their growth. In general, the energy sector is no stranger to government subsidies. According to one independent study, between 1950 and 2010, the US government provided more than $850 billion in energy subsidies, with 47 percent given as tax incentives followed by regulation and R&D at 19 percent and 18 percent, respectively.[170] The oil and gas sectors received the most financial support over this time period in the form of tax incentives, representing 80 percent of total funds allocated across the energy industry.[171]

Government investment in renewables increased significantly under the Obama administration. In 2009, the American Recovery and Reinvestment Act brought $90 billion in clean-energy investments and incentives to the market.[172] Most notably, the Act authorized a 30 percent tax credit for more than 180 advanced energy manufacturing projects; provided $25 million to fund more than 100,000 wind, solar, geothermal, and biomass projects; extended production tax credits for wind, geothermal, and hydroelectric generation; and boosted funds to DOE's guaranteed loan program for clean energy projects.[173] The Act also provided $10 billion to efforts to modernize the grid and ensure reliability.[174] The result has been a significant shift in the last ten years in federal subsidies away from fossil fuels and toward renewables. In 2017, 65 percent of federal energy tax incentives went to renewables while only 26 percent went to fossil fuels.[175]

Past subsidies for renewable energy have helped push wind and solar technologies down the learning curve, lowering costs and improving their economic attractiveness. However, the influence of such subsidies may be waning as costs come down dramatically for solar and wind, making them the potential low-cost option even in the absence of subsidies. With that said, extending incentives to grid integration solutions, such as solar plus storage and smart grid technologies, will accelerate broader adoption of wind and solar.

Invest in Storage

There is a growing consensus that a 100 percent renewable electric grid is possible—*but* only with the support of energy storage to address concerns around wind and solar intermittency. Industry estimates suggest that when solar and wind generation constitutes over 40 percent of total generation, there is a real risk of blackouts and brownouts without reliable storage solutions. Application is a key indicator of which energy storage solution will be more effective. Unlike generation, which has one purpose, storage offers multiple uses for "in front of the meter" and "behind the meter" applications.[176] Storage used for the former case is primarily deployed for frequency regulation. With the rise in intermittent renewables like wind and solar, there will be an increasing need for peaker plant replacement, transmission grid support, and distribution services. Storage deployed for "behind the meter" applications is more nascent, but increased ownership in electric vehicles is accelerating the growth trajectory.

Several storage technologies are vying for a place in the energy market. Some of the more commercially viable options are Li-ion batteries, flywheels, compressed air, and pumped hydro. Pumped-storage hydro stations have been in use for decades and currently represent 95 percent of US grid storage.[177] However, the price to build new stations is high and the time needed for construction is long. Mechanical energy storage systems such as flywheels (storing electricity as kinetic energy using a spinning rotor) and compressed air (heating and expanding compressed air stored underground to create electricity) hold promise but are also challenged by short duration (flywheels) and size of infrastructure (compressed air caverns). Each of these storage solutions has the potential to play a role in a decarbonized electric grid.

Today, Li-ion is the leader in storage deployment for short-term duration needs (one to four hours), representing more than 90 percent of the market.[178] Between 2013 and 2019, Li-ion prices dropped 73 percent. According to Lazard, the estimated LCOE for Li-ion chemistries that offer four-hour duration ranges from $132 to $245/MWh, unsubsidized.[179] Lazard estimates the LCOE for natural gas peaker plants is between $151 and $198/MWh.[180] Where energy storage really starts to compete is when it is paired with a PV system; the LCOE for PV plus energy storage is estimated to be between $81 and $140/MWh.[181]

Significant investment is going toward commercializing other long-term duration solutions. Hydrogen is emerging as an energy storage technology of interest. It has the highest energy content of any fuel and its stable chemistry means you can store energy longer. The idea is to use excess electricity generated by wind and solar to make hydrogen, through electrolysis, and then use that hydrogen to store and deploy electricity when needed. According to NREL, hydrogen storage of more than one-week duration could be cost-effective in the near future if capital costs decline and long-term storage is compensated for its contribution to a more reliable electric grid.[182] Utility-scale hydrogen storage is still in the R&D phase, but there is some excitement around a potential "hydrogen economy," in which a network of solutions is created by demand in other industries (for example, fuel cell vehicles, manufacturing processes) that could quickly bring down the cost of hydrogen storage.

In the United States, there have been efforts to extend tax incentives to energy storage, but so far these efforts have not resulted in any standalone storage incentives. Incentives for storage packaged with solar are available through the federal energy investment tax credit and have helped to accelerate the adoption of energy storage. However, there are limitations to what qualifies, and even with the incentives, the pairing is still quite expensive. Energy-storage-focused incentives aligned with cost and technologies available could speed deployment, and the economics are strong for these technologies longer term.

Natural gas peakers are not just bad for the environment, they are also a bad investment, as they are expensive to maintain and sit idle most of the time, only being called upon to address short periods of high demand (peaks). These are just a few of the many reasons that utilities are opting to choose energy storage over building new gas plants. Between 2013 and 2018, energy storage capacity grew from next to nothing to more than 300 MW of capacity.[183] In 2020, the US energy storage market was estimated to be 1.2 GW and is predicted to grow to 7 GW by 2025, driven by large-scale utility procurement.[184] Just how much energy storage do we need to support a completely decarbonized electric grid? NREL scientists estimate that at least 120 GW of energy storage would be needed across the United States to support an 80 percent renewable energy-powered system.[185]

Modernize the Grid

The intermittency that comes with wind and solar generation sources presents a challenge for an electric grid designed to dispatch base-load sources available twenty-four hours a day. As electricity generation becomes more distributed and the amount of renewable energy coming online grows, there is a critical need for a smarter, more nimble electricity grid. Renewable technologies will reach a generation ceiling without changes to grid infrastructure. At the core of grid modernization is the need for two-way communication, advanced metering, and responsive pricing. Consumer choice in the source of electricity delivered is complicating what used to be a simplified demand-supply decision made and controlled by the utility.

As the industry has been shifting away from a centralized-utility model, there has been an explosion of innovative activity at the grid edge. Digital technologies on the grid such as smart switches and sensors and artificial intelligence are providing the flexibility and system reliability needed to support the increase in distributed energy sources. Grid edge computing can provide predictive maintenance (detecting system anomalies and equipment failure), remote inspections, and cyber security in addition to providing real-time insight into the shifts in supply needed to manage the influx of multiple intermittent energy sources.

The electric grid as we know it today hasn't changed much since its inception. The purpose of the grid, and the driving motivation for utilities serving it, was to provide cheap, reliable access to electricity. Customers didn't ask for much more. New FERC orders created in the years that followed PURPA aimed to increase access to renewables, reduce grid congestion, provide incentives for energy storage, and ensure reliability. These orders facilitated the shift from centralized to more distributed generation. As states became deregulated, utilities were forced to step out of the generation business and focus on transmission and distribution services.

Choice in electricity source is changing the dynamics of the utility-customer relationship. Customers are looking for more customized services and holistic solutions from their energy suppliers. They want a cleaner energy mix and more specificity around source. Providing this level of specificity has required innovation in the way the industry tracks, buys, and sells electrons on the grid. Unless you are generating the electricity on-site, once the electrons are added to the grid, there is no way to identify them as "green." Renewable Energy Certificates (RECs), which track each MWh of renewable generation that can then be sold or traded to comply with renewable portfolios standards or support corporate claims of investment in clean energy, address this challenge. The REC and electricity delivered represent two different revenue streams, assigning social and environmental values to clean energy generation.

Each REC is assigned a unique identification number and tracked to avoid double counting. RECs are traded through a centralized clearinghouse (that is, a centralized ledger), which adds complexity, cost, and risk to the transaction process. Distributed ledger technologies (DLTs) are being explored, which offer an open-source database that operates across a computer network to authenticate and record transactions in real time, allowing for direct transactions between two parties and eliminating the need for centralized control. Instead of the current practice of each party in the transaction maintaining their own copy of the REC, DLTs encrypt the data and track an REC's full chain of custody, avoiding the need to reconcile across the parties. "Prosumers," or households that produce and consume electricity, might be able to benefit financially from such peer-to-peer trading systems. Community microgrids using peer-to-peer trading platforms are enabling prosumers to sell electricity, creating a distributed network of energy sources. How does the electric grid, and those operating and maintaining the balance needed to ensure reliability, respond to this level of distributed generation?

This is a work in progress. Organizations such as the Solar Electric Power Alliance are working to develop standards for distributed energy resource management systems, which will facilitate communications between these resources and utility systems. One of the biggest challenges is the reluctance of companies to join an open standard software platform, choosing proprietary solutions over industrywide collaboration. But the challenge goes even deeper: the traditional utility business model needs to change as well, from one that rewards revenue based on generation to one that rewards services while continuing to ensure reliability and security on the grid.

Grid modernization is in an era of ferment, and while the flurry of innovative activity in this space is promising, more progress is needed at a faster pace to provide the standardization and support needed for renewables to dominate the generation landscape.

Secure Abundant Supply

One challenge that may slow the growth of renewables is rising costs due to shortages of necessary components, such as rare earth elements in wind turbines and solar panels. These shortages may be caused by simple resource scarcity or global trade barriers. Trade barriers became an issue in 2011, when prices for rare earth metals spiked after China, which represented 98 percent of global production, restricted its exports. These restrictions were lifted by 2015, but in response, the industry began looking for other sources for rare earths and substitutes.[186] While new rare earth deposits have been found around the world, it can take a decade to create an extraction and processing supply chain that can compete with China. Rare earths, despite their name, are abundant; the challenge is extracting enough of the metals to make them economical. Industry and governments are looking at potential mitigation strategies regarding rare earths, ranging from reuse and recycling to material substitution and increased mine production.

Organizations such as the US DOE Ames Laboratory's Critical Materials Institute are leading research "on technologies that make better use of materials and eliminate the need for materials that are subject to supply disruptions."[187] Five specific rare earth elements have been identified by DOE as critical to clean energy development: dysprosium, terbium, europium, neodymium, and yttrium, as well as lithium and tellurium. The Institute is conducting research on potential substitutes for these elements. In 2020, the Institute announced $4 million in new projects that seek to "unlock domestic sources of cobalt, improve conversion of rare earth oxides to metal, and improve recovery of critical materials from Li-Ion batteries."[188] These projects were chosen with the hope of establishing a domestic supply chain.

For wind turbines, dysprosium and neodymium are used in in permanent magnets to produce high-performing generators.[189] For solar cells, silicon is abundant and widely available, and therefore not seen as a threat to further growth. However, some solar cell types do use rare earths and may be subject to shortages. One example is thin film, which uses indium and tellurium. Copper, used in many electronic controls and wiring, including wind and solar, could also be affected over the next twenty years, as demand for the metal increases along with demand for electric vehicles and other electronics.[190]

Battery energy storage also faces potential challenges with regard to the supply of cobalt and lithium. Cobalt, which can represent from 10 to 20 percent of the cost of lithium batteries, doubled in price in 2017, and suppliers are indicating shortages in existing stock, driven primarily by the rise in electric vehicle demand.[191] There is work under way in the electric vehicle industry to replace cobalt all together in new battery designs. This work should benefit energy storage. At the end of the day, the relative economic favorability of renewables versus alternatives like natural gas will depend on low-cost production, which itself requires an abundance of low-cost supply of materials, including the solar panels and wind turbines themselves. While the market may solve these sourcing issues on their own, governments can have an impact on the likelihood of supply disruptions and ease the diffusion of renewables.

Innovate Renewables

Of course, many of these interventions may be unnecessary if the costs of renewables and batteries continue their current trajectories. One could imagine a world by 2030 in which renewables in combination with battery storage are clearly the lowest-cost solutions for electrical generation. The quicker we can get there, the better, as transforming global electricity generation will take decades given that building out new capacity and retiring existing capacity will take time, especially as new coal and gas plants continue to be built around the world.

Of course, there are no guarantees that current technology trajectories in renewables and storage will be sustained. We need to continue concerted efforts to innovate solar, wind, and batteries technologies. While there is disagreement, some scientists believe that solar PV has the potential to mimic dynamics seen in the microprocessor industry commonly referred to as Moore's Law, after Intel founder Gordon Moore, who observed that microprocessor capacity doubled roughly every eighteen months. Such exponential improvements in sustainable technologies would benefit from investment by both the private and public sectors. Federal subsidies of R&D, sponsored university research, and corporations all have a role to play in continuing the impressive gains in renewables and storage.

In the end, as long as the wind blows and the sun shines, renewables seem poised to become increasingly attractive, decarbonizing the electric utility sector. It is simple economics—as renewables plus storage decrease in price, they will become the low-cost, and thus preferred, option for generating electricity. The question is how long will this technology transition take? Various institutional players can accelerate or hinder this disruption. Their choices are critical, and 2050 is looming ahead.

CHAPTER 3

THE TRANSPORTATION SECTOR

O THE AVERAGE PERSON, transportation is perhaps the most visible source of greenhouse gas emissions. Whether driving our own automobiles or observing trucks barreling down the road, we are constantly reminded of the environmental costs of our modern transportation infrastructure. Yet, surprising to some, the transportation sector accounts for only 14 percent of global greenhouse gas emissions[1] and 28 percent of US emissions.[2] Substantial for sure, but only one piece of the emissions pie. Yet decarbonize we must if we are to achieve our 2050 goal.

In the United States, close to 60 percent of transportation emissions come from light-duty vehicles such as automobiles and pick-up trucks. Another 23 percent comes from larger delivery vehicles and semis, 9 percent comes from aircraft, 3 percent from shipping and boats, and 2 percent from rail.[3] Similar breakdowns are found in many other regions and countries. For example, close to 72 percent of transportation emissions in the European Union come from vehicles, with the remaining 28 percent coming largely from aviation and maritime emissions.[4] Clearly, when it comes to the transportation sector, vehicles—automobiles, in particular—make up the largest share of carbon emissions.

For this reason, we focus the bulk of our analysis on the automobile industry, and by extension, the broader vehicle industry, including heavy trucks. While we recognize the importance of innovation across all transportation subsectors, technologies and levers discussed for automobiles are applicable to decarbonization efforts in other transportation subsectors as well. For example, advances in battery technology driven by electric cars is spurring interest in the possibility of electrifying airplanes. With that said, there are important differences between these subsectors, and we will revisit airplanes, rail, and shipping at the end of the chapter.

Central to decarbonizing the automotive industry is removing greenhouse gas emissions during the use of these vehicles, which increasingly looks likely to occur through electrification if it is to occur at all. We include in the realm of electrification both battery-powered electric vehicles and hydrogen-fuel-cell-powered electric vehicles. We do not analyze potential upstream carbon emissions from the need to create electricity to power batteries or create hydrogen to power fuel cells nor the potential for greenhouse gas emissions during the manufacturing of vehicles. These greenhouse gas emissions are discussed in our chapters on energy (Chapter 2) and industrials (Chapter 4), respectively. In this chapter, we focus exclusively on greenhouse gas emissions during use.

We focus our analysis on fundamental shifts in the underlying technology used for transportation toward zero-emitting sources. We would be remiss if we did not recognize that there have been numerous efforts by various states and municipalities to reduce the carbon footprint of transportation by reducing the demand for transportation services. These include urban planning initiatives to reduce the need to commute and to drive to residential and commercial destinations. These also include investments in public transportation, carpooling and HOV lanes, and bike paths to reduce the use of private automobiles. These are all critical levers to help lower the carbon footprint of transportation on the path to decarbonization by 2050. We choose to focus on the end-state: assuming demand for transportation services, regardless of level, how can net-zero emissions be achieved?

ELECTRIC VEHICLES:
THE ONE-HUNDRED-YEAR-OLD "NEW" TECHNOLOGY

The automobile industry is arguably in the midst of a major disruption, one that will likely unseat previous industry goliaths and have significant impacts on other sectors. Electric vehicles, powered either by batteries or fuel cells, have attracted the interest of innovators, customers, and policy makers alike. The rise of the electric vehicle has brought into the market a number of intrepid start-ups, including Tesla in the United States and BYD in China. Established auto manufacturers are scrambling to bring new all-electric models to the market.

Concern about the impact of fossil fuels on the climate is driving policy makers to push for widespread adoption of electric vehicles. At the 2017 Marrakech Climate Change Conference, eight nations, Canada, China, France, Japan, Norway, Sweden, the United Kingdom, and the United States, signed a declaration of commitment to increase the share of electric vehicles in government fleets.[5] Several European countries, including the UK, France, Denmark, and Norway, have announced gasoline and diesel bans between 2025 and 2040.[6] China, the world's largest vehicle market, in 2017 announced plans for putting regulations in place that will ban the sale of all fossil-fuel vehicles (although timing is still under discussion).[7] In the US, California and more than a dozen other states are moving forward with zero-emission-vehicle strategies.

Often forgotten in the push for zero-emission cars is that electric vehicles dominated the US market in the late 1800s during the initial advent of automobiles. Due in part to health and environmental concerns that manure from horse-drawn carriages created on city streets during the late 1800s, people looked to the newly invented automobile as a "clean" alternative. Early automobiles varied greatly in their design and included electric-, steam-, and gasoline-powered offerings. Early steam- and gasoline-powered technologies were off-putting—steam required long start-up times and gasoline-powered engines required a hand crank to get started and were dirty and noisy. Meanwhile, electric cars were clean, quiet, and easy to operate, and electricity was becoming more widely available.

But the dominance of the electric car was short lived. In 1908, Henry Ford introduced the Model T, the first mass-produced and affordable gasoline-powered vehicle. By 1912, the gasoline-powered car cost only $650 compared to electric vehicles with prices almost three times that amount. By 1920, the cost of the Model T was cut in half due to assembly line production. Charles P. Kettering's invention of the electric starter, national expansion in road infrastructure, and the discovery of Texas crude oil put gasoline-powered cars firmly in the lead.[8] Gradually, electric vehicles lost out to gasoline internal combustion engines, eventually going extinct by 1935. Over forty years passed before interest in electric vehicles began to rise again.

In 1975, the US government imposed new standards for sales-weighted vehicle fleet fuel economy (27.5 mpg by 1985), largely in response to the 1973 oil embargo, forcing the automobile industry to innovate. During this time, the first production catalytic converter was introduced, scrubbing tailpipe emissions, and was quickly adopted due to new federal regulations on air pollutants.

A renewed interest in electric car technologies emerged, facilitated by the 1975 Electric and Hybrid Vehicle Research, Development, and Demonstration Act under which the US government partnered with industry to improve batteries, motors, controllers, and other hybrid-electric components.[9] Manufacturers such as General Motors (GM) began developing electric car prototypes. The technology, however, was hampered by limited performance compared to gasoline-powered cars—maximum speeds of 45 mph and a driving range of around forty miles.[10]

In the 1980s, with a new administration in the White House, automobile manufacturers lobbied to lower CAFE (car average fuel economy) standards to 26 mpg. But the innovation engine continued to hum, with manufacturers working to improve designs for electronic ignition and introducing electronic fuel injection, valve timing, and lift technologies, increasing fuel efficiency and further reducing tailpipe pollutants. By 1990, the 27.5 mpg level was restored, while new vehicle average fuel efficiency had actually surpassed this limit, reaching 28 mpg.[11]

The Energy Policy Act of 1992 and the 1993 Partnership for New Generation of Vehicles initiative continued to support alternative-fuel vehicle innovation. The 1993 industry partnership initiative resulted in three hybrid-diesel cars, developed by GM, Ford, and Chrysler, all of which reached fuel efficiencies greater than 70 mpg. The initiative was criticized by some for its diesel fuel focus, but the research and development led to several breakthroughs in technology, including reductions in lighter-weight component costs and advancement of Li-ion batteries and fuel cells.[12] The Energy Policy Act set requirements of federal fleets to acquire alternative-fuel vehicles and provided authority to the US Department of Energy (DOE) to create the Clean Cities initiative with the goal of providing resources and support to regulated and nonregulated fleets looking to adopt alternative fuel approaches.

The 1990s also introduced a new zero-emission-vehicle mandate put forth by the California Air Resources Board (CARB), opening the door once again for electric cars. The mandate required that 2 percent of vehicles sold in California have zero emissions by 1998, 5 percent by 2001, and 10 percent by 2003.[13] By the mid-1990s, other states had begun to adopt the standards, and automakers worked to modify existing gasoline models. GM was the first to introduce an electric vehicle in response to the CARB standards. GM's EV-1 model, introduced in 1997, could compete with gasoline-powered cars on speed (0 to 60 mph in nine seconds) and price ($35,000), but offered suboptimal ranges between

70 and 90 miles along with a fifteen-hour charge time.[14] Car battery R&D efforts ramped up as the industry moved from lead acid to nickel metal hydride (NiMH) technologies that promised longer ranges, and other companies became interested in pursuing electric options.

GM launched a leasing program in California, putting a thousand cars on the road, but by 2002 had discontinued EV-1 production, citing low consumer demand and profits.[15] GM repossessed and crushed all of the cars on the road, donating a few to museums. Due to challenges posed by automakers in meeting the timeline and lawsuits filed against CARB, zero-emission standards were relaxed and the scope expanded to hybrids.[16] The documentary "Who Killed the Electric Car?" places blame on several parties, including automakers, oil companies, and consumers. GM was accused of lobbying against the mandate even while producing the EV-1 model.[17] Once again, electric cars disappeared from the market.

HYBRIDS: THE BRIDGE BETWEEN PAST AND FUTURE

The first decade of the twenty-first century saw an explosion of innovative activity around fuel efficiency as federal regulations tightened, gasoline prices increased, and consumer interest in alternative-fuel vehicles grew. In 2000, after success in the Japanese market, Toyota introduced its Prius hybrid model to the United States and worldwide. Not only was the Prius one of the first mass-produced electric hybrids, it came with a reasonable price tag—just under $20,000 at retail.[18] At the end of that first year Toyota had sold 5,500 cars, and by 2005 Prius annual sales exceeded 100,000 in the US.[19] Interestingly, Toyota was not the first to market. A few months before the Prius, Honda released its Insight hybrid car in the US. Offering an impressive 53 mpg, Honda seemed poised to be the market leader. Its two-door and covered-rear-wheel design, however, lost to the Prius's more family-friendly four-door design and expansive cargo space despite the Prius's lower 41 mpg EPA rating, suggesting that form and function reign when it comes to consumer choice.[20]

Recognizing increasing consumer interest, other companies began to more heavily invest in hybrid technologies, and the number of hybrid electric-vehicle-class US patents filed in 2000 doubled by 2002.[21] Over the next five years, Chevy, Lexus, Ford, Mercury, Saturn, GMC, and Cadillac all introduced at least one hybrid model. Annual US hybrid vehicle sales exceeded 350,000 by 2007,[22] or 3 percent of total new car sales (up from 0.17 percent in 2000).[23] Gasoline prices continued to rise, breaking $3 per gallon in May 2007,[24] and hybrid sales in the

United States continued to rise alongside these increasing costs. By July 2008, the gasoline price had reached a record high of $4.11 per gallon,[25] and the US entered into a recession created by the subprime mortgage crises and collapse of the housing bubble. In 2009, total vehicle production in the US dipped to its lowest level since 1960.[26] While hybrid sales also saw a slight decrease, overall demand remained fairly steady due, in part, to high gasoline prices.

President Obama's announcement in 2009 of revised CAFE standards—set at 35 mpg by 2020 under the Energy Independence and Security Act—only further fueled interest in hybrids. Starting in 2010, customers purchasing hybrid vehicles received a federal income tax credit up to $7,500. More stringent CAFE fleetwide average standards followed in 2012—54.6 mpg by 2025 along with a CO_2 limit for passenger cars. US hybrid sales responded, increasing by 60 percent compared to 2011 (see Figure 3.1).[27] From 2000 to 2018, manufacturers introduced into the US market more than a hundred hybrid models across all car types—cars, trucks, and SUVs.[28]

Yet despite buy-in from car companies and federal incentives, US sales of hybrids began to slow. Market share for hybrids held relatively constant around 3 to 4 percent of annual automotive sales in the decade after 2007, but the rate of growth began to tail off and mirror overall industry growth.[29] A number of reasons have been advanced for this slowdown in the rate of growth of hybrids in the United States. Some industry analysts point to improvements in gasoline engine efficiency. The continued decline in gas prices over this time period may have also served as a deterrent to customers not necessarily committed to environmentally friendly purchases.[30] The green customer segment could simply be tapped out, while mainstream purchasers continue to be reluctant to make the switch. Finally, commercialization of plug-in electric vehicles may have contributed to slower hybrid sales.[31]

Automakers continue to invest in, and introduce, new hybrid designs, including Toyota, Honda, Ford, and Kia/Hyundai.[32] With their pricing and fuel efficiency, as well as a growing inventory of available models, hybrids continue to compete with gasoline models and challenge battery-powered electrics for alternative vehicle market share. Even with this renewed interest, hybrid vehicles in the United States represented only 2 percent of total US sales in 2019.[33] Worldwide, hybrid sales have been growing at a faster rate, particularly in Asian and European markets. Government incentives and standards are helping to create demand. For example, in the European Union, new CO_2 emission performance standards that went into effect January 1, 2020, and more stringent levels set

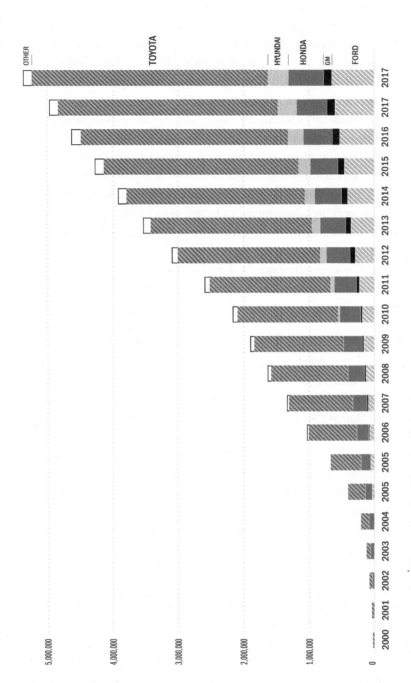

FIGURE 3.1. Cumulative US Hybrid Sales by Company

Source: Transportation Research Center at Argonne National Laboratory, accessed March 9, 2021, anl.gov/es/light-duty-electric-drive-vehicles-monthly-sales-updates

for 2025 and 2030, have given hybrids a boost. New car registrations for hybrid vehicles had tripled to 6 percent of all EU vehicle registrations in 2019, from 2 percent in 2016. China is expected to see an increase in hybrid sales as well, due to recent changes to redefine petrol-electric hybrids as low-fuel-consumption vehicles.[34] Worldwide, predicts JP Morgan, hybrids will represent 20 percent of sales by 2025 and nearly 40 percent by 2030.[35]

Ultimately, while hybrids have done a great job at pushing widespread adoption of alternative drive trains, they may see their demise at the hands of electric vehicles. While Toyota has had more than a decade to learn from and improve its power-split powertrain design, seeing a 10 percent improvement with each generation of the Prius, other companies have not seen similar advancements.[36] Ironically, the next big advancement in hybrid vehicles will likely be tied to improvements in battery technologies, and those improvements may be more beneficial to battery-powered electric vehicles, which are closing the gap on hybrids. Hybrids are increasingly looking like a bridge between traditional gasoline and electric designs as consumers become more comfortable with alternative-fuel vehicles.

BATTERY-POWERED ELECTRICS: DISRUPTIVE AT LAST?

Increased consumer demand for hybrids opened the door once again for electric, but as in many other mature industries, the larger, established manufacturers weren't the ones to take the lead in innovation. Enter Tesla Motors. Founded by Martin Eberhard and Marc Tarpenning, Tesla unveiled its first serial production battery electric car, the Roadster, in 2006. With financing from the chairman of the board, Elon Musk, the Roadster would be the first highway-legal mass-produced all-electric car in the United States, offering consumers a travel range of two hundred miles per charge at a hefty $110,000 price tag. The company sold 2,250 Roadsters by 2012.

In 2008, Musk became CEO of the company, and he brought with him a long-term vision for Tesla. His initial strategy was to use the profits from the Roadster to develop future models that appealed to a broader customer base, improving the design and driving down manufacturing costs along the way. In 2008, Tesla unveiled the Model S, a more affordable family sedan that seated seven people and came with a $50,000 base price. In 2009, Tesla joined forces with Daimler AG for a 10 percent stake in the company. But like many car companies coming out of the recession, Tesla struggled to stay afloat and in 2010 received a $465 million loan from DOE to help the company scale production.

That year Musk won the Automotive Executive of the Year Innovator Award and the company went public, the first automobile manufacturer in the United States to do so since Ford in 1956.[37]

Tesla was not alone. Fisker Automotive, a start-up automotive company founded in 2007, promised to build the first commercialized plug-in hybrid. The company secured millions in funding over the next two years, including a $587 million loan from DOE through the Advanced Technologies Vehicle Manufacturing Loan Program. Of the total DOE funding, $169 million was initially given to Fisker to complete its first vehicle, the Karma, with one caveat: the company had to meet a February 2011 commercial production milestone. Fisker missed this deadline, and in June 2011 DOE issued a draw stop notice, essentially cutting off funding. The company pushed forward and in July delivered its first models to a chosen few investors and high-profile parties, including Al Gore, followed by a retail offering before the end of the year.

Unfortunately, in the years that followed, the Karma was plagued by battery fires and recalls, among other technical issues, and Fisker ended up in bankruptcy by 2014.[38] Often in these situations, one company's demise leads to another's opportunity. Chinese auto parts company Wanxiang purchased Fisker's assets in 2014 for $149 million, as well as the assets of the battery company A123, which manufactured the defective cells in 2013, and rebranded the company as Karma Automotive. In the fall of 2016, the company revealed its first model, the Revero, and announced plans to build a manufacturing facility in China capable of producing fifty thousand electric vehicles.[39] In May 2017, Wanxiang officially launched production of the Revero and distributed vehicles to Karma dealer showrooms.[40] After some not so favorable reviews, the company ditched the original design and in 2020 introduced a new version, Revero GT, which uses a hybrid drive train and sells for $130,000.[41] This model will be an exclusive offering (five hundred models produced) while the company works on future electric drive train designs.

Tesla and Fisker were two promising start-up companies new to the automotive industry, offering cutting-edge technology and poised to lead the industry toward an electric future. Why did only Tesla survive? Many industry experts say that it was Tesla's focus on developing battery, electric motor, and system control technologies in-house that gave them the advantage, both in terms of cost to manufacture and performance, over other companies that were outsourcing. Today, Tesla is seeing even more benefits of this early focus as the company expands to other battery systems, closing the electric car loop with solar and home charging. Fisker's focus on simply making a beautiful car that would appeal to the luxury buyer while outsourcing battery and other manufacturing put much of the quality control in the hands of its vendors. Six years later, Henrik Fisker has not only introduced his first mass-market electric car (Fisker Ocean) but appears to have learned from past mistakes, developing new battery technologies in-house.[42]

As is often the case, the efforts of entrepreneurial entrants attracted the interest of industry incumbents. Soon, established automakers were offering electric vehicles. In 2010, Chevy and Nissan released their own battery electric cars, the Volt (plug-in hybrid) and Leaf (battery electric). GM would redeem itself after a disappointing first attempt with the EV-1 more than a decade prior to the release of the Volt, winning several awards for its design including the 2011 North American Car of the Year and 2011 Motor Trend Car of the Year.[43] Positioning the Volt as an extended-range electric vehicle suggests that GM recognized consumers' electric car range anxiety and made the safe bet to offer a hybrid solution. The Volt offered forty miles in electric mode and an additional three hundred miles in gasoline mode.

The Nissan Leaf received global recognition, including the 2011 European Car of the Year, 2011 Japan Car of the Year, and 2011 World Car of the Year.[44] The fifty-eight-mile-range Leaf would surpass the Volt in electric mode but without a vast supporting charging infrastructure would be characterized as a "second car" or "car for getting around town." In addition to fuel efficiency, early adopters liked its family-friendly hatchback design and roomy interior.[45] With the ability to quickly scale production, Chevy and Nissan would lead Tesla in sales of plug-in and battery electric vehicles for several years by offering vehicles at a lower price point and by leveraging their existing dealer network.

In his 2011 Presidential Address, Barak Obama set the goal to be the first country to reach one million electric cars on the road by 2015. This was an aggressive plan but one that was backed by $2.4 billion in government funds for R&D on electric cars and batteries.[46] Several states offered additional incentives such as rebates or state income tax credits. Further, nine states—Connecticut, Maine, Maryland, Massachusetts, New Jersey, New York, Oregon, Rhode Island, and Vermont—joined California by 2013 in implementing new zero-emission vehicle regulations, with a goal of reaching a 15.4 percent sales target by 2025.[47]

Other automakers would add to the list of plug-in and battery electric vehicles available, including Toyota, Ford, BMW, and Honda. Around this time, Chinese and European governments were laying out their own emission-reduction plans and offering incentives for alternative fuel vehicles. Over the next few years, corporate innovation and support from the US, Chinese, and European governments—representing more than 50 percent of global passenger car sales worldwide[48]—coupled with investments in technology improvements, expansion of the fueling infrastructure, and falling prices, would provide battery electric vehicles the market conditions needed to seriously compete with fossil fuels for the first time in a hundred years (see Figure 3.2). And while the hype is certainly around battery electric technology and Tesla, another electric car technology is quietly emerging—fuel cells. With Toyota and other Asian-based manufacturers investing heavily in fuel cells, and many carmakers looking at both technologies, a battle for electric vehicle market share could unfold over the next decade.

In 2013, battery-powered electric vehicles got a boost when the Tesla Model S won the Motor Trend Car of the Year Award, beating out other gasoline models and putting a stake in the ground for all-electric vehicles. One year before, Tesla had unveiled its new Model X, the first battery electric SUV. In 2013, the company paid back its DOE loan.[49] In mid-2014, the company announced plans to introduce the significantly less expensive Model 3, which would have a starting price of $35,000. Sales of battery electric cars and plug-in hybrids in the United States continued to climb, and by 2015, with almost thirty models to choose from, US consumers had purchased a cumulative 395,000 vehicles.[50] The Model S topped the list of battery electric vehicle sales in 2015, and by the end of that year the Model X was delivered to customers.[51] Then, on March 31, 2016, Tesla unveiled the long-awaited Model 3 with plans to deliver in 2018. Prior to the announcement, Tesla already had 110,000 pre-orders.[52]

Seeing the success of Tesla, other automakers began introducing battery electric options. Since 2012, BMW, Daimler, GMC, Honda, Mitsubishi, Ford, Fiat, Toyota, and Volkswagen have introduced at least one battery electric model in the United States.[53] By 2016, the Model S had distanced itself further from the Nissan Leaf, and with the help of the Model X, Tesla represented more than 50 percent of US electric sales.[54] By January 2020, Tesla had shipped 367,500 cars globally over the previous twelve months. In the US, sales of Tesla's Model 3 were nearly double that of the iconic BMW 3 series gasoline vehicle.[55]

In an attempt to help grow the market for electric vehicles, Tesla decided to open-source more than two hundred patents to any company that wished to design and sell battery electric vehicles. In an interview with USA Today in 2014, Elon Musk suggested that Tesla had fielded interest in their patents from

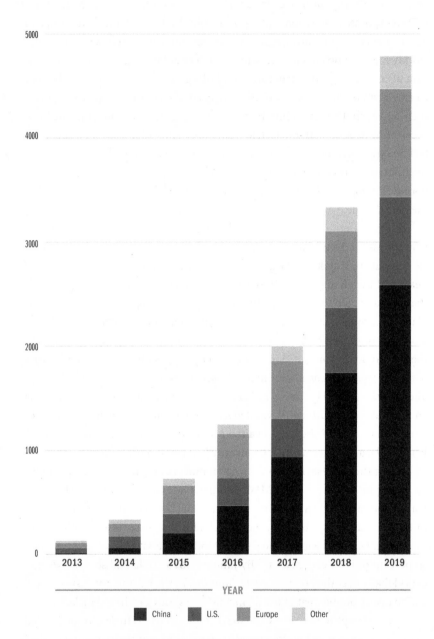

FIGURE 3.2 Cumulative BEV Sales in Selected Countries (in thousands)

Source: IEA, "Global EV Outlook 2019, https://www.iea.org/reports/global-ev-outlook-2019

other established carmakers.[56] Perhaps the biggest beneficiaries of Tesla's patent policy were more-specialized, start-up companies new to the automobile industry such as Faraday Future and Lucid Motors, both of which hired former Tesla engineers for product design and are using cylindrical cell designs similar to Tesla.[57]

Today, lithium ion (Li-ion) is the dominant technology used in plug-in vehicles and next-generation hybrids. The batteries are known for their efficiency, high power to weight ratios, low self-discharge, and temperature performance. The NiMH battery, known for its power and longer life cycle, had dominated the hybrid market but is not expected to compete with Li-ion's high energy densities and lightweight footprint. The global Li-ion battery market is seeing significant growth due largely to the rise in demand for electric vehicles. In 2018, electric vehicles represented nearly 40 percent of the Li-ion market. According to Bloomberg New Energy Finance, global Li-ion battery demand will grow from just over 200 GWh annually in 2019 to nearly 2,000 GWh annually by 2030, driven largely by electric passenger vehicles.[58]

To date, Asian manufacturers have dominated production of Li-ion batteries. Panasonic, through strategic partnerships with Tesla and Toyota, and LG Chem, in partnership with Chevrolet, lead production along with Samsung and CATL, who are tied to BMW and Mercedes. [59] Tesla is not far behind in terms of production capacity. The company's Gigafactory 1 earned the top spot for largest megafactory in 2019, and its Gigafactory 3 is up and running in China, producing fifty thousand Model 3 cars in the first six months of 2020, surpassing all other Chinese manufacturers.[60] Overall, Benchmark Minerals Intelligence estimates that sixty-eight new plants are planned to be built by 2028; just four years ago, this number stood at four megafactories.[61]

Critical to the success of battery electric vehicles is *range*. Energy density, which is the amount of energy stored within the battery expressed in watt hours per kilogram (Wh/kg), drives range. The higher the energy density the further the vehicle can travel between charges. Since first being commercialized in 1991, Li-ion energy density doubled from 100 Wh/kg to 200 Wh/kg in 2010.[62] In 2020, the Tesla Model 3 came equipped with a Panasonic 2170 battery with claims of a 260 Wh/kg density rating.[63] To truly compete with gasoline, electric cars need to offer batteries with higher densities—at least 350 Wh/kg[64]—and longer range. Tesla is hard at work designing a battery that will match this density, with Elon Musk hinting that a mass-produced high-quality 400 Wh/kg battery may be available before 2025.[65]

Gasoline vehicles typically have ranges of 300 to 400 miles (that is, before refueling), and today many hybrids offer ranges of 300 to 500 miles and beyond. Most of the battery electric cars available today have ranges of less than 250 miles, with a few exceptions.[66] Tesla is one of those exceptions; at the low end, the 2020 Model 3 (standard) offers a range of 250 miles while the Model S (long range) boasts a range of 402 miles. This is an area in which many manufacturers have focused investment.

Price continues to be a barrier for battery-powered electric cars seeking parity with gasoline models in terms of range. Models such as the Nissan Leaf and Ford Focus compete on sticker price but fall short on range (less than 200 miles), whereas the Tesla X and S models start to compete in terms of range (300-plus miles) but cost triple the price of the average small or mid-size car on the market in 2020 ($20,000 to $25,000 Kelley Blue Book). Of course, range and price are not the only points of comparison; performance is also very important. Take the Tesla Model 3 and BMW 330i, which Musk has used as a fair comparison.[67] They are similar in price ($35,000 and $38,750 for base models, respectively) and performance (the Model 3 can go 0 to 60 mph in 5.6 seconds and the 3 series in 5.4 seconds), but the Model 3 falls short on range at 250 miles. Upgrading to a more powerful battery extends the range to 322 miles but at a $46,000 price tag.

However, as efficiencies improve and production capabilities grow, battery pack prices are rapidly decreasing, falling 20 percent from 2010 to 2011 and again in 2012, followed by another sharp decrease by 50 percent in 2015 (see Figure 3.3).[68] McKinsey & Company analysts believe that the price needs to get down to $100/kWh to be competitive with gasoline vehicles on price. Industry analysts like BloombergNEF estimate average battery pack prices to be close to $100/kWh as early as 2023.[69] BloombergNEF predicts that the cost of electric vehicles, driven largely by falling battery prices, will fall below gasoline vehicles by 2026.[70]

Increased investments and pricing signals for the metals and minerals needed to manufacture Li-ion batteries seem to support battery electric vehicle market growth estimates. However, there is some uncertainty in whether these critical Li-ion battery inputs can supply the growing electric vehicle market longer term. Lithium, which is naturally abundant, saw prices jump 10 to 15 percent between 2014 and 2015 in response to the increase in demand for electric vehicles. Prices for lithium carbonate, the type most commonly used in electric vehicles, doubled between 2016 and 2017; however,

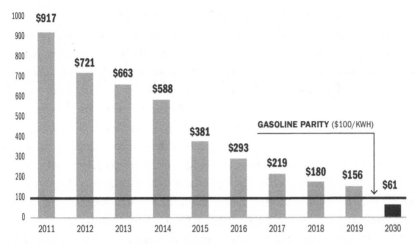

FIGURE 3.3   Lithium-Ion Battery Pack Costs Worldwide, 2011–2019 (in dollars per kwh)
Source: Statista, February 15, 2021, statista.com/statistics/883118/global-lithium-ion-battery-pack-costs/

prices soon after started to decline due largely to cuts in Chinese subsidies and an influx of lithium supply, notably from Australia, which holds the majority of hard rock (spodumene, from which lithium is sourced) mines.[71] However, some analysts blame bottlenecks in downstream conversion (to carbonate) in China for the oversupply, and that the market will balance out.[72] Looking forward, lithium supply is expected to triple by 2025, yet this may not keep up with electric vehicle demand, which could increase ten-fold over the same time period.[73]

One metal that could threaten the rapid growth of electric vehicle production is cobalt, which is widely used in Li-ion batteries to help extend range. In 2017, investors were buying up cobalt resources in anticipation of increased global electric vehicle manufacturing over the next decade, driven primarily by China's market and longer-term shortages of the metal. The increase in cobalt demand coupled with tight supply drove prices up to a ten-year high in 2018. High prices attracted more suppliers, driving prices down below 2016 levels by 2020. The cobalt market is now in a state of oversupply.[74] More than 70 percent of cobalt is supplied by the Democratic Republic of Congo and Zambia, where regional instability and supply chain disruptions threaten global supply.[75] In addition to general uncertainty in the region, an analysis done by MIT suggests that unless improvements are made in refining methods and recycling rates, we could see a global cobalt shortage.[76]

However, the concerns around cobalt availability may be moot, as manufacturers are moving away from cobalt. In 2020, Panasonic shared its plans to commercialize and produce a battery for Tesla within two to three years.[77] In fact, all of the top producers are reducing cobalt in their designs. The challenge in finding a cobalt replacement is in identifying another metal that not only is widely available and low cost but also provides the user with the same performance (range) as Li-ion batteries that use cobalt. Manufacturers typically use nickel-cobalt-aluminum or nickel-manganese-cobalt combinations in batteries.

One of the replacements being pursued is lithium iron phosphate (LRP). CATL is rumored to be making one for Tesla, and the chemistry is already being widely used by Chinese electric vehicle manufacturers, including BYD.[78] LRP batteries aren't new, yet in the past they have not promised the same level of performance; after years of R&D investment, that is no longer the case. CATL announced more recently that its new battery pack will offer users a lifetime of 1.2 million miles, but at a 10 percent premium.[79] In 2020, researchers at UT Austin identified a new class of cathodes that uses high nickel content along with manganese and aluminum, which they believe will provide manufacturers with a low-cost, no-cobalt high-performance option. The team formed a new start-up called TexPower to bring the new cathodes to market.[80]

Another alternative receiving a lot of attention is the solid-state battery, which offers a much higher energy density than Li-ion but also higher cost and failure rates after repeated charging. Samsung has indicated that it has a battery in the works that offers a five-hundred-mile range and five-hundred-thousand-mile lifetime on its solid-state battery.[81] Toyota is even getting into the solid-state battery electric vehicle game. The company has a solid-state battery prototype in the works but faces the same challenge as Samsung regarding lifetime. Toyota is also looking at new materials to introduce into the battery design to address this issue.[82] While solid-state batteries seem promising, they are likely years away from mass commercialization.

The biggest challenge to "range anxiety" of battery electric vehicles is the lack of a charging infrastructure, which contributes to consumers' fear of being stranded somewhere without a station. Battery electric vehicles today offer significant mileage between charges, but a patchwork of stations doesn't provide the consumer confidence needed to go on long trips. Thanks to government and private investments, the number of electric charging stations in the United States jumped from 3,394 in 2011 to 36,600 stations in 2020.[83] This is in addition to home charging systems that are available to the customer at the point of vehicle sale. Home access to charging, supported by existing electric power infrastructure already being provided to the residence, is another benefit of battery electric cars, allowing the homeowner to charge the vehicle overnight.

Rather than wait for charging infrastructure to be built by others, Tesla has built its own network of electric-car-charging stations. By the beginning of 2017, Tesla alone had built more than 5,400 superchargers worldwide.[84] By 2020, there were 1,971 supercharger stations available, with more than 17,000 supercharger stalls in the United States, Europe, Asia, and the Middle East.[85] Superchargers help to address time to recharge, another perceived barrier, offering forty-five to fifty minutes to charge 80 percent compared to several hours for other chargers.

As battery electric sales grow worldwide, countries are ramping up charging infrastructure to support this growth. According to the International Energy Agency, in 2019 there were 7.3 million charging outlets available worldwide.[86] Of these outlets, more than 85 percent were private, light-duty vehicle slow chargers in homes, multidwelling buildings, and workplaces. Although publicly accessible chargers represented a smaller share, the category experienced a growth of 60 percent in 2019, driven largely by China, which hosts 82 percent and 52 percent of the inventory for fast and slow chargers, respectively.[87] Decarbonization targets established around the world have played an important role in the growth in infrastructure. According to IEA's 2020 Global EV Outlook Report, "17 countries had announced 100% zero-emission vehicle targets or the phase-out of internal combustion engine vehicles through 2050."[88] The report further suggests that under a more aggressive scenario in line with Paris Accord goals, 250 million electric vehicles could be on the road by 2030, which would require an electric vehicle charging network to grow 4 to 10 percent across China, the United States, and the EU.

FUEL CELLS: PLAYING THE LONG GAME

Battery electric vehicles are not the only zero-emission technology in the market. Fuel cells, which have been used in space exploration since the 1960s, are also receiving investment. They gained attention in 2003 when President George W. Bush announced a $1.2 billion initiative to support fuel cell technology development and distribution, citing energy independence as well as environmental concerns. Critics argued that this was not a move in the interest of innovation but rather a way to protect automakers from more stringent fuel efficiency standards. By 2009, President Obama had greatly reduced the US government's investment in fuel cell R&D to $68 million, electing instead to put more money toward battery electric vehicles, which appeared to hold more immediate promise.[89] Even so, innovation and industry investment continued forward, and DOE has continued to support fuel cell R&D despite the reduced budget. More than 580 patents and thirty new fuel cell technologies entered the market in 2016 with the help of DOE funding.[90]

Fuel cell vehicles combine intake air (oxygen) and hydrogen to create a chemical reaction, sending electricity to the motor, which powers the car. The only by-product of this reaction is water, which exits out the tailpipe. Today, most of the hydrogen produced is through a process called steam-methane reforming, with natural gas as the source. Compared to battery electric cars, fuel cell electric cars offer higher energy densities and thus longer ranges as well as shorter refuel times (minutes compared to hours). Some manufacturers are betting that these benefits, along with declining manufacturing costs as more companies enter the space, will allow fuel cell technology to compete with battery electric and gasoline competitors longer term.

In 2020, there were three fuel cell electric car models available for sale or lease in the United States: Toyota's Mirai, Hyundai's Nexo, and Honda's Clarity. These vehicles offer ranges that go head-to-head with the Tesla models (310-plus miles range) and compete with gasoline models (ranging from 312 to 380 miles range). In 2017, Audi, BMW, Ford, Daimler/Mercedes Benz, General Motors, and Lexus were reported to have concept fuel cell cars developed or plans under way.[91] However, as of 2020, most of the efforts to develop fuel cell passenger vehicles have been put on hold or discontinued due to concerns around cost, especially as Li-ion battery prices continue to drop.[92] BMW is one of the companies that are continuing to pursue fuel cell designs, announcing that a mass production vehicle will be available after 2025.[93]

Industry partnerships are forming around fuel stack development that could drive down the cost of these systems, making fuel cell technologies more price competitive. In 2017, GM and Honda announced a joint venture, Fuel Cell System Manufacturing, with plans to start producing next-generation fuel cell stacks by 2020.[94] Also in 2017, thirteen companies joined together to form the Hydrogen Council to discuss and promote the use of hydrogen as a fuel source, and in Japan, carmaker heavyweights Toyota, Honda, and Nissan signed a Memorandum of Understanding that provides for the collaboration needed to expand the hydrogen fuel infrastructure in that country.[95] After just three years, the Hydrogen Council has grown to ninety members, including several major automakers. With the hope of stimulating the fuel cell electric car market, Toyota announced in 2015 that it would share more than 5,600 hydrogen fuel cell technology patents with other companies in the industry for free.[96] Toyota is continuing to benefit from its short-term success in hybrids, but longer term the company's success in retaining its market share in the global alternative vehicle market is riding on more widespread advancements in hydrogen technologies.

Between 2012 and 2017, fuel cell patents accounted for 29 percent of all renewable energy patents issued in the United States, second only to solar at 42 percent.[97] The leaders in fuel cell patents during this period were GM and Toyota, with more than 750 each. Honda and Samsung were close behind, with over 500 patents each. Other auto industry stakeholders such as Panasonic, Hyundai, Nissan, Ford, and Daimler had patents as well.[98] The total number of annual fuel cell patent applications has been declining since 2010, when there were 1,263 submitted to the United States Patent and Trademark Office.[99] A similar trend is being observed with patents issued around the world. In 2015, the number of fuel cell patents dropped by 40 percent and growth has been flat since.[100] This could be a sign that the industry is slowly moving away from R&D toward commercialization. Of course, this could also signal that manufacturers are shifting their focus away from fuel cells and putting resources into battery electric vehicles, which hold more immediate promise. While the total number of fuel cell applications has slowed, the trend in investment supports the stated commitment of Asian manufacturers in bringing this technology to market; in 2019, Toyota, Honda, Nissan, and Hyundai had claimed the top four spots in total fuel cell patents.[101]

Fuel cell systems have a way to go before we see mass diffusion in the marketplace. One of the biggest barriers is cost. Improvements in fuel cell research and manufacturing processes have driven fuel cell system costs down. According to DOE, high-volume automotive fuel cell system costs fell almost 50 percent between 2007 and 2016 to $53/kW (in 2002 the cost was $275/kW); the target for commercialization is closer to $30/kW. Onboard hydrogen storage is also still too high, coming in at $15 to 18/kWh; the commercialization target is $2/kWh.[102] As a result, the Toyota Mirai base model retails for $57,000 while the electric Nissan Leaf starts at $29,000. The price to refuel is also a barrier. In 2019, the average price of hydrogen fuel in California was $16.51/kg.[103] The Mirai 2020 holds about 5 kg of hydrogen, which equates to more than $80 per fill-up. This is more than a two-fold increase in fueling costs compared to gasoline vehicles. Battery electric vehicle charging ranges from $10 to $15 for a full charge.

To compete, Toyota has positioned the Mirai as a leasing opportunity at $339 per month, offering no-cost maintenance for thirty-five months and a complimentary $15,000 fuel card to attract customers. In California, fuel cell vehicles qualified for a $4,500 rebate in 2020. Toyota sees the opportunity for hydrogen longer term in both grid energy storage and ease in scalability to other sectors (a challenge that current Li-ion batteries will face over time), as well as the similarity to current fueling infrastructure. Being first to market isn't new to Toyota, a company that prides itself on innovation and green ideals, but unlike the first-generation Prius, the cost of the Mirai, and fuel cell technologies in general, will be initially prohibitive to widespread adoption.

The biggest challenge to fuel cells, from a climate change perspective, is to find decarbonized solutions to hydrogen generation. To truly decarbonize transportation using hydrogen, natural gas cannot be part of the solution. There is a cleaner alternative, water electrolysis, by which electricity is used to split water into hydrogen and oxygen. Powering the water electrolysis with renewable energy achieves what many refer to as green hydrogen. Water electrolysis is not a new technology, yet in 2018 it represented less than 5 percent of hydrogen being produced globally.[104] Cost has been a key barrier to commercialization.

Mass production using renewables could help to bring the cost of clean hydrogen down. In 2018, the cost to produce hydrogen from renewable-sourced electricity was $3.00 to $7.50/kg compared to natural gas as the source, at $0.90 to $3.20/kg.[105] IEA estimates that by 2030 the cost to produce clean hydrogen could be reduced by 30 percent with continued decline in renewable energy pricing and increasing production.[106] An analysis released by the Hydrogen Council suggests that the cost of electrolysis will fall to $1.60 to $2.40/kg by 2030, driven by "industrialization of manufacturing, improvements in efficiency and operation and maintenance, and availability of low-cost renewable energy sources."[107]

In 2019, the Clean Energy Ministerial announced a new hydrogen initiative that aims to "drive international collaboration on policies, programs and projects to accelerate the commercial deployment of hydrogen and fuel cell technologies across all sectors of the economy."[108] Countries participating include the United States, Canada, Japan, India, Korea, Netherlands, Norway, Saudi Arabia, and the European Union. While the focus of the initiative is on industrial, energy, and commercial transport applications, investing in fuel cell technologies and infrastructure within these industries will help to reduce the costs of clean hydrogen for passenger vehicle applications.

Of course, for automobiles, the production of clean hydrogen needs to be distributed through a vast network of hydrogen filling stations. There are several companies working to bring electrolysis-powered hydrogen filling stations to market, targeting regions or countries that have favorable government fuel cell vehicle incentives and strategies. Fueling stations are nascent in their design and still expensive to build. Unlike battery electric, a national hydrogen fuel network doesn't exist in the United States and will need to be built at considerable cost and time. Germany, France, Japan, and Korea all have targets to increase the number of filling stations to support growth in fuel cell vehicles sold. In 2019, IEA estimated that there were 470 hydrogen refueling stations worldwide.[109] With a target of ten million fuel cell vehicles on the road by 2030, the Hydrogen Energy Ministry has also set a target for fueling stations at 10,000.[110]

In the United States, there were fewer than fifty hydrogen filling stations in operation in 2020, most of which are found in the greater Los Angeles and San Francisco/Silicon Valley areas of California.[111] California often serves as a market entry point for cutting-edge technologies and ideas, as well as tougher regulations, and often other progressive states soon follow suit. This will take time, however, and likely will require government incentives. It is unclear whether the work done through the Hydrogen Initiative will accelerate hydrogen commercialization more broadly in the US market. More likely, fuel cell vehicles will be more broadly adopted in other countries well before mass commercialization in the US.

Just as hybrid gasoline-electric cars have helped to bridge the gap between gasoline and electric, a hybrid gasoline-hydrogen car could do the same for fuel cell vehicles. Adding hydrogen gas to the air intake of an internal combustion gasoline engine can improve combustion efficiency—reducing fuel consumption and increasing range—while helping to build out the fueling infrastructure needed for fuel cells to compete longer term. This approach could also offer automakers a more cost-efficient way to reduce carbon emissions of current internal combustion engine designs. Fuel delivery could be done at existing gas stations if expanded to store hydrogen gas, providing ease of adoption for consumers weary of fuel-switching.

In 2013, Aston Martin, in partnership with Alset Global, demonstrated a prototype hybrid hydrogen Rapide S that could operate on gasoline, hydrogen, or both fuels. The car successfully completed the ADAC Zurich Nürburgring twenty-four-hour race and was recognized as the 2013 PMW Powertrain of the Year. Alset Global continues to promote its patented technology to automakers on the company's website, but further research suggests that little progress has been made toward wider adoption as companies like Toyota and BMW push forward with 100 percent hydrogen fuel cell designs. However, the opportunity for this technology may be in bringing along reluctant automakers and consumers, helping them to make a longer-term transition to hydrogen as opposed to preceding fuel cell technologies in the switch to a hydrogen economy.

Another interesting hybrid concept is the plug-in hydrogen hybrid. Announcements were made by Hyundai and Daimler in 2017 around battery electric-hydrogen SUVs being developed under luxury brands Genesis and Mercedes Benz. The GV80 fuel cell and GFC F-Cell models were the first plug-in hydrogen drive train concepts to be introduced. In these designs, the electric battery has a limited range and the fuel cell is being used to extend driving between charges. Could this be a bridge between the shorter-term growing electric infrastructure and longer-term hydrogen market? More likely it's a result of manufacturers who have committed to 100 percent electric drive trains who are looking for interim solutions while the fuel cell infrastructure continues to build out. After selling a small number of GFC F-Cell models overseas, Daimler has since abandoned production and Genesis has yet to bring the fuel cell hybrid design to market.

PAVING THE ROAD FORWARD FOR ELECTRIC VEHICLES

Today, battery electric vehicles are well ahead of fuel cells on many dimensions of merit with the notable exception of range, which is quickly improving. Some manufacturers, however, see fuel cell vehicles as the likely winner long term, citing technical challenges that Li-ion batteries will face as manufacturers tackle the challenge of range (in other words, the bigger the density, the larger the battery). Fuel cells do not face the same size-weight challenges. As these new technologies move into larger car footprints, it seems that fuel cells have the advantage. However, work is under way to develop lighter-weight, high-density batteries that could challenge fuel cells.

With regard to supporting infrastructure, battery electric is well ahead of fuel cells yet one could argue that shorter charge times and the customer's comfort with a gasoline fueling routine and a station infrastructure that is more closely aligned with traditional gas stations gives fuel cells an advantage. Industry investment is beginning to provide some clarity on the future of electric vehicles, with most of the automakers following Tesla's lead on battery electrics though with some notable exceptions such as Toyota, Honda, and Hyundai continuing to push hydrogen fuel cells. Electric vehicles could play out as a classic standards battle along the lines of Betamax versus VHS and Blu-ray versus HD-DVD in video imaging. It's clear that the market is shifting but less clear which technology will win. Perhaps the market is shifting toward a mixed-fuel infrastructure, in which there is a place for battery and fuel cell electric vehicles as well as gasoline and diesel, depending on region and application.

To date, battery-powered electrics have been the clear market leader in electric light-duty vehicles. In 2017, worldwide battery electric vehicle sales surpassed the one million mark. Just two years later, annual sales increased to 2.1 million vehicles. In 2010, the number of electric cars on the road was estimated at 17,000 worldwide; by 2019, the stock of electric cars had increased to 7.2 million, with China, Europe, and the United States representing 91 percent of inventory.[112] While the 2020 pandemic slowed sales temporarily, the market for battery electric vehicles is quickly expanding. All evidence points to battery electric vehicles entering the increasing growth phase of the technology S-curve and thus increasing the likelihood of a major technology disruption.

Which companies have benefited the most from this market shift? Initially Renault, which has a controlling interest in Nissan, led global battery electric vehicles sales volumes in 2014 and 2015 (see Figure 3.4). In 2016, Tesla took over the number one spot with its Model S, which with Nissan's Leaf, and BMW's i3 represented the top three electric models sold worldwide. With the release of the more cost-friendly Tesla Model 3, Tesla pulled well ahead of the pack in the United States and globally. In 2019, the company sold over three hundred thousand Model 3s in one year, putting the company ahead of fast-growing Chinese manufacturers BYD and BAIC.[113] While Tesla is clearly benefiting from its own efforts, arguably a win for the company is a win for battery electric cars and all the companies that are offering battery-powered vehicles.

While sales of electric vehicles were estimated at just 2.5 percent worldwide in 2020,[114] we expect to see a sharp increase in sales with China and Europe in the lead as a result of government regulation and/or subsidies. With the expectation that battery electric vehicles will be cost competitive with gasoline by 2025, Bloomberg's 2020 Electric Vehicle Outlook projects that electric vehicle sales will represent 10 percent of global sales by 2025, 28 percent by 2030, and 58 percent by 2040.[115] There will be more than 116 million electric vehicles on the road by 2040, which is impressive but represents only an 8 percent share of inventory.[116] There are some reasons to believe that these estimates greatly understate the likely diffusion of electric vehicles. As we've seen in other product

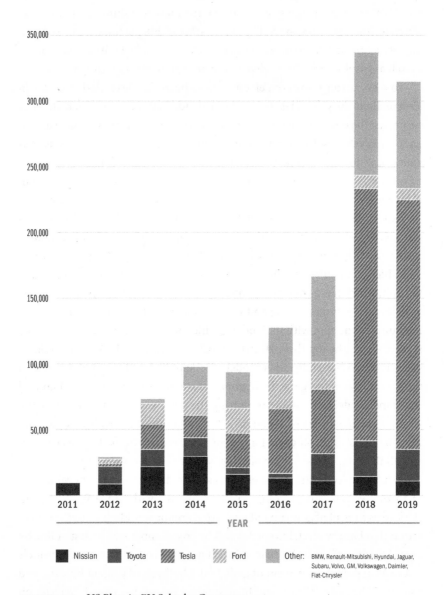

FIGURE 3.4 US Plug-in EV Sales by Company

Source: Alternative Fuels Data Center, updated January 2020, afdc.energy.gov/data/10567

categories, once a new dominant design takes hold, transition can occur surprisingly quickly.

Overall, analysts predict a slower market-growth trajectory for fuel cell electric cars, at least in the short-term, due to cost and infrastructure challenges. According to several market research sources, sales of fuel cell vehicles (passenger, buses, and other) were fewer than 10,000 in 2020 compared to battery electric vehicles, which were 2.2 million in the same year.[117] One market study estimates that cumulative fuel cell vehicle sales are projected to reach 22 million by 2032.[118] While this growth is impressive, fuel cells will have a hard time competing with the projected 116 million in annual battery electric vehicle sales by 2040. While fuel cell vehicles have been slow to take off in the United States, countries strategic to Toyota, Honda, and Hyundai (Japan and Korea) are offering government incentives, spurring some interest in those regions. Global alliances are forming more widely in support of the deployment of fuel cell vehicles and supporting infrastructure. However, for fuel cells to take off, investments must also be made in supporting infrastructure and continued R&D to bring the technology costs down in addition to incentives for new vehicles.

WILDCARD DISRUPTORS: AUTONOMOUS VEHICLES

While the battery-versus-fuel-cell-technology battle wages on, there is another technology that could further disrupt and dictate the future direction of the automobile industry—autonomous driving. The idea behind autonomous driving has been around since the 1940s, but it wasn't until the US Department of Defense's Defense Advanced Research Projects Agency Grand Challenge that the industry took the concept more seriously as an investment opportunity. The goal of the competition, held between 2004 and 2007, was to create the autonomous vehicle of the future. Attracting participants such as Google, Cisco Systems, and Stanford, each year of competition brought improvements in the technology and increased interest from the IT and auto industries. Years later, in 2010, Google launched its Driverless Car Program, which reached the two-million-miles-driven mark by 2016.[119] By 2020, Google's Waymo had entered into partnerships with Fiat Chrysler Automotive, Tata's Jaguar Land Rover, Renault Nissan Mitsubishi, and Volvo to incorporate their automated driving solutions into their car designs.[120]

The competition in autonomous vehicles is diverse, from incumbent car manufacturers to major tech companies to entrepreneurs—in 2020, more than 250 companies were working to make autonomous driving a reality.[121]

Three manufacturers—Toyota, Ford, and GM—own the most autonomous vehicle patents.[122] Partnerships are forming between car manufacturers and ridesharing companies, suggesting an initial focus on dense, urban areas. In 2016, Volvo entered into a venture with Uber to launch a fleet of self-driving ridesharing vehicles.[123]

Several barriers must be overcome before autonomous cars will be more widely embraced, including liability, privacy standards, road safety, and licensing and testing standards. Even with these challenges, the rate of adoption is expected to happen relatively quickly. Several car companies, including GM, Volvo, Nissan, and Ford, have announced that autonomous vehicles will begin appearing on highways as soon as 2021; Tesla is already incorporating autopilot capabilities into its cars, and Elon Musk has claimed that a fully autonomous option is imminent. After launching a self-driving pilot with two hundred cars in Pittsburgh, Tempe, and San Francisco, Uber announced that after one year the company had reached the one-million-miles-driven mark;[124] yet even though the pilot has been largely accident free, Uber pulled all self-driving vehicles after a fatal accident in Tempe in 2018 and is revisiting its market strategy. Waymo is taking its time introducing its automated taxi service, Waymo One, to consumers, launching an Early Rider program (exclusive to four hundred members) in Phoenix and putting trained drivers in the front seat. This program was stalled in 2020 due to COVID-19 and concerns regarding the trained driver.[125] Earlier in 2020, the US Congress was working on a bill to regulate autonomous driving. However, this bill was set aside due to the COVID-19 crisis, leaving companies to work with individual states.

What are the implications for zero-emission vehicles? Battery-electric cars are a good candidate for autonomous technology for several reasons, including ease of computer operation (that is, electronic controls versus mechanical) and recharging without human interaction. We will likely first see the technology become popular in ridesharing applications, with these companies choosing electric powertrains due to lower fuel costs and greater reliability. According to a Securing America's Future Energy press release in 2017, "58 percent of autonomous light-duty vehicle retrofits and models are built over an electric powertrain, while a further 21 percent utilize a hybrid powertrain."[126] One of the challenges with pairing autonomous driving with electric vehicles is that the computing power required by the sensors and controls can end up draining the battery, affecting range. For example, analysis shared by Ford suggests that as much as 50 percent of a battery electric vehicle's range would be used by autonomous driving, air conditioning, and other entertainment features.[127] The company has signaled that its gasoline hybrids will be the first to be equipped with these controls.[128] Other companies such as Tesla and GM are moving forward with battery electric autonomous vehicles. Longer term, analysts agree that there are inherent benefits to pairing autonomy with electric vehicles.

Broader consumer adoption will take a while, but within cities there will be not only a more rapid shift from gasoline to electric but also a decrease in car ownership overall. Even without autonomous technologies, this shift is already happening, as the number of new car sales slows and use of public transportation increases in urban centers. This trend is even occurring across the car-centric United States; according to the American Public Transportation Association, public transit ridership has grown 28 percent compared to 1995 numbers.[129] According to IHS Markit, the number of autonomous vehicles will surpass fifty thousand in 2021 then increase to thirty-three million globally by 2040.[130] IHS Markit agrees with the assumption that initially most of the autonomous vehicles will be found in urban centers and used by ridesharing companies. A shift to ridesharing may increase the demand for transportation services as it lowers costs, increasing the miles traveled per person. As for the emissions implications, it is hard to say. This increase in use may be offset by an acceleration in the shift to electric vehicles.

THE UPSHOT: ELECTRIC WILL DECARBONIZE
THE AUTOMOBILE INDUSTRY, BUT WHEN?

We believe that zero-emission electric vehicles represent the likely future of the automotive industry. We hypothesize that hybrids, despite their success in the United States and globally, will phase out over time as electric vehicle technology improves and range anxiety subsides. The battery electric car is emerging as the early leader but continues to face barriers of cost and range performance. Hydrogen fuel cells ease range anxiety and offer a fueling infrastructure more compatible with current practice but face significant cost barriers regarding the fuel stack system and fueling infrastructure. A battle for electric is emerging, with manufacturers like Toyota betting on fuel cells and others, like Tesla, leading the charge on battery electric. Both manufacturers have offered open-source technology patents to spur further investment in their technologies of interest. We are in an era of ferment during which a dominant design for electric vehicles has yet to emerge. It remains possible that a mixed-technology infrastructure might emerge, with consumers choosing the battery electric vehicles and companies using both fuel cell and battery electric technologies for more diverse fleets.

Autonomous technology is providing further disruption, bringing in startups and more established IT companies that until now played a small role in car design. Ridesharing and technology companies are now major players in this industry, and interesting partnerships are starting to develop across sectors. As would be expected, strategic mergers and acquisitions are emerging and are likely to accelerate. With this merging of the IT and automobile industries will come a major disruption to the business model. More customers will decide against owning a car, and automakers will need to choose whether they will focus on car production or move into a role of longer-term customer engagement via digital communication platforms. Although autonomous technology is fuel-neutral, the battery electric car is a natural partner in creating the next generation smart car.

All in all, electric vehicles are moving up the technology S-curve as improvements in performance correspond with increasing penetration in the market. The irony is that growth in electric vehicles will decrease demand for fossil fuels, which will drive down the price of gasoline and which in turn could undermine the justification of purchasing an electric vehicle. However, the cost of use—the price of electricity versus gasoline—already strongly favors electric vehicles in most markets today. In the United States, the average cost of use per year is $1,117 for gasoline and only $485 for electricity.[131] The main barrier to ownership is the purchase price, which is largely driven by the cost of batteries or fuel cells. As the technology improves and these costs decline, there are reasons to believe that electric vehicles will be the low-cost option for consumers.

In addition, there are indications that these vehicles are being purchased for reasons beyond just the purchase price. The overall cost of ownership is proving lower, given that electric vehicles require little maintenance as they are relatively simple machines—basically electric motors and a power source—as compared to internal combustion engines that require fuel injectors, cooling systems, transmissions, and exhaust systems. They have driving performance advantages such as quick acceleration, maximum torque from a standstill (valuable for towing), and a low center of gravity that improves handling driven by the weight of the battery. And of course, for some consumers, the environmental benefits of electric vehicles provide personal utility that can justify a higher purchase price.

As demand grows for electric vehicles, competition among manufacturers will intensify. As new entrants and incumbent firms race to develop electric vehicles, a competitive shakeout is looming on the horizon. Forbes conducted a mapping study in 2017 and identified more than seventeen hundred start-ups vying for a place in the new automobile market, thanks to electrification, artificial intelligence, mobility, and the connected car experience.[132] With so many companies competing for the future of the automobile, we will see many failures—including likely some well-established incumbents in the industry. A standards battle looms between battery electrics and hydrogen fuel cells, further intensifying competition. There will be new partnerships formed, acquisitions will increase, and many bankruptcies will be filed. These are all to be expected as the industry is disrupted.

Historically, the automobile industry has moved slowly when it comes to disrupting itself. However, the entry of hundreds of start-ups, willing to take risks with new ideas, is pushing the industry forward more quickly. Rumors of solutions from Apple, Microsoft, and IBM alone suggest disruption may happen quickly. The technology sector tends to move much more quickly than other sectors, with companies releasing new generations of products each year. Many existing automobile manufacturers recognize the need to nurture this kind of forward thinking and have set up their own innovation incubators, including GM Ventures, BMW Start-up Garage, Honda Xcelerator, and Toyota Innovation Hub.[133]

With such turbulence and innovation occurring in automobiles, it appears that the sustainable disruption of transportation is imminent. The important question though may not be if, but how long this disruption will take place. Time is of the essence. Even if all new vehicle sales in the world were electric, it still would take a decade, at very least, for the turnover in existing vehicle fleets to fully decarbonize transportation. Interventions, by both the public and private sectors, will be necessary to decarbonize transportation by 2050, especially when we consider the other subsectors of transportation such as planes, trains, and ships.

There is both promise and concern for transition to a zero-emission future in aviation, rail, and maritime shipping. For rail, global electrification is well under way, with 75 percent of passengers already traveling on electric trains.[134] IEA predicts that global rail transport will be close to electrified by 2050. The exception is North America, which will continue to rely on diesel for freight rail absent a shift in policy.[135] In the shipping industry, electrification is a challenge,

as the weight of Li-ion batteries sufficient to power large ships would be un-
manageable at current densities.[136] Ammonia, hydrogen, and advanced biofuels
are emerging as leading technologies toward industrywide decarbonization.[137]
Given the international nature of maritime shipping, the International Maritime Organization (IMO) has taken the lead on setting goals for reducing GHG
emissions: reduce carbon intensity 70 percent and total GHG emissions by
50 percent by 2050 compared to 2008 emissions.[138] However, according to IEA,
the projected reductions from current and proposed IMO policies fall short of
these goals, and uptake of alternative fuels would only be at 3 percent by 2040
under the current framework.[139]

Aviation, while currently a small contributor to global transportation emissions, is growing in terms of carbon footprint. According to IEA, demand for
air transport has doubled since 2000 and aviation emissions grew by 32 percent
over the last five years.[140] Efficiency improvements made between 2000 and
2016 avoided a potential 70 percent increase in energy consumption.[141] In 2010,
the International Civil Aviation Organization issued a resolution that set an
annual 2 percent efficiency improvement target between 2013 and 2050. There
is a collective effort industrywide to use alternative biofuels; however, in the
United States biofuel use was estimated at 0.1 percent in 2018.[142] Several airlines,
including Airbus,[143] are exploring electrification, but it's questionable whether
battery technologies can scale to support longer routes without adding too much
weight to the aircraft. All-electric planes tested and flown to date have been
limited to smaller designs. To decarbonize by 2050, aviation may need to take a
page out of the electric vehicle handbook, starting with hybrid-propulsion systems that offer range and low-carbon performance but avoid concerns around
added weight when scaled.

HOW CAN WE DECARBONIZE
TRANSPORTATION BY 2050?

If time is of the essence, how might we accelerate the adoption rate of zero-
emission vehicles and transportation? As discussed in Chapter 2, putting a
price on carbon is a commonly recommended antidote to our climate challenges. For automobiles, the simplest solution arguably is to increase gas taxes.
Raising the cost of gasoline should drive more consumers to prefer electric vehicles. Clearly, this can drive purchasing behavior and help advance the diffusion of electric vehicles. Raising taxes on gasoline is not without its challenges
in the United States and abroad, however. Politically there is resistance to rais-

ing the price of such a critical component of families' and many businesses' budgets. So what other levers are available?

Increase or Extend Subsidies

If federal incentives for new plug-in vehicle purchases are discontinued, we could see slower growth of electric vehicles in the United States over the next few years. Efforts by the Trump administration to roll back funding to federal agencies that historically have been critical to innovation and continued improvement in technologies like fuel cells and batteries threatened to slow progress further. However, the overall impact could be limited, as demand from Asia and Europe will continue to drive incentives to innovate and improve electric vehicles to parity, or better, with fossil-fuel vehicles.

An analysis conducted by the UC Davis Plug-in Hybrid and Electric Vehicle Research Center suggests that even with the existing battery-powered-vehicle momentum, purchase incentives remain critical for stimulating demand for electric vehicles.[144] In the United States, a maximum $7,500 federal tax credit is available for battery electric and plug-in hybrid vehicles bought after 2010. As initially passed by Congress, the credit begins to phase out once the manufacturer reaches two hundred thousand units in cumulative sales. In February 2021, a new six hundred thousand sales cap was proposed under the Green Act, which would allow companies like Tesla and GM, who have met the initial cap, the opportunity to leverage these incentives with their customers. Fuel cell vehicles' eligibility for a federal tax credit (max $8,000) was to expire in 2017 and then again in December 2020; however, it was extended through December 2021. Industry sales data suggest that these incentives are helping to increase electric vehicle sales. The UC Davis study warns that if incentives are pulled back too early (that is, before late majority buy-in), it could have a negative effect on widespread market adoption.

Perhaps the best example of impact through government incentives can be seen in China and Europe. In Europe, diesel emerged as a frontrunner as countries looked to reduce carbon emissions through more fuel-efficient diesel engines. Significant cuts in the diesel sales tax boosted sales of diesel vehicles, from 10 percent in 1990 to 60 percent market share in 2011.[145] Yet diesel fell out of favor by consumers and policy makers due to increased concerns over other environmental pollutants attributed to diesel use (such as NOx) as well as the distrust created by Volkswagen's misleading emissions claims on their diesel cars. In 2011, policy makers turned to alternative fuel vehicles to help them meet carbon-emission-reduction goals, offering tax incentives on qualifying hybrid and electric vehicles—in just five years, sales grew from eight thousand in 2011 to eighty thousand by 2016.[146] More recently, Europe strengthened and extended its New Energy Vehicle and CO_2 emission standards. By 2019, the electric vehicle share of European sales was 3.5 percent.[147]

China saw an incredible surge in demand due to government incentives. Launched in 2010, government subsidies paid directly to Chinese automakers drove down the price of electric cars for consumers and resulted in explosive growth in hybrid and electric car sales. The subsidy program was limited to Shanghai, Shenzhen, Hangzhou, Hefei, and Changchun, where incentives of $7,000 to $8,700 were paid out per vehicle produced and sold. The government also committed to funding charging station infrastructure and battery recovery networks in these cities.[148] Incentives were extended in 2012, and the Chinese market saw an explosion in new car sales—from a mere nine thousand in 2012 to more than two-hundred-and-fifty thousand in 2016.[149] More recently, China extended its alternative fuel subsidies and strengthened its New Energy Vehicle and CO_2 standards. By 2019, electric vehicles in China represented 4.9 percent of sales.[150]

Build Out Charging Infrastructure

Both battery and fuel cell electric vehicles will benefit from continued investment in infrastructure. This is also an area in which state and federal funds could be targeted. In November 2016, the Obama administration announced several actions to help expand the US alternative-fuel-charging network, including the creation of forty-eight national electric charging corridors covering twenty-five thousand miles of highway by the US Department of Transportation (DOT).[151] DOT then released a call for location nominations from state and local officials. After four rounds of nominations (2016–2019), the Federal Highways Administration's Alternative Fuel Corridor program reported a hundred nominations that included portions of 119 Interstates and comprised forty-nine states.[152]

The private sector may prove the most important conduit for building out infrastructure. Tesla has invested in building out its own charging infrastructure to help allay fears of range anxiety. Electric utilities and entrepreneurial entrants are capitalizing on the market opportunity to sell electricity through chargers. Commitments from corporate entities to change commercial fleets over to electric vehicles could accelerate the buildout of charging infrastructure, similar to the push of large technology companies to purchase renewable electricity. All in all, we would expect that private markets will adjust to meet the demand for chargers in the same way that gasoline stations proliferated during the rise of ICE vehicles a century ago. From a public policy perspective, lowering barriers to siting and building out new charging infrastructure by private entities may be the most helpful lever to pull.

Power Electrification with Renewables

To be clear, "zero-emission vehicles" are only zero emission to the extent that charging infrastructure or hydrogen production are done with no emissions. Thus battery electric vehicles must rely on zero-emission technologies in electricity generation, such as renewable energy, to truly claim zero emissions. In many areas, coal is the dominant feedstock for electricity generation. As for fuel cells, water electrolysis offers a truly emission-free solution in fuel cells, but until costs for this technology significantly decrease, there will be continued reliance on natural gas to generate hydrogen fuel. Even with water electrolysis, electricity is necessary and will require sources such as renewables to drive zero emissions.

Efforts in the energy sector to expand renewables and build a nationwide storage network offer battery-powered and hydrogen fuel cell vehicles the opportunity to serve as a cross-sector solution, further increasing demand for electric vehicles. Many companies, including auto manufacturers, are working on bringing vehicle-to-grid (V2G) solutions to market, by which the electric vehicle battery could be charged and discharged to support building energy needs and even the larger electric grid. As utilities start to lay out their grid modernization plans, V2G offers a new pathway to engaging consumers and generating revenue while ensuring that they retain control of what will be hundreds of new points of bidirectional charging. Tesla likely had exactly this in mind when it acquired Solar City and changed its mission from "accelerating the world's transition to sustainable transportation" to "accelerating the world's transition to sustainable energy." Continued investment in R&D to innovate electric vehicles and the underlying technology are critical to driving further adoption and disruption of gasoline-powered vehicles. Government subsidies for research can be an important catalyst.

Incentivize Early Retirement

One way to remove gasoline-powered cars from the road more quickly is to provide a financial incentive for their early retirement and subsequent replacement with a new electric model. The idea of paying consumers to retire older cars isn't a new one. Following the 2008 recession, a new initiative called the Car Allowance Rebate System was signed into law as part of the larger auto industry bailout. The "Cash for Clunkers" program aimed to take out of service pre-1984 models with ratings of 18 MPG or less, with the intent to not only help boost the auto industry but also reduce environmental impact. Car owners who participated in the program were given vouchers ranging from $2,900 to $4,500 to purchase new, cleaner vehicles.[153] The program was a success in that it resulted in nearly seven hundred thousand new car sales, but American automakers saw only a small percentage of these sales and the spike was only temporary as federal funding was quickly depleted. The initiative also received some criticism that it only benefited wealthier Americans.[154]

In 2019, Senator Chuck Schumer (D-NY) proposed a revamped Cash for Clunkers program that would pay consumers between $3,000 and $5,000 to turn in their gasoline-powered cars and purchase a new electric (fuel cell or battery) or hybrid vehicle.[155] Perhaps learning from the first initiative, Schumer proposed $454 billion over a ten-year period, providing additional dollars to low-income consumers and limiting the program to American carmakers.[156] In addition to consumer rebates, the plan sets aside $45 billion to support electric-vehicle-charging infrastructure and $7 billion to help American companies shift production from gasoline to electric models. If enacted, the plan is estimated to replace 25 percent of the existing gasoline vehicle inventory by 2030.[157] The plan as currently proposed could accelerate a longer-term and more sustainable shift toward broader vehicle electrification; however, electric vehicle prices must continue to come down if they are going to compete with hybrids for the incentives.

Overall, we believe that rapid maturity and decreasing costs of electric vehicle technologies as well as a strong global demand, particularly in Asia, will drive a transition to electric vehicles. However, decarbonization of the automobile industry will take time simply because we have so many existing fossil-fuel cars on the road to replace. Meeting a 2050 target for decarbonization is possible but will be challenging. It will require continued investment and growth that at least matches what we have seen in the last few years, especially when it comes to aviation and shipping. Make no mistake—a low-carbon transportation sector is in the future and electric will get us there; it's just a matter of what technology and when.

CHAPTER 4

THE INDUSTRIALS SECTOR

S | INCE THE DAWN OF MODERN SOCIETY, industrial manufacturing has been a key driver of economic growth. During the Second Industrial Revolution (1870–1914), steel and cement manufacturing, along with railroad expansion, provided the means for mass production and delivery of lower-cost goods, giving rise to urbanization and an improved quality of life for millions. Yet this industrialization has come at a cost. Historically, carbon emissions have been correlated with the expansion of the industrials sector. Data provided by the National Oceanic and Atmospheric Administration show that prior to the Second Industrial Revolution, the average daily global atmospheric CO_2 measured 280 ppm. Shortly after the Second Industrial Revolution, emissions began to rise, reaching 315 ppm by the 1950s, then accelerated to surpass 400 ppm by 2015.[1] Industrialization, not just in the United States but in developing economies, has contributed to this increase in emissions. Manufacturing requires significant amounts of thermal energy, and for decades, fossil fuels have served as the primary energy source (Figure 4.1).

In total, the industrials sector accounts for 22 percent of greenhouse gas emissions in the United States and 21 percent of global emissions.[2] *Industrials* refers to a broad array of industries that mine, refine, and manufacture many of the materials and products in the global economy. Given the breadth and diversity of this sector, we focus on three industries in this chapter: steel,

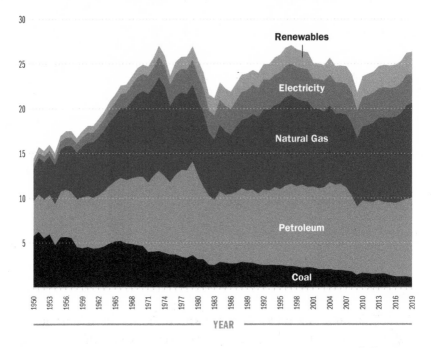

FIGURE 4.1   US Industrial Sector Energy Use by Source, 1950–2019 (in quadrillion Btus)

Notes: Includes energy sources used as feedstocks in manufacturing products. Electricity is retail purchases. Renewables are mainly biomass.

Source: US Energy Information Administration, *Monthly Energy Review*, Table 2.4, June 2020

cement, and petrochemicals. These industries were chosen because they represent the largest share of "scope 1" industrial carbon emissions, which are those produced *in situ* as opposed to those created through the use of electricity supplied from an electric utility (covered in Chapter 2). Together, the steel, cement, and petrochemical industries are responsible for nearly 65 percent of global scope 1 CO_2 emissions from the industrials sector and 20 percent of total global carbon emissions.[3]

There is often quiet resignation to the idea that national economies cannot grow without some increase in emissions. However, in recent years, we have seen a potential decoupling of economic growth and carbon emissions. In 2016, IEA first released data that showed a two-year flattening in carbon emissions at the same time economic growth was positive.[4] More recently IEA found that in in advanced economies like the United States, economic growth averaged 1.7 percent while energy-related emissions fell by 3.2 percent in 2019.[5] The power sector, driven by the adoption of renewable technologies, was responsible for 85 percent of this reduction.[6] Manufacturing operations are more complex, but there are innumerable areas in which improvements in energy efficiency and raw material choice can help to reduce the carbon footprint of a facility.

Energy represents the highest operating cost for industrial manufacturers. Companies already have a natural incentive to reduce these costs. Over the past decade, a flattening out of emissions has been observed in developed countries[7] as a result of energy efficiency improvements and fuel-switching from coal to natural gas as the price of natural gas has come down.[8] However, the real challenge is in developing countries, led by China and India, who have seen sustained economic growth and continue to rely heavily on coal in industrial processes. These rising countries, and the ones following right behind them, will ultimately determine the global rate of decarbonization.

Industrials, such as steel, cement, and petrochemicals, are beholden to commercial customers that demand cheap, reliable, and readily available products. Profit margins are often slim and investment in new innovation is risky. Clean technologies exist, but many are far from commercialization or face barriers to scaling. Most of the energy savings observed to date have been the result of optimizing operations and reducing cost. There has been little incentive for manufacturers to innovate or adopt low-carbon technologies.

While the 2050 goal may seem far away, shifting a sector this big and diverse will be challenging. Let's consider the three biggest emitters—steel, cement, and petrochemicals—in turn.

STEEL: ELECTRIFYING THE PROCESS

Steel is a critical industry in the global economy, serving as an important input to everything from buildings to autos to appliances. Steel production dates back to the thirteenth century BC, but came into broad commercial application with the invention of the Bessemer process, named for inventor Henry Bessemer, who developed a novel steelmaking process that blew air into molten iron, thereby removing impurities through oxidation. Variations of the Bessemer design were introduced over the next hundred years, addressing concerns around purity of the steel, fuel consumption, and productivity. The basic oxygen furnace (BOF)—derived from the Bessemer design, introduced in Europe, and commercialized in the 1950s—dominates global production today (Figure 4.2).

Global steel production reached nearly 1.9 billion tons in 2019.[9] With the exception of the 2008 recession, worldwide steel production has steadily increased

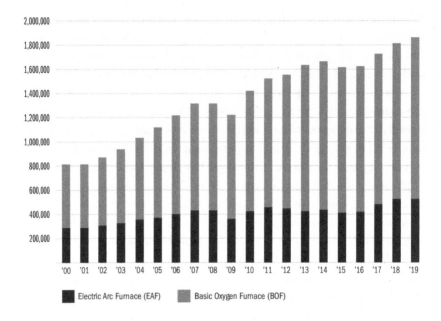

FIGURE 4.2   Global Crude Steel Production, 2000–2019 (in tons)

Source: "World Steel in Figures 2020," World Steel Association, https://www.worldsteel.org/steel-by-topic/statistics/World-Steel-in-Figures.html.

over the last twenty years, driven largely by China. According to the World Steel Association, China alone represented 86 percent of the global growth in production experienced between 2002 and 2016, accounting for 70 percent of the increase in consumption.[10] In 2019, Chinese steel continued to dominate in both production and consumption at just over 50 percent.[11]

In the United States, steel production has seen a steady decline over the last ten years, driven by competitive foreign pricing and increases in imports.[12] The fall of American steel was a long, multidecade process. Following World War II, European and Asian steel industries began to rebuild, embracing new BOF steelmaking. US steelmakers, instead of exploring new technology, continued to use open-hearth furnaces to produce steel. It wasn't until the 1960s that the big three US manufacturers—US Steel, Bethlehem Steel, and Republic Steel—began building BOF plants.

By that time, it was too late. Europe, Japan, and China were growing by leaps and bounds in production, utilizing not only BOF but also electric arc furnace (EAF) technologies, what is commonly referred to as "mini-mills." US manufacturing had lost its foothold. By 1991, US Steel had been dropped from the Dow Jones Industrial Index, and Bethlehem Steel followed in 1999. As other steel companies went out of business, US Steel consolidated and survived, accompanied by a relative newcomer to the industry, Nucor Steel, which embraced EAF mini-mills in the 1960s.

Distributing more than $1 trillion to society, and employing over six million people around the world, the steel industry is an important contributor to the global economy.[13] The top five steel producers worldwide are ArcelorMittal (Germany), China Baowu Steel Group (China), Nippon Steel Corporation (Japan), HBIS Group (China), and POSCO (South Korea).[14] The top ten companies represent a quarter of production globally.[15] Nucor Corporation, now the largest US steel manufacturing company, ranks 14th globally.[16] Other US manufacturers include US Steel (ranked 27), Steel Dynamics (ranked 47), and AK Steel. Once the leader in steel production, the United States today represents just under 5 percent of global steel production and sits fourth behind China (53 percent), India (6 percent), and Japan (5.3 percent).[17]

Today, BOF and EAF steelmaking processes dominate the industry. The BOF is the key component of an *integrated steel mill* that transforms iron ore into finished steel products. Iron ore is placed into a blast furnace along with coke (a reducing agent) and flux (materials, such as limestone, to collect impurities). The resulting hot metal, or pig iron, is transferred to the BOF along with a small amount of steel scrap and flux, and the iron ore is reduced to liquid steel.[18] The final step is casting and rolling the steel into specialty products. Today, the BOF process and integrated mills are used to produce 72 percent of global steel.[19]

The EAF process emerged in the 1960s. Initially developed for the production of small-batch specialty steels, EAFs were able to meet the thermal demand needed for steel production by running electricity through charged material. Using scrap metal exclusively, EAF manufacturing bypasses the iron-ore processing step in BOF integrated mills. Steel scrap is introduced into the EAF and melted using electrodes that deliver an electric arc through the scrap, raising the temperature to 1,600 degrees Celsius to make steel.[20] Once the molten steel comes out of the furnace, the finishing steps are the same as in BOF operations: transfer to secondary refining to adjust chemistry; casting; and rolling. Further processing may occur during these steps that requires reheating, usually provided by natural gas boilers and furnaces.[21] EAFs allow for the building of mini-mills, which tend to be smaller than integrated mills and can be started and stopped on short notice. This offers operators more flexibility in terms of locating the mills and varying production based on demand. Today, EAFs and mini-mills make up 28 percent of global steel production.[22]

Steel production contributes approximately 6.7 percent of global CO_2 emissions.[23] Most of this is from BOF integrated steel mills. The iron-making process alone represents 70 to 80 percent of CO_2 emissions from BOF steel manufacturing,[24] with most of those emissions coming from the coke used as feedstock.[25] There are also emissions from fuel combustion, as the blast furnace is typically heated by natural gas, oil, or coal.[26] Last, the chemical process within the BOF produces CO_2 emissions when the oxygen removes carbon from the molten iron and steel scrap, either mixing it with incoming air at the furnace's mouth or flaring it after gas cleaning.[27]

In contrast, minimal CO_2 emissions from EAFs and mini-mills come from the melting and refining processes, as carbon is driven off the charged material and carbon electrodes. Some EAF plants use oxy-fuel burners that burn natural gas and oxygen, transferring additional heat to the scrap metal. With that said, EAFs require a significant amount of electricity to operate. The largest emissions from EAF mini-mills come from the fuel used to produce electricity for the furnace, especially if that fuel is coal. On average, the total energy required to produce molten steel in an EAF is 425 kWh/ton,[28] or 127 million kWh/year, which is equivalent to the electricity needed to power nearly twelve thousand homes in the United States. However, this is also one of the great advantages of EAF mini-mills, as coal and other fossil fuels could be replaced by low-carbon energy sources, thereby greatly reducing net emissions from EAF plants.

In the United States, the shift from BOF to EAF has largely happened already, with the share of EAF production close to 70 percent today.[29] Lower capital costs, flexibility in operation in response to market demand, and favorable scrap pricing have driven this transition.[30] The difference in cost between BOF and EAF mills comes down to raw or scrap material prices and capital expenditures. Iron ore and coal represent most of the cost to operate BOF mills, but these are variable. Similarly, steel scrap represents most of the cost to operate an EAF mill, and this price is also variable. However, when comparing fixed capital costs, those of EAF are about half those of BOF.[31]

It's a different story in China, where BOFs represent 90 percent of steel production.[32] With just over 50 percent share of worldwide steel production, and continued reliance on coal as a dominant fuel source, China has heavily influenced the global carbon footprint of steel and could influence the pace at which the global shift to cleaner steel manufacturing will happen. Rapid expansion of

BOF integrated mills in China reduced EAFs' share of the global market starting in 2000, driven largely by tight supplies of power and scrap.[33] According to some industry experts, this is expected to change with the increased access to electricity and domestic scrap supply resulting from the rapid growth in Chinese steel consumption over the last two decades, as well as stricter environmental regulations and a looming national carbon trading scheme.[34]

Market analysts have long predicted a slowing of China's explosive economic growth in the coming years and a resulting slowdown in new steel production. Amid concerns about oversupply and its ability to meet domestic emissions targets in 2018, China announced a reduction in steel production.[35] Expansion of steel production capacity in the country was strictly prohibited in 2019 and again in 2020. However, some analysts predict that the shift from BOF to EAF in China is only a matter of time, citing stricter government environmental regulations and the low cost to set up and operate EAF mills, as well as their ability to respond quickly to fluctuating market demands.[36]

So how can 100 percent decarbonization in global steel production be achieved by 2050? The World Steel Association reports that the steel industry has reduced its energy intensity per ton of steel produced by 61 percent over the last sixty years.[37] In 2020, the carbon intensity average was reported at 20 GJ/ton, down from 50 GJ/ton in the 1960s.[38] Modern integrated steel mills, employing best practices using currently available technologies, are operating near maximum energy efficiency.[39] According to IEA, the minimum energy needed to produce steel using pig iron is 10.4 GJ/ton of steel. Current state-of-the-art blast furnaces use 12.0 GJ/ton.[40] The differential between state-of-the-art and global-average carbon intensity suggests an opportunity for continuous improvement, yet even if these BOF technologies are adopted, we will not get to zero emissions with BOFs.

Decarbonization opportunities are limited because the pig iron used in the BOF process contains 4 to 5 percent carbon by weight due to the inclusion of coal or coke as a reducing agent. The DOE is currently working on several alternatives to the blast furnace and BOF processes, which would reduce the steelmaking carbon footprint but won't eliminate carbon emissions completely as long as molten iron continues to be a critical part of the process.[41]

One possibility for decarbonization is to substitute charcoal for coking coal. The coal used in iron-making acts as a reducing agent, an energy source to drive the process, and a carbon source that remains with the steel. Charcoal, made from wood or other biomass, could serve as an alternative renewable fuel source that would meet all of these needs. In fact, charcoal was the first fuel used in early steelmaking. Steel manufacturers are experimenting with the idea once again. ArcelorMittal's company BioFlorestas is growing and maintaining a forest of eucalyptus for use in one of its Brazil plants, supporting the small amount of pig iron needed to supplement the EAF-dominant steelmaking operation.[42]

However, while biomass is renewable, it continues to emit some carbon dioxide when processed and burned, albeit less than fossil fuels. In addition, the growing demands for steel production would need to be balanced with the impacts to forests as well as the challenges in transporting biomass to the mills. Deforestation is already a hot-button issue around the world because, among other reasons, it contributes to global warming by removing carbon sinks (natural environments that absorb CO_2 from the atmosphere). Biomass as a fuel is only zero carbon if the trees burned are offset by a carbon sink. The BioFlorestas eucalyptus forest serves as a case study in effectively balancing production needs with sustainability, but it is only for one operation; the question is, can it be scaled? While biomass is a legitimate option for replacing coal and decarbonizing steel manufacturing, it is not likely to significantly reduce the global carbon footprint.

One technology that holds promise is hydrogen flash smelting. R&D is currently being funded by DOE in partnership with ArcelorMittal, US Steel, and others. With flash smelting, hydrogen (or natural gas) can be used as the reducing agent instead of coal and is applied directly to the iron ore. When compared to the average blast furnace, hydrogen flash smelting reduces CO_2 emissions by 96 percent[43] and avoids the coke-making and sinistering processes needed for iron-making.[44] Scientists in Europe are exploring a similar process called hydrogen direct reduction, which is similar to natural-gas direct reduction iron (DRI) methods.[45] DRI uses natural gas or hydrogen to react with iron oxide, without melting it, producing sponge iron nuggets or briquettes to be used primarily in EAF processes. However, these technologies are still in the scale-up and demonstration phases and would require the hydrogen to be produced by electrolysis, with electricity provided by a zero-carbon energy source, to truly decarbonize the process. At least one steel manufacturer has this in mind. ArcelorMittal announced in late 2019 a project to design the first industrial-scale DRI plant in Hamburg, Germany, eventually to be powered by renewable energy such as wind farms off the coast.[46]

A better option for more quickly decarbonizing steel production would be to accelerate the adoption of EAF mini-mills. However, a complete shift to

100 percent EAF steel production is challenged by (1) steel quality, due to the continued demand for high-quality specialized applications that cannot be met by EAF steel because of steel scrap contamination; (2) access to large sources of electricity to power EAFs, which is particularly challenging for developing countries; and (3) continued economic growth, creating demand for steel that outstrips the supply of scrap. The end-of-life recycling rate for iron and steel is encouraging, with a global range of 70 to 90 percent suggested by the United Nations Environment Programme in its 2011 "Recycling Rates of Metals" report.[47] More recent data suggest the rate is 80 to 90 percent.[48] Yet a sufficient supply of scrap steel remains the main barrier to broader EAF adoption.

EAFs cannot currently satisfy demand for infrastructure expansion without adding virgin steel into the mix. The quality of steel scrap and the steel produced in EAFs has improved over time, yet there are some specialty steels that require a purer iron-sourced steel. To broaden the range of products produced in EAFs, and to adjust to the availability of scrap metal and variable pricing, manufacturers are incorporating DRI into their steelmaking processes.[49] DRI-enhanced EAFs offer a cleaner source of iron, lowering the residual elements and improving the quality of steel produced, while avoiding the more carbon-intensive iron-making process by replacing coke with natural gas. DRI-EAFs are allowing these mills to more directly compete with BOF mills that use pig iron. In the future, hydrogen sourced from renewables using electrolysis could replace natural gas.

Even if we could produce the steel needed using EAF and electrification, the electricity must be provided by zero-carbon sources to decarbonize. In China, most of the EAF steel mills are powered by coal plants.[50] In the United States, the availability of electricity from zero-carbon sources depends largely on where mills sit geographically. For wind and solar, the large amounts of electricity needed to power EAF mini-mills is a barrier and will likely require a dedicated power plant.

CEMENT: MOVING AWAY FROM PORTLAND

Cement is the second key industrial process that will require significant decarbonization in order to achieve global carbon emission targets by 2050. The production and use of cement dates back to the time of the ancient Egyptians, but Portland cement, used widely today, wasn't invented until 1924 when Joseph Aspdin filed a patent for the process, which used finely ground clay and limestone in calcination. Twenty years later, Isaac Johnson improved upon

Aspdin's formula, mixing chalk and clay at much higher temperatures to create the clinker needed to make modern Portland cement.[51] Clinker is the result of sinistering limestone and other minerals into lumps or nodules, which then forms cement paste with the addition of water. Aspdin named the combination Portland cement after limestone found in Portland, England.[52]

Today, Portland cement is the most commonly used cement globally for concrete, mortar, stucco, and nonspecialty grout. This is due to the high availability of low-cost limestone, shale, and other naturally occurring materials used in Portland cement.[53] The cement manufacturing process begins with the quarrying of limestone, clay, and other materials. The rocks are then crushed to a size of 2 to 5 cm, fed into a rotary kiln, and heated to about 2,500 degrees Fahrenheit. As the material travels through the kiln, elements are released in the form of gas, namely CO_2. The remaining materials bond together to make clinker. To achieve the temperatures needed for the kiln-heating process, cement plants have traditionally burned coal, natural gas, or oil. The hot clinker is transferred to coolers prior to being mixed with gypsum, which slows the set time of the cement, and ground into fine powder. The heated air collected in the coolers is sent back to the kiln in an effort to improve burning efficiency and reduce fuel combustion.

Cement can be made using either a dry or a wet process. In the wet process, the clay is washed first to remove adhering organic matter. The resulting slurry, which can contain up to 40 percent water, provides for a more homogeneously blended material. However, adding moisture to the materials then requires more energy to drive off the water, in addition to the elements, within the kiln—specifically, 350 kg of coal per ton of cement produced.[54] The dry process grinds the materials separately then mixes them according to the required proportions. Compared to the "wet" process, the dry process uses only 100 kg of coal per ton of cement produced.[55] Modern dry cement plants incorporate suspension preheaters that use the hot gas from the kiln and hot air from the coolers to preheat the raw materials, thus reducing the energy needed for clinker production. Newer plants incorporate a precalcinator kiln, which further heats the raw materials to 85 to 95 percent decarbonization prior to entering the rotary kiln.[56] Upgrading to a precalcinator generally offers plant operators increased capacity while reducing fuel consumption and thermal nitrogen oxide (NOx) emissions.[57]

Fuel savings influenced the shift to dry process manufacturing in the United States, which increased from 38 percent market share in 1975 to 70 percent by 2001.[58] Today, more than 90 percent of US cement is manufactured using the dry process.[59] Similar trends have been seen worldwide. In Europe, the use of dry production increased from 78 percent in 1997 to 90 percent by 2007.[60] Dry production plants dominate the industries in the top four producing countries,[61] the United States, China,[62] India,[63] and Vietnam.[64] While the shift to dry production appears to have largely happened globally, there are cases where wet plants continue to contribute significantly to production. For example, in Russia, ranked eighth in production in 2019, wet process cement plants continue to operate.[65]

Due to the high cost of shipping and other transportation, the US cement distribution channel is largely limited to domestic customers.[66] However, the US market also depends heavily on imports, as domestic production is insufficient to cover demand. Canada provides the bulk of US imports, given its close proximity.[67] US exports are predominantly to Canada and Mexico, again due to close proximity to operations, but revenues are less than 2 percent.[68] Concrete is mostly used in construction-related activities, including infrastructure, utilities, public works, and residential and private nonresidential construction projects. Therefore, growth of the cement industry relies on the health of the construction market.[69] In the United States, the cement industry experienced consistent growth between 1990 and 2008, reaching an all-time high in 2005. However, the 2008 recession brought a sharp decline of 35 percent in production in 2009, and the industry has recovered slowly, only most recently returning to 2000 levels.[70] Market analysts predict a modest decline in US production in 2020 and 2021 due to the COVID-19 pandemic, but that growth will return in 2022, with support from publicly and privately funded infrastructure improvements.[71]

We see similar industry dynamics around the world, with production recovering post-2008 and starting to slow in the last five years.[72] In the last ten-plus years, China has seen a significant increase in production in response to rising domestic demand for concrete to support urbanization. With twenty million people moving into cities every year, there are estimates that half of China's infrastructure has been built since 2000.[73] More than half of global production in 2019 came from China (see Figure 4.3).[74] Production started to slow in response to overcapacity concerns, and according to industry sources, this trend is expected to continue over the next few years, eventually declining to a level similar to production in developed countries. However, China is looking to infrastructure to drive its economic recovery following the COVID-19 pandemic, and as a result, its demand plateau will likely get pushed out another three to five years.[75] Overall, industry analysts predict continued growth worldwide driven largely by continued urbanization in developing countries.[76]

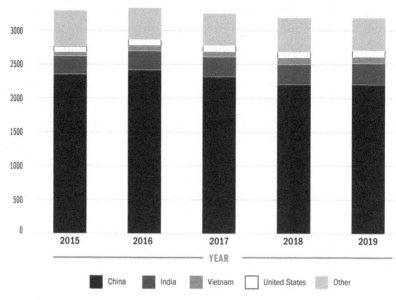

FIGURE 4.3   Global Cement Production by Country, 2015–2019 (in mega metric tons)

Source: Statista, accessed March 11, 2021,
https://www.statista.com/statistics/267364/world-cement-production-by-country/

Global companies are expanding their operations in an effort to increase revenues and profits outside the domestic market. Cement is largely a commodity product, with little differentiation, which results in a highly competitive market. Expanding the customer base requires global companies to establish operations in other countries. In the United States, acquisition of domestic operations has been the path forward for global expansion. More than 75 percent of US clinker capacity is owned by companies headquartered outside of the country,[77] with CRH (Ireland), Cemex (Mexico), LafargeHolcim (Switzerland), and HeidelbergCement (Germany) leading in revenues.[78] LafargeHolcim is the largest cement producer, operating in ninety countries.[79] Anhui Conch (China), China National Building Materials, HeidelbergCement, and Cemex round out the top five global companies.[80]

Cement accounts for 7 percent of global CO_2 emissions,[81] the majority of which arise from the chemical reactions involved in converting limestone to calcium oxide. The bulk of the remaining emissions are from on-site fossil-fuel combustion, with a smaller share from electricity consumption (about 10 percent).[82] The carbon intensity of global cement manufacturing has declined over the years due largely to reduced clinker factor (the proportion of Portland clinker in the cement mix) and energy-efficiency improvements.[83] According to a 2016 report issued by the PBL Netherlands Environmental Assessment Agency and the European Union's Joint Research Centre, decreasing average clinker factor resulted in a 20 percent decrease in carbon emissions per ton of cement produced compared to that made in the 1980s.[84] While significant progress has been made on reducing energy intensity, research into low-carbon materials is still largely in the testing and demonstration phases.

Coal continues to be the fuel and feedstock of choice for most cement plants in the United States. According to the Portland Cement Association, coal and coke represent nearly 70 percent of the fuels consumed on-site, followed by alternative fuels (15 percent), electricity (11 percent), and natural gas (6 percent).[85] Coal is also the dominant fuel source globally (70 percent), while oil (16 percent), natural gas (8 percent), and alternative fuels, including biomass (6 percent), account for smaller portions of the mix.[86]

Opportunities for decarbonizing cement manufacturing lie largely in the kiln-heating process (in other words, fossil-fuel combustion and limestone calcination) and the grinding and milling processes (electricity).[87] Similar to the steel industry, the electricity used in cement manufacturing is a small portion (roughly 10 percent) of its energy consumption.[88] Manufacturers are incorporating state-of-the-art technologies, such as high-pressure grinding rolls and vertical rolling mills (used to grind materials to a fine powder); these offer 50 to 70 percent electricity savings relative to the current practice of using ball roller mills.[89] To decarbonize this industry, the focus needs to be on fossil fuels and raw materials.

Since coal is still a significant share of fuel consumption globally, we first look at the potential for fuel-switching to a less carbon-intense fossil-fuel source. The EPA estimates that switching from coal to natural gas could reduce CO_2 emissions in the US cement industry as much as 40 percent.[90] A global shift to natural gas for clinker production would have a significant impact, but it won't get us to zero carbon, obviously. Alternative fuels, including biomass, have potential in this industry, with many companies already using them for clinker production. However, as previously mentioned, biomass is not a zero-carbon solution and comes with concerns around deforestation. Also, caloric content must be taken into account when assessing biomass for fossil-fuel substitution. Most organic materials have caloric contents of 9 to 16 GJ/ton of cement, and 18 to 20 GJ/ton of cement is required for cement kiln firing.[91] Some blending of other materials is needed to meet the thermal needs of the kiln. In the European Union, plastics, mixed industrial waste, and tires represent nearly 70 percent of alternative fuels used in plants.[92] Many cement plants in the United States are also using tires and other waste fuels in their manufacturing process. According to industry sources, tires are the closest substitute for coal with regard to the energy required to sufficiently heat the kiln.

Using waste fuel for cement manufacturing has the added benefit of addressing growing waste-management issues. In Poland, taxes imposed on landfills forced waste-management companies to look for other options. Faced with potentially high incinerator construction and operation costs, waste-management companies saw an opportunity in cement manufacturing and entered into long-term contracts to process alternative fuels. Today, Poland's alternative fuel substitution rate is above 60 percent, with several cement plants reaching 85 percent.[93] In the United States, average landfill tipping costs (price paid for dumping waste) are still relatively cheap at $55/ton.[94] However, this average has risen every year since 2010, and in the Pacific Region, the cost to landfill reached $73/ton in 2019.[95] As these prices continue to rise, and landfill space becomes scarce, similar partnerships could form between waste management companies and cement plants.

Alternative fuel use in cement plants faces other barriers, including public acceptance; local regulations; complex permitting processes; and costs of collection, transportation, and processing. Supply chains would also need to be established; in the United States, these waste streams are often provided through individual partnerships as opposed to a network of distribution. And, to be clear, while biomass is renewable and waste-to-energy supports a circular economy, using them as fuel still emits CO_2 in the production process. These alternatives may reduce carbon emissions but will not entirely eliminate them.

Even if the thermal process is decarbonized, the CO_2 emissions coming from the chemical reaction to make Portland cement need to be addressed. Given the direct relationship between clinker factor and CO_2 emissions, lowering the clinker-to-cement ratio can go a long way toward decarbonization. Ordinary Portland cement can contain up to 95 percent clinker, with gypsum making up the remainder. Manufacturers have been adding other materials to lower the clinker factor, making sure that strength and durability are not threatened by lowering that ratio. In 2014, the average global clinker-to-cement ratio was down to 65 percent,[96] yet according to IEA, this ratio has increased each year since reaching 70 percent, driven largely by overcapacity and changing standards in China.[97]

Clinker substitutes include natural pozzolans (silicon-based materials that react with hydraulic lime at room temperature) such as clays, shale, and sedimentary rocks; finely ground (unheated) limestone; silica fume (a pozzolanic material and by-product of silicon or ferrosilicon alloy production); granulated blast furnace slag (a by-product of steel and iron production); and fly ash (dust-like particles from coal-fired power plants).[98] Blended cements also offer other performance benefits, such as increased strength and durability.

However, there are limits to the quantity of substitute materials used in concrete. For example, the American Concrete Institute establishes limits for the use of supplementary cementitious materials, which range from 25 to 50 percent of total material mass, depending on the substitute materials used.[99] The limits established are based on ASTM International standards for cement, concrete, and aggregates.

One alternative that is gaining momentum in the United States is Portland-limestone cements (PLCs), known as Type 1L cements. PLCs offer similar performance to Portland Type I (general use) cements with a 10 percent savings in carbon emissions. Finely ground limestone is blended with the Portland cement in the final milling stage. ASTM standards were revised in 2012 to define PLCs as having 5 to 15 percent limestone by mass (compared to the previous 5 percent requirement).[100] Considered a new technology in the United States, PLCs have been used for decades in Europe, which caps limestone addition at 35 percent.[101] According to industry sources, it has taken years of meeting with state officials, in particular Department of Transportation representatives, to build acceptance of PLCs, and many states are still not on board.

According to a 2016 report by Allied Market Research, green cement (defined by Allied as cementious materials made from industrial waste) represented less than 5 percent of total global production.[102] North America, Europe, and Asia-Pacific represented 86 percent of this market.[103] In 2019, fly-ash-based green cement dominated the global market, with a market share of 40 percent.[104] Industry analysts predict that the green cement market will continue to grow, led by major cement manufacturers and driven by adoption of green building certifications, including Leadership in Energy and Environmental Design (LEED).[105] According to data supplied by the industry in 2017, PLC sales are growing in the United States but represented only 1 percent of total production. Widespread adoption of supplemental cementious materials can greatly reduce cement's carbon footprint, but the regulatory and performance constraints around Portland substitution will limit their potential impact. To achieve total decarbonization, we need a drop-in replacement for Portland cement.

While still in the very early stages of R&D and demonstration, low-carbon cements and concretes offer significant disruptive potential. These alternatives must offer the same strength, durability, and consistency as Portland varieties but without the carbon emissions associated with their manufacturing. Efforts to create substitutes to Portland cement are under way, but early in commercialization. One example is Solidia Cement, which uses the same raw materials, manufacturing equipment, and processes as Portland cement, but its chemistry requires less limestone. As a result, the raw materials are heated at lower kiln temperatures, reducing CO_2 emissions associated with fuel burning and limestone calcination; the company estimates a 30 to 40 percent reduction in greenhouse gases and other pollutants compared to ordinary Portland.[106] In addition, the Solidia concrete curing technology uses CO_2 instead of water, which reacts with the solidia cement to make calcium carbonate and silica, hardening in less than twenty-four hours and consuming otherwise emitted CO_2.

Carbon capture and utilization holds promise for the cement industry. In addition to Solidia, several companies are looking at the potential for using CO_2 to enhance or replace cement and concrete products while lowering carbon footprints. CarbonCure Technologies offers a solution that injects captured CO_2 into the ready-mix concrete process, replacing some of the Portland cement needed for the mix. The company estimates a 5 percent reduction in cement binder[107] and compressive strength gain of 10 percent.[108] Carbicrete replaces Portland cement with steel slag, adding CO_2 to the wet concrete to strengthen the mix during the curing process. A cement plant that substitutes a cement-based process with Carbicrete could see thirteen thousand tons of CO_2 emissions avoided or sequestered.[109] Carbon Capture Machine and Carbon Upcycling UCLA (CO_2NCRETE) are researching the use of CO_2 to create novel binding materials to replace Portland cement.[110]

One group of concretes, geopolymers, are leading alternatives for commercialization. Geopolymer concretes use silicon and aluminum found in thermally activated natural materials, such as fly ash and blast furnace slag, with an activating solution to create a hardened binder with performance similar to Portland cement concretes. Zeobond's E-Crete and Wagner's Earth Friendly Concrete, both commercially available, can reduce carbon emissions by 60 percent and 80 to 90 percent, respectively, compared to ordinary Portland cement.[111] In most cases, low-carbon cements and concretes perform better than Portland cement in terms of durability, fire resistance, and other industry metrics. However, these novel alternatives do not yet have the long-term performance data needed for an industrywide shift away from Portland cement. For example, the first geopolymer concrete building, the University of Queensland's Global Change Institute, was built in 2013.[112]

Alternatives to Portland cement show promise, but the cement industry is large, and adoption of new technologies requires years of rigorous testing. Performance must be proven not only in a lab setting but also in the field with decades of data. According to industry discussions, alternatives that are commercially available are too expensive; without a significant increase in customer demand and changes to standards set by the likes of ASTM, an international standards organization, and state department of transportation specifications for roadways that allow for these alternatives, adoption will be slow.

PETROCHEMICALS:
THE HUNT FOR ALTERNATIVE FEEDSTOCKS

Petrochemicals are ubiquitous in modern life. Decarbonizing this rapidly growing industry will be challenging, yet critical to significantly reducing carbon emissions. Petrochemicals and their derivatives are used to make plastics, rubber, detergents, insulation, solvents, fertilizer, furniture, clothes, and electronic equipment, to name just a few applications. Scientific discoveries around polymer chemistry in the 1920s laid the groundwork for today's petrochemical industry, and World War II created initial demand for large-scale petrochemical production. Two decades later, the fast pace of economic growth in the United States provided consumers with new wealth, and petrochemicals offered an opportunity to achieve a higher standard of living at lower cost.

By the 1960s, petrochemical manufacturing had expanded to Europe and other parts of the world, led by companies such as ExxonMobil and BP, which built facilities in close proximity to their oil refineries.[113] The oil price shock of the 1970s slowed consumer demand for products made with petrochemicals in western economies and shifted production to developing countries with access to oil reserves such as in the Middle East. By the 1970s, most of the technological advances in polymer chemistry in use today had been achieved. The 1980s brought the discovery of linear low-density polyethylene, a stronger, more versatile, and lower-cost bulk polymer. R&D efforts then shifted from product innovation and focused instead on improving processes to reduce energy consumption and increase yields and efficiencies.[114]

The 2008 global recession resulted in a significant decrease in petrochemical production in developed countries, but growth continued in emerging countries such as China and India. China shifted from the region's biggest importer to the world's largest producer by 2016.[115] Over the last fifteen years, the petrochemical industry has seen significant growth, led by ethylene production, which increased by fifty million metric tons,[116] growing 4 to 5 percent annually between 2000 and 2016.[117] Overall, plastics manufacturing in particular has experienced consistent, significant growth (see Figure 4.4). While only about 9 percent of oil production went to plastics manufacturing in 2020, the demand forecast suggests that it could represent 45 percent of total oil demand growth.[118]

In the United States, 99 percent of petrochemicals are manufactured using crude oil or natural gas as feedstock, and more than 60 percent of petrochemicals are bought by plastic, resin, and synthetic rubber manufacturers.[119] The shale-oil boom in 2010 revived US production of petrochemicals, and low natural gas pricing will continue to pave the way for growth over the next five years, according to industry analysts. New capacity growth in the United States is expected to outpace the Middle East and China, which rely on naphtha (a liquid rich with hydrocarbons distilled from oil refining) for petrochemical production.[120] Downstream demand over the next five years from the new construction and packaging industries is expected to drive production of petrochemicals.

The petrochemical industry is largely regional in terms of trade and distribution, but shifts are being observed within some major producing countries. In 2000, only 5 percent of petrochemicals produced in Europe were exported.[121] By 2018, the export share of production had increased to 29 percent.[122] In the United States, neighboring countries Canada and Mexico continue to represent the largest share of exports; however, more recently China has emerged as an important customer. Overall, the chemical industry has enjoyed two decades of growth due primarily to demand for products in developing countries such as China; however, according to industry analysts, while growth will continue, the decade ahead will be more challenging as demand in China slows and global concerns around issues such as circular economy grow in popularity.[123]

Petrochemical manufacturing represents approximately 7 percent of global CO_2 emissions.[124] According to the US EPA, carbon emissions from petrochemical production have increased by 33 percent in the United States since 1990.[125] The most common classes of petrochemicals are olefins, aromatics, and

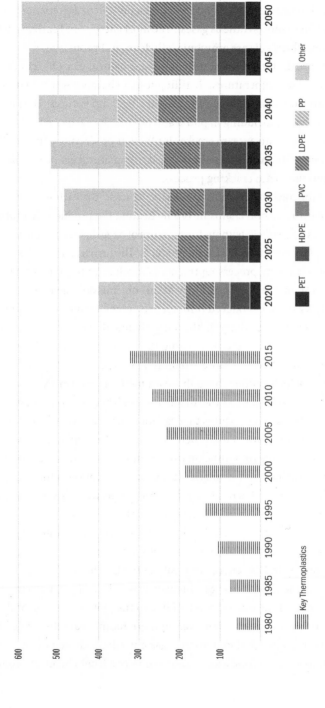

FIGURE 4.4 Global Production of Key Thermoplastics, 1980–2050 (in metric tons)

Source: IEA, "The Future of Petrochemicals," October 2018, iea.org/reports/the-future-of-petrochemicals

synthesis gases. The primary petrochemicals within these classes are ethylene, propylene, butadiene (olefins), benzene, toluene, xylene (aromatics), and ammonia and methanol (synthesis gases). The most energy- and carbon-intensive, high-volume chemicals are ammonia, ethylene, and propylene.[126]

Olefins are derived primarily from oil and natural gas. Oil refineries heat crude oil at high temperatures, distilling it in a chamber where hydrocarbon products are boiled off and recovered at varying temperatures. The lighter hydrocarbon chains, including naphtha and ethane, are recovered at lower temperatures and fed into a steam cracker for further processing to make ethylene and propylene. Ethane may also be sourced from natural gas processing plants and fed into the steam cracking process.

The steam cracking chamber breaks, or "cracks," the carbon-carbon bonds within the hydrocarbon chains by briefly heating the products in a furnace at 1,500 degrees Fahrenheit, without the presence of oxygen, creating the intermediate chemicals needed to make useful products. The furnace, or pyrolysis, section of the steam cracking process represents as much as 73 percent of total energy use and is responsible for the majority of carbon emissions generated on-site.[127]

Synthesis gases are produced through a steam reforming process (ammonia) or coal gasification (methanol). The basic chemical reaction needed to make ammonia isn't thermal driven, avoiding the need for cracking. However, significant amounts of heat energy are required to source the hydrogen needed for the reaction, which is done through steam methane reforming using natural gas. The currently practiced thermochemical Haber-Bosch process requires high temperatures and pressures that call for large-scale, centralized reactions to make economic sense. Fossil fuels provide the thermal energy needed for this process, resulting in significant carbon emissions. China is the only country producing olefins and aromatics from coal gasification, a thermochemical process that breaks it down into its chemical properties. This is largely due to the country's access to abundant, low-cost coal.[128]

Efforts in the petrochemical industry to reduce energy intensity (ratio of energy use to output) and carbon emissions have slowed the growth of emissions. According to IEA, energy intensity of the US chemical sector improved by 39 percent and greenhouse gas intensity was reduced by 10 percent between 1997 and 2007.[129] Emissions leveled off due to the global recession and slowed growth across the industry; however, in more recent years there has been an absolute increase in total greenhouse gas emissions, driven by increases in carbon emissions.[130] Worldwide carbon emissions from chemical production nearly doubled between 2000 and 2018. As the global market for plastics continues to grow, more significant reductions will be needed to offset the increase in emissions inherent in industry expansion.

Overall, energy consumed in petrochemical plants can be broken down to three sources: fuel combustion, 60 percent; steam energy consumption, 35 percent; and power consumption, 5 percent.[131] Steam cracking is the largest single point of opportunity for carbon emission reduction. Naphtha steam cracking is more energy intensive than natural gas and therefore produces more carbon emissions. Yet substituting one for the other isn't that easy. While gas crackers are less complex, less costly, and less energy intensive, their production is largely limited to ethylene. Naphtha crackers also produce by-products like propylene that are important constituents of consumer products today.[132] State-of-the-art steam cracking furnaces have thermal efficiencies around 94 percent.[133] There is little to be gained from further efficiency measures. To truly have an impact on carbon emissions, either the energy source for steam cracking needs to shift to electric or biomass fuels or the thermal-driven cracking process needs to be replaced altogether by an electrochemical one.

Biomass could serve as a substitute for fossil-fuel energy sources and feedstock. Sugars from sugarcane, sugar beets, grain starches (such as corn and wheat), and lignocellulose (plant dry matter), along with vegetable oils from palm, soybean, and oilseeds, offer promise. For industrials overall, biomass represented 90 percent of renewable heat consumption globally in 2019.[134] However, the biomass share of total industrial energy demand for heat is less than 10 percent.[135] Industries in which biomass waste is produced as a by-product of operations (for example, pulp and paper) are best positioned to adopt bioenergy technologies, creating a "waste to energy" closed-loop industrial process.[136] In the case of petrochemicals, biomass is up against the highly integrated relationship between petrochemicals and the oil and gas industry, as well as low fossil-fuel prices. Harvesting and transporting crop waste to make petrochemicals is expensive as well as logistically challenging. Furthermore, use of biomass at an industrial scale could have a negative impact on the global food supply as well as biodiversity.

Another approach to reducing carbon emissions is substituting existing chemical processes and feedstocks. Looking at the most carbon-intensive petrochemicals—ammonia, ethylene, and propylene—two new technologies offer promise: electrolysis and oxidative dehydrogenation. For ammonia, the opportunity for decarbonization comes at the hydrogen-sourcing stage. Hydrogen, which reacts with nitrogen to produce ammonia, is currently derived from natural-gas reforming. This is a process through which methane reacts with high pressure steam to produce hydrogen and CO_2. As discussed in Chapter 3, another way to make hydrogen is electrolysis, in which electricity is used to split water into hydrogen and oxygen. The process could thus be powered by renewable energy sources, eliminating all carbon emissions. Electrolysis is not a new technology, but it is cost-prohibitive and far from commercialization in petrochemicals. According to IEA, producing hydrogen from electrolysis is twice the cost of gas steam reforming.[137] More promising is hydrogen's potential role across several critical industries, including the transportation and energy sectors, which may help to support further R&D and drive down the price of the technology.

For ethylene and propylene, avoiding the steam cracking step would eliminate a significant share of carbon emissions. Oxidative dehydrogenation is a chemical process in which oxygen is introduced to react with ethane and propane to make ethylene and propylene, with water as a by-product. This seems simple enough, but a catalyst is needed to control the reaction, and while there has been research in this area, one has yet to be identified.

Bioplastics, or plastics derived from plant feedstock instead of petroleum, show some promise for reducing carbon emissions and offer the added benefit of being biodegradable. Research published by Carnegie Mellon in 2017 suggests that carbon emissions could be reduced by 25 percent through a shift from traditional plastics to corn-based bioplastics.[138] Yet there might be some unintended consequences for agriculture and the environment if bioplastic manufacturing were scaled up. There are also cross-contamination challenges with the traditional plastics recycling stream and higher costs, which can be 20 to 50 percent more expensive due to the complexity of processing the plant feedstock.[139]

Compared to cement and steel, the focus of the petrochemical industry has been on rapid growth and streamlining processes to reduce production costs. Expansion of the US industry provides an opportunity to more cost-effectively incorporate new, clean technologies that will prove more costly down the road in retrofitting existing plants. Yet as long as oil and gas prices are low, and regulatory pressures absent, there is little incentive for change.

WILDCARD DISRUPTORS:
THE FOURTH INDUSTRIAL REVOLUTION

Many experts believe we are in the midst of the Fourth Industrial Revolution, defined by the fusion of technologies that blurs the lines between the physical and digital worlds. The World Economic Forum's Klaus Schwab characterized this revolution as one that will disrupt almost every industry at unprecedented speeds.[140] New technology developments in data analytics, artificial intelligence, advanced robotics, and the Internet of Things have the potential to optimize resources and increase manufacturing productivity.

IBM uses the term *cognitive* when describing the manufacturing plant of the future, with a vision of real-time data analytics to maximize throughput, reduce equipment downtime, and minimize energy costs.[141] Some studies have suggested emissions reductions of 25 percent resulting from digitization of processes, real-time monitoring of equipment and systems, and advanced data analytics.[142] Some companies are even embedding digital sensors in cement and steel to monitor their resilience in structures.

For manufacturing, waste—of energy or materials—raises costs. Focused investment continues to be directed toward improving operations and increasing productivity. Consumer pressure on companies to be more transparent and environmentally conscious when making products is also influencing change on the factory floor and in supply chains. The new technologies could assist companies in addressing challenges, but they could also make problems worse if not implemented responsibly.

One example is additive manufacturing (AM), or 3D printing, which uses digital information to apply successive layers of raw material to produce a product. A benefit of AM is the ability to place printers close to customers, reducing the transportation needed to ship products and thus emissions associated with the supply chain. AM also reduces material waste compared to conventional processes that start larger and subtract material through cutting. AM has the potential to replace current thermal-driven manufacturing processes for industries such as steel and cement, driving down carbon emissions.

However, some industry analysts caution that AM can be more energy intensive than conventional manufacturing. If the electricity is supplied by clean energy sources, then the emission gains will be realized. Today, AM is mostly aimed at smaller, specialized applications, and it is not yet known whether it is capable of replacing mass-produced industrial processes. As 3D printer prices drop and applications scale, we could see significant disruption across the industrials sector. Whether this will help or hurt efforts to reduce carbon emissions is yet to be determined.[143]

More broadly, as the industrials sector adopts smarter manufacturing technologies and systems, the need for additional computing power will grow. Data collection, housing, and analytics, along with sensors and digitalization of processes, could actually increase the industrials sector's impact on the electric grid at the same time that core functions are being decarbonized. As industries look to streamline and electrify operations, companies should be mindful of impacts outside of factory walls. Governments can play a critical role in ensuring that standards and incentives are put in place to ensure that the expansion of Fourth Industrial Revolution technologies doesn't negate the strides being made to reduce carbon emissions across these industries.

THE UPSHOT: INDUSTRIAL DECARBONIZATION IS UNLIKELY WITHOUT INTERVENTION

Industrialization has contributed to both the modern world in which we live and the environmental challenges we face today. As we progress into the Fourth Industrial Revolution, the industrials sector has an opportunity to reverse these impacts, by harnessing existing (and innovating new) technologies that use resources more efficiently and reduce reliance on fossil fuels. Data and automation also could help facilitate a shift toward more efficient operations in general. As the IT and industrial worlds collide, will industries within this sector be able to reinvent themselves and stay cost-competitive? Without public intervention, will carbon emissions ever become more than a reporting requirement? Can these industries continue to grow sustainably?

According to IEA, increasing population and urbanization patterns, coupled with infrastructure development needs, will drive new demand for cement and concrete. Cement production will grow 12 to 23 percent by 2050 from the current level.[144] Demand for green cement (blends) is expected to grow significantly over the next decade due to several factors, including increased demand from governments to reduce carbon emissions. Analysts' predictions range from 10 to 15 percent CAGR increase in green cement global production.[145] In comparison, CAGR growth of the overall global cement industry is estimated at 7 to 8 percent.[146] This is encouraging but doesn't go far enough to decarbonize this industry without novel low-carbon cements.

The steel industry has long claimed to be green because of the high percentage of recycled steel used in the manufacturing process. However, with any significant growth in demand comes the need for new steel, which is more carbon-intensive than EAF-produced steel. IEA projects that global demand for steel will increase by more than one-third through to 2050, driven by the buildings and transportation sectors.[147] Yet reports of overproduction and oversupply as well as expected new sources of recycled steel from developing economies bode well for EAFs. Market analysts expect that there will be a trend toward higher EAF production worldwide, driven primarily in response to government efforts to reduce overall carbon emissions.[148]

Expanding economies such as China have helped to drive demand for plastics, and thus petrochemicals. Consumers in developed countries such as the United States are acquiring more goods and devices that incorporate plastics. Even clean technologies like lightweight vehicles, wind turbines, and solar panels are creating a new market segment for plastics. Low oil and natural-gas prices are boosting new petrochemical plant construction in the United States and the Middle East. The path forward to a significant reduction in carbon emissions seems to include switching from coal to natural gas; increasing energy efficiency; and requiring carbon capture, utilization, and storage (CCUS) for remaining emissions.[149] Alternative feedstocks and recycling are expected to play a lesser role in the transition, yet these options are the only ones that truly move the industry toward decarbonization.

HOW CAN WE DECARBONIZE INDUSTRIALS BY 2050?

Substituting for steel, cement, and plastics will be difficult. These industries and the products they produce are the backbone of global infrastructure growth and new product development. The sector overall is challenged by the fact that it is made up of dozens of industries, all requiring different inputs and feedstocks. Even within industries there can be hundreds of different methods used for manufacturing. For example, there are 130 different industrial processes that can be used to manufacture the eighteen most carbon-intensive chemicals, with these processes being specific to any one company.[150] Carbon pricing could provide industrywide incentives to innovate and adopt low-carbon technologies without being prescriptive, but many political hurdles face its implementation in the United States and globally. Electrification of manufacturing processes could significantly reduce the need for fossil-fuel heating across the sector but is challenged by the scale of the demand. To significantly decarbonize this sector by 2050, other solutions need to be identified.

Focusing primarily on the steel, cement, and petrochemical industries, which represent more than 60 percent of industrial carbon emissions, is a good start. Of course, this does not negate the need to address carbon-intensive operations within other industries that collectively could present a growing problem. Developing industry-specific strategies could enable customized solutions based on operational needs and be more effective. For example, IEA is moving the dialogue forward through its technology roadmap series on key industries, such as steel and cement, which identifies the priority actions that governments, industry, financial partners, and civil society need to take to advance clean technologies in these areas in support of achieving international climate goals.

Support from the government in the form of R&D investment could further accelerate technology adoption and commercialization. Lack of government support may slow progress, but investment by private industry could still push forward key industrial solutions. One example is the Breakthrough Energy Coalition, led by Microsoft's Bill Gates, which brings together private investors, global corporations, financial institutions, and academic institutions to support innovative clean technologies at every stage of development, from discovery to development to deployment. Manufacturing is one of the "grand challenges" identified by the coalition, and targeted technology solutions include low-greenhouse-gas chemicals and steel, low- or negative-GHG cement, and low-GHG industrial thermal processing.[151] Yet the commercialization of new technologies will take time, and while some industries, like steel, have technologies at the ready, others, such as petrochemicals, have yet to identify alternatives. The road is long for industrial decarbonization, and unfortunately it appears to stretch beyond our 2050 target.

For many of these industries, downstream influencers could make the difference. While each industry within the industrials sector may face different decarbonization challenges, there is a common thread across all of them. Industrial manufacturers are producing commodity products destined for use by downstream market actors that drive price and volume, which in turn are driven by consumer demand. This consumer demand has more recently included preferences for greener products, influencing the choice of materials used in manufacturing. Private companies looking to establish themselves as good environmental stewards are asking more from their supply chains and have the buying power to influence change. Apple's efforts to decarbonize the aluminum industry is a great example (see "Spur Demand for Green Substitutes" further on). This is only one of several levers that need to be pulled for industrials to have a chance of meeting the 2050 decarbonization goal. In the following, we explore each of the potential influencers and discuss the opportunities and barriers to their success.

Subsidize Innovation

In the United States, the industrials sector represents roughly one-third of total natural gas consumption. What would it take to shift the entire sector to electrification, similar to what we have seen in the steel industry? For steel, it took investment by an industry outsider, Nucor, using a radically different steelmaking process, which was being applied in Europe but yet to be explored in the United States. At the time, electricity was cheap and scrap metal was a fraction of the cost of iron ore, and as a result Nucor was able to undercut other US steelmakers on price. Today, Nucor is the largest manufacturer of US-produced steel, and electrified steel represents the majority of steel produced in the country. Similar disruption is needed across dozens of industries within the industrials sector, each contending with its own market dynamics and challenges.

Often, it is too risky for private companies, particularly incumbents, to invest significantly in R&D within highly competitive commodity markets. Many low-carbon solutions are in the early stages of technology development for several industries, including cement and petrochemicals, and public investment could provide the funding and expertise (such as national labs) needed to pilot solutions, perfect designs, and drive down the cost of these new technologies. Once these technologies are cost-competitive, private industry can more easily deploy and scale the solutions. This type of government intervention has proven to be successful in the past. For example, as discussed in Chapter 2, US government investment in early wind and solar energy development and demonstration projects paved the way for commercialization. Today, clean energy is increasingly becoming cost-competitive with coal and natural gas on the electric grid.

Yet clean technology R&D was precisely the area of research targeted for cuts by the Trump administration. The Office of Energy Efficiency & Renewable Energy (EERE), where much of this research takes place, was in danger of receiving 70 percent less funding in 2018 compared to 2017.[152] As a result of bipartisan support and a decision to raise the spending cap, EERE's FY18 budget landed 11 percent higher than FY17.[153] Once again science was targeted for significant cuts in the requested FY19 budget, including 70 to 100 percent for DOE programs that focus on low-carbon technologies; however, the final approved budget granted the agency additional funding.[154]

The uncertainty of future government funding provides an opportunity for private investors with a keen interest in climate change and technology innovation to step into a critical funding role. Some public-private industry partnerships are forming to provide shared investment in the most challenging industries. These partnerships may provide private industry access to agency laboratory resources and expertise and/or governments might leverage private funding to support R&D and commercialization of technologies of shared interest. Efforts such as the Breakthrough Energy Coalition can pick up where government agencies fall short, more quickly funneling private investment into promising new technologies.

Power Electrification by Renewables

Electrification is only clean if the electricity generation is carbon-free. Industrials have two choices: (1) purchase green electricity off the electric grid through a third-party power producer located near the plant, or (2) install clean energy on-site, where the plant fully owns and operates the power-producing asset. Given their flexibility in siting, wind and solar are best positioned to support industrials. Yet deploying wind and solar to meet the energy-intensive demands of industries such as steel, cement, and petrochemicals is fraught with challenges.

The temperatures demanded by energy-intensive industries are too high for today's commercially available solar thermal technologies. Most plants implementing solar projects use nonconcentrating technologies, which do not deliver useable heat over 100 degrees Celsius.[155] Concentrated solar technologies have the potential to reach temperatures up to 400 degrees Celsius, which can support medium to high heating processes. A concentrated solar system uses mirrors to concentrate the sunlight into a receiver, converting the light into heat. Typically, this heat is then used to generate electricity, but it can also be stored and used to heat industrial processes. However, concentrated solar arrays are geographically limited to areas with good direct normal irradiance (the amount of solar energy falling perpendicular to the panel, measured in watts/m2). Solar towers, which also use mirrors to concentrate sunlight, can reach higher temperatures (500-plus degrees Celsius) but have been deployed only in the electric power sector to date.

R&D efforts are under way to create thermal solar solutions that can better serve the industrials sector. For example, the SOLPART initiative, funded by the European Union and several cement companies, was tasked to develop a new solar technology capable of producing a high-temperature concentrating solar process suitable for particle calcination in energy-intensive industries. At the end of the four-year initiative (December 2019), a pilot-scale reactor was built and tested for mineral calcification.[156] Researchers claim that by using the solar technologies developed through the initiative, plant owners could see a reduction of 40 percent in greenhouse gas emissions.[157] However, the 800 to 900 degrees Celsius achieved by these technologies fall short of the 1,500 degrees Celsius needed to make clinker. Raw material substitution will be necessary to lower the thermal demand of these processes and bring it within concentrated solar's reach.

A promising new concentrated solar technology has emerged to address this problem with the support of Bill Gates and other private investors. The Heliogen solar system uses mirrors, sensors, and high-tech computing to precisely focus sunlight on a particular spot (tower or transmission pipe), heating it up to the desired 1,500 degrees Celsius.[158] The company was launched out of Idealab, a technology incubator, in 2019 and by 2020 was looking for industry partners to deploy the technology. [159]

Yet focusing only on energy-intensive industries alone would be a mistake. There is a shift happening within the industrials sector that merits consideration when setting the path to decarbonization. Data provided by IEA suggests that while industries with high-temperature heat demand, such as the three covered in this chapter, drove thermal industrial demand in the past, industries with low- and medium-temperature heat demand (operations requiring thermal sources under 400 degrees Celsius) will propel 75 percent of industrial growth between now and 2040.[160] While efforts should continue to address the high demands of industries such as steel, cement, and petrochemicals, solar technologies available today could be deployed in less-demanding industries (for example, computer and electronic products, pharmaceuticals, machinery).

Even if renewables could meet 100 percent of industrial thermal and electricity needs, these energy sources are further challenged by location, scale, and land availability. A petrochemical company operating a plant built on the Gulf Coast to be close to oil refineries would be hard-pressed to find a sufficiently large site conducive to solar within the region. Industrial facilities require large amounts of power to operate. The US DOE National Renewable Energy Laboratory estimates that it takes 2.8 acres of land to generate 1 GWh of solar per year, and 3.5 acres for concentrated solar.[161] To give a sense of scale, Lightsource BP entered into an agreement with utility Xcel Energy and EAF steel manufacturer EVRAZ to build a 300 MW solar plant that will exclusively deliver electricity to their Rocky Mountain, Colorado, facility.[162]

The company claimed that 95 percent of the mill's annual energy demand will be met by the more than seven hundred thousand solar panels planned for the sixteen-acre site.[163]

Price Carbon

For industrials, capturing carbon emissions will be a critical piece to decarbonizing the sector. Yet adoption of carbon-capture technologies has been slow, largely due to the fact that there are limited market incentives or regulatory pressures to incorporate them into industrial operations. Observed carbon-emission reductions over the years are attributed to efficiency improvements or fuel-switching from coal to natural gas, driven by an interest in reducing energy costs, which make up the largest share of operational expense. For these industries to consider CCUS, we need to place a price on carbon; otherwise, there is no economic incentive to adopt it.

There is a significant additional cost to incorporating CCUS technologies into industrial operations. Industries in this sector are very familiar with the idea of capturing by-products, such as heat and steam, and putting those back into the process to increase efficiencies and reduce costs. Carbon emissions don't offer the same efficiency improvements for the plants emitting them, nor do they provide a means for recovering the capital expense. What are the most viable options for creating a demand for CO_2 and motivating manufacturers to adopt CCUS technologies?

Carbon emission trading could motivate industrial manufacturers to explore clean technologies. In the United States, California has a cap-and-trade program that covers industrial facilities. It includes industrial plants that emit twenty-five thousand metric tons or more of CO_2-equivalent. While overall the state has observed declining carbon emissions under the program, some industries emitted more than their baseline through the purchase of offsets. According to one study, cement plants increased their carbon emissions by 75 percent in the first three years (2013–2016).[164] A carbon tax might provide the pricing certainty needed for industry to make longer-term investments in clean technologies.

Creating a market for selling the actual CO_2 emissions could also motivate investment in CCUS. For example, in addition to enhanced recovery, CO_2 is used by the food and beverage industry, and in agriculture to stimulate plant growth in greenhouses. As discussed earlier in the chapter, CO_2 can also be used in cement and other building materials. What is the price that will move industry? Modeling suggests a carbon tax of $100/ton CO_2 combined with CCUS technologies could significantly decarbonize steel and cement industries.[165] Most carbon prices today fall significantly short of this value.

Create Tax Incentives

Federal tax incentives can defray the initial cost of purchasing and installing a CCUS system. Increasing the demand for CCUS technologies could create new markets for CO_2 and lower the cost for deployment. In 2018, Congress extended tax credits to carbon-capture projects that would begin construction within six years. Along with the extension, Congress increased the credit amounts. The previous measure offered credits of $10/ton of carbon captured and used for enhanced oil recovery and $20/ton of carbon captured and put in geological storage or used in other ways. The new measure increased these credits to $35/ton and $50/ton, respectively.[166]

For some industries, the new tax credit will greatly reduce the cost of carbon capture. In the electricity industry, carbon-capture costs are about $60/ton for coal plants and $70/ton for natural gas plants. In the industrials sector, plants that manufacture petrochemicals like ethanol and fertilizers, where carbon capture costs $9/ton to $30/ton, will benefit the most from these credits.[167] For steel and cement plants, these incentives will do little to sway decision making. Carbon-capture costs for these industries are estimated to be closer to $100/ton.[168] Also, there are other costs to consider, including transportation and storage costs, that are an additional $11/ton of carbon.[169]

If subsidies could reduce the fixed costs of CCUS adoption, customer demand for CO_2 could provide a further catalyst for industrial manufacturers to embrace CCUS. There are many ways in which CO_2 could be used to enhance and substitute other manufacturing processes. The largest application of captured CO_2 today is enhanced oil recovery (EOR), in which the CO_2 is injected into the ground to facilitate oil and gas extraction. Of course, the longer-term profitability of EOR will depend on oil and gas pricing. Other potential applications include turning CO_2 into chemicals, fuels, and products. Selling CO_2 as an input to other industries holds promise, particularly if consumer demand for greener products continues to grow.

We already see some examples of this happening across several industries. One example is HeidelbergCement's plant in Germany that uses algae to absorb its CO_2 emissions, then sells the algae as a food additive to agricultural companies.[170] Another example is Newlight Technologies, which uses carbon from greenhouse gases and converts it into plastics, fibers, and other materials. Carbicrete, mentioned earlier, uses CO_2 with steel slag during the cement curing process.

Spur Demand for Green Substitutes

The manufacturing of industrial components is driven by demand for the finished products in which they are used. More than 60 percent of steel made in the United States is sold to companies in the nonresidential construction and automobile industries.[171] For cement, 70 percent of the volume produced is sold to ready-mix concrete companies, while 10 percent is sold to precast-concrete manufacturers,[172] both of which are influenced by the demand for new construction. For petrochemicals, demand comes from dozens of industries from health care to IT to automobiles, many of which sell consumer-facing products.

In the building industry, construction companies are beholden to building codes and standards. These standards can drive demand for new technologies, such as more effective and efficient insulation and lighting, but can also stifle innovation if too prescriptive, as in the case of cement when Portland may be included in specifications. This makes it difficult for new low-carbon cements to enter the market. Voluntary certification and labeling programs, such as LEED for buildings, can also drive demand for greener materials. For example, slag cement used in new construction can contribute to thirteen LEED points.[173]

Shifts in the automobile industry have had a significant impact on steel innovation. As car manufacturers work toward more fuel-efficient designs to meet new federal standards, steel has met some competition from aluminum, carbon fiber, and other lightweight materials. This has motivated research into lighter-weight steel alloys reducing the amount of steel needed. Through innovation, steel has been able to reduce its carbon footprint while retaining its leading spot as the most common metal used in automobile manufacturing today.

The buying power and influence of global corporations has the potential to shift entire industries. One example is Apple. In May 2018, aluminum manufacturers Alcoa and Rio Tinto launched a joint venture, Elysis, to further develop and scale a new smelting process that replaces carbon material with an advanced conductive material. The new process releases oxygen instead of carbon dioxide. This unlikely partnership between two aluminum giants was facilitated by Apple, which was looking for opportunities to further reduce its own carbon footprint. Apple provided technical support and funding to the development process, along with financial contributions from Alcoa, Rio Tinto, and the governments of Canada and Quebec.[174] In 2019, the company bought the first ever commercial batch carbon-free aluminum from the venture, which has plans to make it more broadly available by 2024.[175]

Growing concerns among consumers around plastics could have an impact on future demand for petrochemicals. While it is unlikely that consumers will have insight into the manufacturing process and thus influence the chemistry used to make these products, an increased demand for higher recycled content or product substitution (for example, wooden toys instead of plastic) could have a direct impact on petrochemical manufacturing. Companies such as Green Toys, Pilot, and Trex are selling toys, ballpoint pens, and deck materials using recycled plastics.

Certification and labeling programs could make it easier for customers to identify, and trust, green products. The success of labeling programs in changing purchasing behavior is dependent on the ability to clearly communicate the benefits of the alternative and provide customers with the assurance that green product performance is equivalent to the conventional product. Recent consumer surveys suggest a readiness to choose green products. According to a CGS 2019 retail and sustainability survey, 68 percent of consumers rate sustainability as important when purchasing products.[176] Accenture released similar findings from its "2019 Chemical Global Consumer Sustainability Survey," finding that 83 percent of consumers "believe it's important or extremely important for companies to design products that are meant to be reused or recycled."[177] However, these surveys also suggest that price continues to be the main driver of purchasing decisions. While there is a small percentage of customers willing to pay more for green products—the CGS survey shows that 35 percent of consumers are willing to pay 25 percent more for green products while the Accenture survey shows that 36 percent would pay more for products made from recycled materials[178]—most consumers, although well-intentioned, will need to see cost parity between green and conventional options.

At the end of the day, we have to accept that wholesale substitution away from core industrials sectors such as cement and steel is unlikely if not impossible. Consider recent advances in structural timber that allow for the building of structures up to seven stories tall. An advance for sure, but as long as we continue to build skyscrapers (or simply buildings taller than seven stories), steel will be in demand. So we should do what we can to reduce the use of major greenhouse-gas-emitting suppliers, but we also need to continue to push technological innovations that eliminate emissions from production of these core industrials sectors. When technological solutions are not available or viable, we will need either direct regulation or a price on carbon to incentivize manufacturers to capture and store CO_2 emissions.

CHAPTER 5

THE BUILDINGS SECTOR

ITIES AROUND THE WORLD are expanding and increasing in density as more people recognize the numerous opportunities that metropolitan areas offer in terms of jobs, education, and services. The United Nations projects that by 2050, 68 percent of the world population will live in urban areas compared to 55 percent today.[1] Growing cities in Asia and Africa will represent close to 90 percent of this increase, with India alone adding 416 million people to cities.[2] Developed countries will see more modest growth—in North America, 82 percent of the population already lives in cities. Some analysts estimate that in order to support global urbanization, thirteen thousand new buildings will need to be constructed every day through 2050.[3]

Each of these buildings comes with a carbon footprint, with emissions resulting from off-site and on-site operations. Emissions tied to building construction are referred to as "embodied carbon," which is defined as "the carbon dioxide that is emitted from the extraction, manufacturing, and transport of building materials."[4] Electricity consumed by the building but purchased from an off-site supplier such as a utility (scope 2 emissions) is another significant contributor to the carbon footprint of buildings. Last, and most important for our analysis, emissions are generated as the result of on-site fossil-fuel consumption, primarily natural gas for heating and cooking (scope 1 emissions).[5]

The Global Alliance for Buildings and Construction (GlobalABC) estimates that the construction and operation of residential and commercial buildings around the world represents 36 percent of final energy use and 39 percent of energy- and process-related carbon emissions.[6] Three-fourths of these emissions are tied to the manufacturing of building materials (embedded carbon) and electricity consumption (scope 2), and the remaining one-fourth is attributed to on-site energy consumption (scope 1).[7] Our focus in this chapter is how to decarbonize the scope 1 emissions (since we addressed building materials in Chapter 4, on industrials, and scope 2 emissions in Chapter 2, on energy).

While our focus is on scope 1 emissions, it is useful to think of building emissions as part of an integrated system. For example, energy efficiency projects are helping to slow the growth of carbon emissions from buildings. Global building energy intensity—or the amount of energy used per square foot of space—is lowering at an annual average rate of 1.5 percent, but floor area continues to grow by 2.3 percent annually, offsetting these improvements.[8] EIA forecasts that global building energy consumption will increase by 1.3 percent each year between 2018 and 2050 without significant changes (Figure 5.1).[9] Maximizing energy efficiency within residential and commercial buildings is a critical step in any decarbonization strategy, but without more aggressive mitigation measures, IPCC estimates that building carbon emissions could double by 2050.[10]

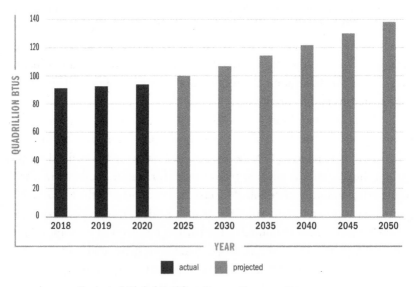

FIGURE 5.1   Projected Global Building Energy Consumption
Source: IEA, "International Energy Outlook 2019, with Projections to 2050, Buildings"

We believe that electrification of building systems, supported by a clean energy grid, is the more likely path forward for building decarbonization. To get there, building operations need to remove all fossil fuels; that is, to eliminate scope 1 emissions. Cases when electrification proves challenging indicate the need to innovate carbon-neutral or even carbon-*negative* solutions that capitalize on the potential for buildings to serve as carbon sinks. As in our previous chapters on transportation and industrials, we do not analyze the carbon emissions tied to off-site electricity generation (addressed in Chapter 2). We do, however, discuss the influence that buildings have in decarbonizing this and other sectors with regard to sourcing green products and services.

RESIDENTIAL: BIGGER IS NOT NECESSARILY BETTER

Residential buildings are a significant source of energy consumption and carbon emissions. According to EIA, US homes and residences represent 16 percent of national energy consumption and 56 percent of building energy consumption.[11] Globally, the residential share of total building energy consumption is a bit higher, at 73 percent.[12] Compared to other critical sectors, residential represents 22 percent of global energy consumption, which places it third behind industrials (32 percent) and transportation (28 percent). The ranking is similar for global carbon emissions, with residential estimated at 17 percent share of the total.[13]

How did we get here? In the United States, residential energy consumption has risen due to several trends, most notably growing floorplans. In 1910, the average home size was 1,398 square feet.[14] By 2018, newly built single-family homes averaged 2,386 square feet.[15] As home sizes grow, so do space heating and cooling demands. Technologies introduced to provide comfort and convenience are contributing to increased home energy use. Air conditioning, first introduced in the 1920s, is now offered in 90 percent of new homes[16] and represents a large portion of the home's energy footprint in the United States today. Once luxuries, appliances and personal electronics such as televisions are found in every home and bring with them their own energy demands.

According to EIA, between 1950 and 2009, residential energy consumption and carbon emissions tripled.[17] During this time, there was a significant shift in the fuel mix found in US homes. In 1950, petroleum represented 26 percent of home energy consumption, followed by coal (25 percent), natural gas (25 percent), and electricity (5 percent).[18] By 2015, electricity represented 47 percent of household energy use and natural gas 44 percent, while petroleum dropped to 9 percent and coal disappeared completely (Figure 5.2).[19]

Globally, we see expanding access to energy and the adoption of new technologies driving worldwide residential energy consumption upward. IEA estimates that electricity consumption by appliances and small plug-load devices, such as TVs and computers, has grown nearly 3 percent each year since 2010.[20] Today, the use of air conditioning is concentrated in just a few countries, but according to IEA, two-thirds of homes around the world could have air conditioning by 2050, with China, India, and Indonesia representing half of those homes.[21] The continued use of natural gas, coal, and oil for heating and cooking in homes around the world also contributes to rising energy consumption and related emissions. Natural gas consumption is rising in developing countries, with China and Africa more than doubling consumption between 2010 and 2016.[22]

In the United States, space heating represents 68 percent of residential natural gas consumption, followed by water heating at 26 percent.[23] Natural gas is the primary heating source in 51 percent of homes.[24] Looking at the data more closely, we see that the share between electricity and natural gas usage differs

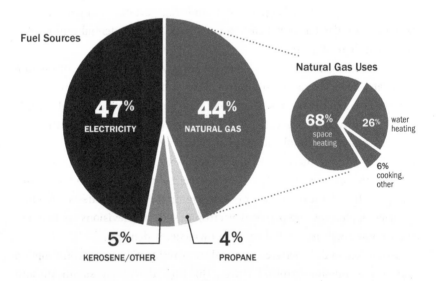

FIGURE 5.2   Breakdown of Energy Consumption in US Homes

Source: "2015 Residential Energy Consumption Survey (RECS): Energy Consumption and Expenditures Tables" US Energy Information Administration, revised May 31, 2018, https://www.eia.gov/consumption/residential/reports/2015/overview/index.php?src=%E2%80%B9%20Consumption%20%20%20%20%20Residential%20Energy%20Consumption%20Survey%20(RECS)-f3

by US climate region. According to EIA's "Residential Energy Consumption Survey," natural gas is the most-frequently used heating fuel in the Northeast (54 percent), Midwest (71 percent), and West regions (59 percent). In the South, electricity is the dominant fuel at 59 percent.[25] In the Northeast, there is also heavy use of oil; the region represents 82 percent of all US homes using oil for space heating.[26]

A quarter of US households are all-electric, and this share is trending upward, most prominently in the South and driven largely by electric space heating becoming common more broadly.[27] In general, new home construction is trending toward warmer regions. The hot-humid climate zone, which covers Florida to Southeastern Texas, has experienced a spike in new construction activities, representing 28 percent of all new homes built since 2000.[28] EIA estimates that over the next thirty years, natural gas consumption will fall by 0.3 percent per year in the United States as a result of a shift in population and housing stock growth to the South and West regions, decreasing the number of heating degree days.[29] During this same time period, purchased electricity is expected to rise 0.6 percent each year as a result of increased demand for appliances and electronic devices as well as an increase in cooling degree days.[30] These predictions bode well for electrification, but unless accelerated, they will fall short of our goal to decarbonize residential buildings by 2050.

Globally, we see a similar share of electricity and natural gas energy consumption.[31] While some households in non-OECD countries (those not participating in the Organisation for Economic Co-operation and Development, including China and India) continue to use coal for space heating, water heating, and cooking, its use in homes will continue to decline.[32] According to IEA, nearly 50 percent of residential energy consumption (in member countries) is tied to space heating, followed by residential appliances and water heating; together, these end uses represent about 75 percent of the total.[33] Rising incomes, urbanization, and increased access to electricity are shifting these economies toward electrification and provide an opportunity to shift heating systems and cooking with it. IEA estimates that worldwide residential electricity consumption will grow by 2.5 percent each year to 2050. This increase will be driven largely by the increase in air conditioner use in hotter, developing countries and rise in demand for appliances and personal devices. However, natural gas consumption is also expected to grow 0.7 percent annually over the same time period, as coal use declines.[34]

COMMERCIAL: LEANER BUT GROWING

Commercial buildings in the United States represent 12 percent of total US energy consumption and 45 percent of total building energy use.[35] Globally, the commercial share of total building energy consumption is quite a bit smaller than residential, at 38 percent.[36] Overall, the energy consumed and related emissions from commercial buildings worldwide are small compared to other critical sectors, at 8 percent and 11 percent, respectively. However, with the expected growth in urbanization, global building floor space is expected to double by 2060 (2.48 million square feet),[37] and energy consumption and carbon emissions along with it. Commercial buildings will be a key driver of this growth.

Commercial building energy consumption historically has been closely tied to new construction. However, increasing square footage isn't the only driver of increasing energy demand. Similar to residential, the introduction of new technologies has played a role. In the United States, electricity consumption rose significantly between 1979 and 2012 due primarily to the introduction of computers, office equipment, telecommunication equipment, and medical and diagnostic equipment.[38] Lighting also contributed to increasing electricity use, and today it is the largest single user of electricity in buildings. As a result of rising electricity use, scope 2 emissions of commercial buildings has increased. Meanwhile, scope 1 fossil-fuel consumption and related carbon emissions continued to rise with square footage, albeit more slowly than electricity. Between 1990 and 2015, scope 1 emissions for commercial buildings in the United States increased by 13.2 percent.[39]

During this time period, commercial buildings in the United States experienced a significant shift away from petroleum and coal to electricity and natural gas. In 1950, petroleum and coal represented 79 percent, and today that share is 9 percent for petroleum and less than 1 percent for coal. Electricity is now the dominant energy source at 49 percent, followed by natural gas at 39 percent (Figure 5.3).[40] Today, commercial scope 1 emissions are driven primarily by the combustion of natural gas for space heating, water heating, and cooking.[41] According to EIA, space heating accounts for nearly 60 percent of natural gas consumption, followed by water heating at 19 percent and cooking at 18 percent.[42]

By 2050, commercial building floor space in the United States is projected to be 40 percent larger than in 2016, resulting in a 20 percent increase in energy demand. Energy efficiency improvements will help to curb the scope 2 emissions tied to increase in electricity use, but scope 1 emissions are projected to

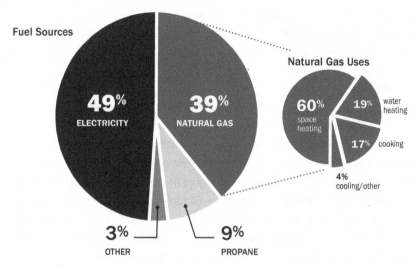

FIGURE 5.3 Breakdown of Energy Consumption in US Commercial Buildings

Source: EIA, "US Energy Facts Explained," updated May 7, 2020; and AGA, "Uncovering the US Natural Gas Commercial Sector," January 2017, https://www.aga.org/contentassets/70b4444e883f479ba0efa91a90140f33/uncovering_the_us_natural_gas_commercial_sector_final.pdf.

increase 20 percent by 2050.[43] Access to clean energy will help to further reduce building scope 2 emissions, but unless we electrify scope 1 emissions, the continued reliance on natural gas equipment and systems will slow the progress of decarbonization overall.

Elsewhere in the world, commercial building energy demand is rising due to increased access to energy grids in developing countries, and proliferation of energy-using devices and appliances. Growth in building floor area has also contributed, 3 percent between 2017 and 2018 and 23 percent since 2010.[44] Floor area additions will be led by Africa, China, India, and North America through 2050.[45]

BUILDING A SOLUTION: ELECTRIFICATION

The challenge to building electrification is not a technological one. Electric alternatives to fossil-fuel equipment are readily available. In the past, some of these electric replacements have faced challenges with performance compared to their gas counterparts. Investment in technology improvements by the DOE and manufacturers to address these challenges has resulted in superior offerings. For example, air-source heat pumps, which extract heat from the outside air, historically have not worked well in regions that experience extreme winters. Cold-climate designs have more recently been introduced into the market that perform effectively at sub-zero temperatures.[46] So why hasn't electrification been adopted more broadly?

Residential

Air-source heat pumps, geothermal heat pumps, heat pump or solar water heaters, and electric or induction ranges are direct replacements for fossil-fuel space heating, water heating, and cooking. While most of these products can be dropped into existing systems, geothermal heat pumps and solar water heaters require a bit more infrastructure. Geothermal heat pumps are essentially refrigerator systems that transfer energy to and from the earth to heat and cool the home. With consistent soil temperatures between 50 and 60 degrees Fahrenheit several feet below the earth's surface, geothermal heat pumps are 25 to 50 percent more efficient than other heating and cooling equipment.[47]

However, geothermal heat pumps are significantly more expensive and require favorable siting, including a significant amount of land to install piping underground. Horizontal piping systems are the most cost-effective and require at least three to five troughs of 130 to 160 feet long, and 12 to 20 feet apart. Installation costs will vary, but an average water-to-air system, which could replace a furnace and air conditioner, will cost close to $20,000 or more.[48] The best opportunity for geothermal heat pumps is in new construction, where the system can be part of the initial site planning, but even in that case, it is an expensive endeavor and may not be suitable for all soil types. While geothermal heat pumps might be the right choice for some, the technology won't be able to lead the electrification shift.

Solar water heaters require a solar collector to be installed on the roof. Liquid within the collectors is piped into the water heater to heat the water. The water heater does not need to be replaced, but a solar storage tank is required with a heat exchanger that is connected to the existing water supply to the water heater. Most systems need a backup for less than optimal cloudy days. Costs for these systems vary, but *Consumer Reports* suggests that payback, even with federal and local rebates, could be ten to thirty years.[49] The cost-effectiveness of a solar water heater is most attractive if part of a larger rooftop panel system, where the added cost is only adding an electric water heater.

Even though air source heat pumps, heat pump water heaters, and electric ranges are readily available, switching fuel source in an existing home is more challenging. Most natural gas ranges, water heaters, and furnaces require a connection to electricity for igniting the gas, but there is work to be done to cap the existing natural gas lines and convert the electricity supply from 120 V to 240 V. These changes can be costly, ranging from several hundred to several thousand US dollars, depending on how many appliances you convert and how difficult it is to update supply lines.

In addition to the cost of fuel-switching, operating costs for electric products compared to natural gas are prohibitive given current low natural gas prices. Replacing natural gas with electric heating and cooking products can mean paying hundreds of dollars more in annual utility bills. As of January 2020, the average price of electricity in the United States was 12.79 cents per kilowatt hour (kWh). Washington Gas, which covers Washington, DC, Maryland, and Virginia and publishes rates close to the national average, shows an operation cost differential on its website of $700 to $800/year when switching from natural gas to electric heating and cooking products.[50] For several of the Northeast states, electricity prices are well above the national average. Yet even in the South and Central United States, where electricity prices are well below the national average,[51] natural gas is two to three times cheaper.[52]

Finally, there is the homeowner's lack of familiarity with electric equipment, particularly in regions where natural gas is the dominant fuel used for heating applications. This is most prevalent in cooking. While the large flame of the gas top burner charring a steak certainly commands an audience, testing conducted by *Consumer Reports* found that electric smooth-top ranges actually perform better overall than their gas counterparts.[53] Indeed, familiarizing yourself with an electric range takes some time, as gauging the right amount of heat and cook time requires some practice. However, if celebrity chefs began using electric ranges and touting their efficiency and performance, would we think differently about gas?

Consumers may be equally hesitant to remove their gas furnace and central air conditioning units, replacing them with an air-source heat pump. In new construction, when you compare the up-front cost of a heat pump with a furnace plus air conditioning, the heat pump is the more economical choice. Prices vary on the basis of location and labor, but on average, a heat pump is about half the cost of the furnace-air conditioner combination.[54] However, if the existing heating and cooling systems are not nearing the end of their design life, the homeowner may be reluctant to take on this additional cost. Heat pump water heaters face the same familiarity challenge, in addition to a higher up-front cost compared to natural gas and standard electric resistance models.

Switching from natural gas to electric equipment will require a little homeowner persuasion and contractor education, and financial incentive.

One analysis conducted by NREL found that when comparing the costs for equipment, fuel, and maintenance over a fifteen-year period, heat pumps are competitive with natural gas options (Figure 5.4).[55] Cold-climate air-source heat pumps are slightly higher in cost, due to lower efficiencies compared to standard air-source heat pumps. The report looks at the Levelized Cost of Service (LCOS), which takes into account capital cost, efficiency, and technology lifetime as well as fuel and maintenance costs, discount rate associated with the adopter, and usage pattern or capacity factor. In simple terms, the LCOS is the cost per unit of service provided over the equipment lifetime.[56] Looking closer at the breakdown, NREL suggests that roughly half of air-source heat pumps and heat pump water heaters are attributed to up-front capital cost.

The Rocky Mountain Institute also looked at the economics of electrifying space and water heating in homes within four regions of the United States: Oakland, California; Houston; Providence, Rhode Island; and Chicago.[57] For new construction in all four regions, electrification of space and water heating reduces the homeowner's expenses over the lifetime of the equipment, or fifteen years.[58] For retrofits, unless the homeowner is already considering replacing their existing furnace and air conditioner, electric technologies will cost more over the equipment lifetime.[59] Electric heat pumps represent less than 3 percent of residential heating worldwide but have the potential to provide more than 90 percent of the water and space heating needed.[60]

Commercial

For commercial buildings, the list of replacement equipment is similar to residential, albeit larger scale: air-source heat pumps, geothermal heat pumps, and heat pump water heaters. Added to this list of alternatives are variable refrigerant flow (VRF) systems, which were invented in Japan in 1982 and now operate in 50 percent of Japan's mid-size buildings and 33 percent of large office spaces.[61] VRF systems use refrigerant to move heat through the building using multiple indoor units attached to one shared outdoor unit. They provide customized heating to multiple zones within the building on the basis of individual space needs. When a heat recovery unit serves as the outdoor unit, the system can heat and cool spaces simultaneously. One of the biggest advantages of VRF systems is that ductwork is not needed, which is a large source of air and energy loss in ducted systems.[62] VRF systems were introduced into the US

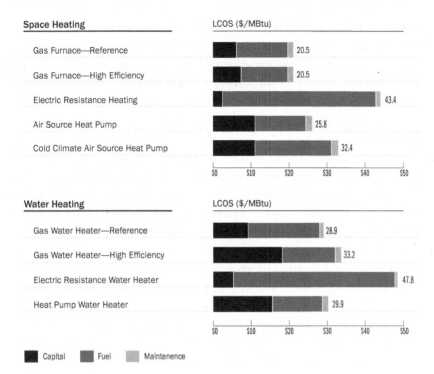

FIGURE 5.4   Levelized Cost of Service in Residential: Heat Pumps vs. Natural Gas

Source: Jadun et al., *Electrification Futures Study: End-Use Electric Technology Cost and Performance Projections Through 2050*, NREL, 2017

market in the early 2000s but are still relatively unknown. In Europe and Asia, these systems represent 80 to 90 percent of installed commercial heating and cooling systems.[63] Today, VRF systems represent 3 to 5 percent of heating and cooling systems in the United States, but it is the fastest-growing category.[64] Some of the barriers include lack of architect and contractor familiarity with the systems and cost and performance uncertainty, given that the technology is still considered nascent.

In general, commercial buildings face similar challenges to those of residential with regard to the costly building upgrades needed to electrify existing buildings as well as higher costs associated with operating an all-electric building, compared to natural gas heating systems. Looking at natural gas-electric technology replacement, NREL suggests that air-source heat pumps are competitive longer term with natural gas space heating but heat pump water heaters are twice as expensive over the fifteen-year equipment lifetime, driven by a high capital expense that represents 60 percent of total cost.[65] VRF systems cost more than traditional systems, but when all mechanical costs are considered, can net out the same cost per square foot of installation.[66] With regard to building operations, today commercial building owners on average spend $1.44/square foot annually on electricity compared to $0.30/square foot on natural gas.[67]

For commercial buildings, total electrification is actually a new concept. In the United States, early ventures into commercial building electrification can be found largely on the West Coast, where aggressive climate goals are being set and pro-electric legislation is being proposed. Tech companies such as Google, Adobe, Tesla, LinkedIn, and SpaceX either have all-electric campuses or plans to build them. These projects are serving as case studies for electrification. Kilroy Realty, which owns and manages more than thirteen million square feet of properties in San Francisco, Los Angeles, San Diego, and the Pacific Northwest, announced that 17 percent of its portfolio is 100 percent electric.[68]

As with residential, new construction projects are paving the way for commercial building electrification. Commercial retrofits also face some unique challenges. First, commercial fossil-fuel systems are larger and more complex than those found in households, and energy consumption must be approached holistically. The scale of the changes that need to be made to an existing building is much larger than upgrading or building a single family home, although both require significant capital expense. There are also notable challenges posed by the commercial tenant-owner split incentives, in which the party investing in electric technologies isn't the one paying the utility bill. In general, commercial building owners are not incentivized for greening their existing stock so the deep energy retrofits (that is, those aiming to reduce energy consumption by 50 percent or more) needed to decarbonize are often not considered. Last, commercial buildings are revenue-producing assets, and asking paying tenants to evacuate while upgrades are made is not an attractive pitch.

THE FUTURE OF GREEN BUILDINGS: ZERO CARBON PLUS

The term "net zero" is used to describe a variety of green building designs. Net-zero-*energy* buildings maximize energy efficiency then produce as much energy on-site as they use annually. Net-zero-*carbon* buildings institute energy efficiency measures and then produce enough carbon-free renewable energy on site, or purchased elsewhere, to meet annual energy consumption. Both building types allow for continued use of fossil fuels on-site.[69] Zero-*carbon* buildings take it a step further, eliminating all fossil-fuel equipment and powering the remaining building operations using only clean electricity or low-carbon fuels. This last category of buildings could be interactive with the grid, providing support for energy storage and load management.

Decarbonizing the buildings sector by 2050 will require electrification of all new construction and deep energy retrofits of existing buildings. However, given the challenges faced in retrofitting existing buildings, 100 percent electrification will be a tall order. To decarbonize existing buildings, a more likely path will be a mix of the green building approaches described earlier. Further, there are significant carbon emissions tied to the construction of buildings that is adding to the problem. The end goal must be zero carbon across all buildings by 2050, but getting there will require us to think differently about the role of buildings in the larger system.

Embodied Carbon

Material selection in new construction can greatly reduce a building's footprint, especially when one considers the material manufacturing process. According to GlobalABC, embodied carbon from building materials and construction represents 11 percent of global carbon emissions.[70] The building shell is where the most progress could be made, with 80 percent of embodied carbon found in the structural materials.[71] Decarbonized steel and cement industries could go a long way to reducing building embodied carbon, but as discussed in Chapter 4, those industries are slow to change. Low-carbon manufacturing processes and materials exist but have not been more broadly adopted due to building code challenges and lack of demand from customers. Builders can play an important role in changing these building codes and demanding low-carbon materials, thus accelerating decarbonization within those industries and reducing the carbon emissions tied to the structure.

The idea of embodied-carbon reduction is a new one, but it is gaining steam. Unlike emissions from building operations that can be further reduced over time by energy efficiency measures and clean energy, embodied carbon is locked in for the lifetime of the building, typically thirty to fifty years. Understanding the opportunities to reduce embodied carbon has been a challenge for many architects, engineers, and policy makers. Environmental Product Declarations are available from manufacturers but not searchable more broadly. Historically, the industry has lacked a robust, single database from which to choose materials and evaluate potential savings. In February 2020, the Embodied Carbon in Construction Calculator was released, which includes a database of more than sixteen thousand materials, including concrete, steel, wood, aluminum, and more.[72] The calculator, initially created by global construction company Skanska and embraced by a nonprofit alliance that includes the American Institute of Architects (AIA), Carbon Leadership Forum, Autodesk, Amazon, and Microsoft, is available for free on the Building Transparency website. In addition to finding materials, the tool provides support for planning and designing buildings as well as verifying performance.[73]

Carbon Sinks

Materials substitution will go a long way to reducing carbon emissions from more carbon-intensive manufacturing processes. In some cases, these material replacements offer more than industrial process decarbonization and reduced embodied carbon; building materials are being developed that actually sequester CO_2 during production and construction. As discussed in Chapter 4, Solidia concrete sequesters CO_2 equal to 5 percent of its weight during the curing process and other companies are looking to inject captured CO_2 to reduce the amount of carbon-intensive Portland cement needed in the final product. In Chapter 6, we will discuss the rise of hemp and the potential for the crop to serve as a carbon sink. Today, "hempcrete" is replacing fiberglass insulation and sheetrock in homes across the United States, created by mixing chipped hemp bark, lime binder, and water.[74] The strong, stone-like substance continues to sequester CO_2 as it cures.[75] This is in addition to the twenty-two tons of carbon sequestered within every 2.5 acres of hemp cultivated.[76]

A new category of building material, mass timber, is becoming more popular as a sustainable replacement for cement and steel. The category represents engineered wood products such as cross-, glue-, nail-, and dowel-laminated timber, which are sourced from smaller, fast-growing trees. Wood is 50 percent carbon dry weight and when harvested and installed into a building will lock that carbon away while the tree planted in its place will pick up where the last one left off.[77] According to one study, a five-story residential building constructed with mass timber can store nearly four thousand pounds of carbon per square foot or "three times more than in the aboveground biomass of natural forests with high carbon density."[78] However, the benefits of mass timber come with some caveats. First, the forests from which the trees are harvested must be sustainably managed and the wood must be preserved and reused upon demolition so that the carbon isn't then released into the atmosphere.[79]

Existing and new buildings can serve as carbon sinks with the addition of a green roof. A green roof system consists of a water-proofing membrane, root repellent system, drainage system, filter cloth, a lightweight growing medium, and plants.[80] Plants naturally absorb carbon dioxide, storing it in their leaves and tissues. One study conducted on typical grass species used on rooftops in Japan found that carbon sequestration ranged from twenty-nine to sixty-five pounds of CO_2 per square foot annually.[81] Green roofs can also reduce building energy use through evapotranspiration, which lowers the heat surrounding the building. One study, which reviewed available literature on the subject, suggests that annual energy savings could be as low as 2 percent and as high as 70 percent, depending on location, roof configuration, installation type, and plant species.[82] Although fairly new in the United States, green roofs have been installed on buildings for decades in other countries.

WILDCARD DISRUPTORS: ROOFTOP AND COMMERCIAL SOLAR

To truly decarbonize, electrified buildings must be powered by clean energy. Otherwise we run the risk of increasing scope 2 emissions while removing scope 1 sources. This can be achieved in two ways: purchasing zero-carbon electricity from a utility or third-party supplier (discussed in Chapter 2) or generating the electricity on-site using renewable energy sources. While several on-site renewable energy options exist (such as biofuel, wind, and geothermal), solar has emerged as the leading technology due largely to falling costs and flexibility in installation.

Even as the price of solar declines, the capital cost to install a solar system continues to be a barrier to broader adoption. The Lazard 2019 analysis of LCOE suggests that while utility-scale solar is cost-competitive with conventional generation technologies, the LCOE ($/MWh) for residential and commercial applications is three to five times that for utility scale.[83] Capital cost is the driver, representing 90 percent of LCOE for both residential and commercial solar, although adding storage to commercial solar increases its cost-competitiveness.[84] As we have seen in utility-scale solar, further investment and scaling of residential and commercial solar technologies will help to drive this cost down.

The federal solar tax credit has helped to defray this cost, allowing building and home owners to claim 26 percent of project expenses as credit on federal tax returns. The tax credit steps down to 22 percent in 2021 and expires in 2022. Many states and utilities offer rebates and incentives for solar installations. In areas that offer net-metering, owners can also receive credits for excess electricity produced but not needed by the building, to use at a later time when the system is not able to meet the demand. As an added benefit, there is some research that suggests solar installations raise the selling cost of homes by 4.1 percent on average,[85] and the general consensus regarding commercial buildings is that solar installations increase property value, although the amount will vary more widely. Combined, these incentives have made solar a more attractive option. Yet adoption has been slower for residential and commercial solar PV installations—17 GW and 15 GW cumulative installed capacity—compared to utility-scale applications, which represented close to 60 GW in 2020.[86]

Requiring solar for all new construction moving forward would help to accelerate adoption. Across the United States, changes in building codes are spurring demand for rooftop solar. For example, California instituted a new building code requirement effective in 2020 that requires new homes and multifamily residential buildings up to three stories high to include solar rooftop panels.[87] Several cities have instituted solar-ready requirements in residential and commercial building codes, with the intent to reduce some of the installation costs associated with adding solar panels down the line.

Perhaps the solar market needs some disruption of its own. New solar technologies are emerging that could compete with more traditional panels or, at the very least, help to bridge the gap to 100 percent electrified, renewable energy buildings. Examples include Tesla's solar roof tiles that offer homeowners solar energy without sacrificing roof aesthetics and solar films applied to windows to create electricity-producing glass. Solar windows show promise for residential and commercial applications.

THE UPSHOT: THE TECHNOLOGY EXISTS, BUT CAN WE MAKE THE TRANSITION IN TIME?

To decarbonize buildings, we have all the technologies we need. Converting scope 1 emissions to scope 2 emissions through electrification and then decarbonizing electrical generation is technically possible and, in many instances, economically viable. Yet according to the World Resources Institute (WRI), less than 1 percent of buildings around the world are zero carbon.[88] As argued in

Chapter 1, the lack of diffusion of green technologies typically reflects underlying economics that make adoption undesirable. In some regions, it has to do with the relative cost of alternatives driven by the local costs of fossil fuels and the specific heating and cooling demands of the region. In many instances, it has to do with the incentives to replace existing infrastructure with high capital cost, though often cheaper cost of use, decarbonized alternatives.

With continued interest in and investment in electrification and other zero-emission alternatives, we would expect for the relative cost of these options to fall versus fossil-fuel-burning technologies. Perhaps even more exciting, the potential for buildings to be net-zero- or even net-*negative*-carbon sources—through sequestering carbon in building materials, creating carbon sinks such as green roofs, or adopting roof-top solar—holds great promise and should see increasing adoption. Even absent any policy interventions, buildings should continue to become greener over time.

The question is whether these trends are on pace to decarbonize buildings by 2050. The simple answer is no. Increasing urbanization across the globe and the demand for new buildings that it fosters creates both opportunities and challenges. As the built environment expands, the total carbon footprint of buildings will grow, all else being equal. However, each new building is an opportunity to eliminate carbon emissions or even create net-negative spaces. The question of whether we decarbonize the built environment hinges on the set of actions that we take, both by public agencies and private organizations, that create the conditions under which green options are adopted.

HOW CAN WE DECARBONIZE BUILDINGS BY 2050?

For buildings, the path to decarbonization seems clear. Unlike in other sectors, the technologies needed to achieve zero carbon are readily available and competitive with less sustainable options. Yet while significant investments have been made in reducing energy consumption within buildings, the industry has only recently started to make the shift toward electrification and zero-carbon construction. As we face the potential for these carbon emissions to be locked in place for the next thirty to fifty years, the time to decarbonize buildings is now. Levers to decarbonize residential and commercial buildings must focus on reducing capital costs, incentivizing adoption, and changing building codes and standards. But first there needs to be a concerted effort to inform developers, builders, architects, homeowners, and tenants on the benefits of electrification and low-carbon materials.

Promote Awareness

With any new commercial building design trend, one of the critical stakeholder groups to get on board is architects. The American Institute of Architects (AIA) is helping to drive awareness and inviting architects to make commitments to green building through their 2030 Challenge. Released in 2006, the AIA challenge sets a goal to be carbon-neutral by 2030 for all new construction, eliminating the use of fossil fuels completely. AIA reports that more than four hundred US firms have committed to the 2030 Challenge.[89] More recently, AIA announced a five-point climate action plan that includes advocating building codes and policies promoting zero-carbon building toward a longer-term goal of net zero by 2050.[90] Architects can help to shape the mission and vision of building construction by incorporating green building principles early in the planning process.

Even with the building architect on board, developers and builders may change plans throughout the construction process in ways that cut costs but unknowingly increase the carbon footprint of the building. Educating these actors will also be important to ensuring zero-carbon plans are carried through to completion. However, as discussed in Chapter 4, builders are reluctant to change and adopt new technologies, particularly with regard to commercial, often requiring decades of performance data to reach a comfort level in adoption. Large-scale building projects that showcase new technologies and materials will be critical to shifting mindsets. One example is San Francisco Airport's new terminal and runways built with CO_2-enhanced concrete that is estimated to reduce emissions by 44 percent compared to standard Portland concrete.[91] These projects are few and far between; to convince commercial builders to change, more case studies and time to prove performance are needed. Strong customer demand could accelerate this shift, but without standardized requirements for zero carbon, projects will be custom and slow to move.

For residential retrofits, the decision to fuel-switch lies in the hands of the homeowner, but even in progressive states, awareness of electric technology options is low. According to a poll conducted by the Sierra Club and several clean energy advocacy groups, while 70 percent of respondents expressed a preference for clean-energy-sourced electricity, 62 percent were unfamiliar with air-source heat pumps and heat pump water heaters.[92] This is where electric utilities can help educate homeowners to understand the benefits of electrification, provide incentives for fuel-switching, and receive the benefits of additional revenue. Some research suggests that green upgrades in general could result in a higher sale price. A National Association of Realtors survey of US homebuyers shows that 68 percent are interested in an environmentally friendly home and 46 percent would pay more for a home with green features.[93] To provide greater transparency to homebuyers, the Council of Multiple Listing Services added new fields to be included in listings, including ENERGY STAR product compliance, renewable energy or storage systems, and sustainable construction materials.[94]

In new home construction, demand must come from potential homebuyers. According to the National Association of Home Builders, one-third of single-family and multifamily home builders surveyed in 2017 indicated that at least 60 percent of their portfolio included green buildings. However, only 30 percent of multifamily home builders and 20 percent of single-family home builders identified themselves as "dedicated green builders" (90 percent of portfolio green).[95] These builders cite customer demand as one of several key drivers for the growth in green building but also indicated the cost premium as being a barrier.

One interesting trend that could accelerate the zero-carbon shift is the relatively new interest in healthy buildings. According to WorldGBC's "World Green Building Trends" poll, 77 percent of respondents cited "improved occupant health and wellbeing" as the most important driver of building green.[96] However, the link between healthy building and electrification, zero carbon is not always a direct one. Most healthy building initiatives focus on air quality, occupant comfort and well-being, and creating a calm environment. For example, the International Well Building Institute's WELL V2 healthy building standard addresses indoor air quality and water quality but does not include low-carbon materials or energy.[97] Making a connection between low-carbon and healthy buildings could benefit both movements.

Adapt Building Codes and Standards

Building codes ensure the integrity of the structure and safety of its occupants and are established by law and enforced by the state and local jurisdictions. While these codes are developed in partnership with industry members and revisited on a regular basis, they tend to be inconsistent from one jurisdiction to the next, creating a patchwork of requirements across the country. Given this, decarbonizing the building industry in the United States through more stringent codes will be challenging.

In 2009, a collaboration between the US Green Building Council, the American Society of Heating, Refrigerating, and Air-Conditioning Engineers (ASHRAE), and the Illuminating Engineering Society produced Standard 189.1: *Standard for the Design of High-Performance Green Buildings, Except Low-Rise Residential Buildings.* ASHRAE Standard 189.1 provided the first green building model standard for building projects seeking to exceed the minimum energy efficiency requirements established by ASHRAE Standard 90.1. In 2012, a similar model code was introduced by the International Code Council (ICC).

Recognizing the competition and confusion being created in the industry, ICC and ASHRAE worked together to release a new, collaborative International Green Construction Code (IgCC) in 2018.[98] The new model code is voluntary and compatible with local energy codes, International Codes, and LEED. The new code provides the "fundamental criteria for energy efficiency, resource conservation, water safety, land use, site development, indoor environmental quality and building performance."[99] IgCC 2018 incorporates ASHRAE 90.1 and includes several provisions that exceed this standard. This level of coordination with industry-accepted standards is a step in the right direction, but adoption of IgCC 2018 has been slow and the requirements do not address zero-carbon operation or materials.

Historically, building codes have been used to address building safety and level the playing field—not pave the way for innovative new products or building approaches. In lieu of more aggressive building codes, voluntary certification programs can bridge the gap between standard practice and cutting edge.

Push Voluntary Certification Programs

Commercial building energy intensity, or the amount of energy used per square foot of space, in the United States decreased by 15 percent between 2007 and 2017.[100] Voluntary energy efficiency programs, such as LEED and ENERGY STAR, greatly contributed to this decline, providing architects, building owners, contractors, and homeowners the tools needed to identify high-efficiency products and design approaches. On average, LEED- and ENERGY STAR-certified buildings use 25 percent and 35 percent less energy, respectively, and generate 35 percent less greenhouse gas emissions.[101]

Continued efforts to reduce energy consumption will be critical to decarbonizing buildings by 2050. There is evidence that these certification programs are helping to accelerate green building, particularly in US cities. According to the fifth annual US Green Building Adoption Index by CBRE Group and

Maastricht University, green certified office space represented 41 percent of market totals across the thirty largest US metro areas in 2018. Chicago ranked the highest, with close to 70 percent of its commercial office space certified.[102]

Over time these certification programs have evolved to address more than just energy consumption. For example, LEED Zero Carbon is awarded to buildings that operate with "net zero carbon emissions from energy consumption and occupant transportation to carbon emissions avoided or offset over a period of 12 months." It does not, however, go as far to eliminate on-site fossil fuels.[103] To decarbonize buildings by 2050, these certification programs must be expanded to recognize buildings that achieve 100 percent electrification.

LEED Zero Carbon and other LEED V4.0 and 4.1 include requirements for embodied carbon. In fact, according to the Urban Land Institute, over a hundred voluntary sustainability certifications recognize embodied carbon as a measure to reduce building carbon emissions.[104] Many tools are also available to assist architects and designers in evaluating product carbon footprints and conducting whole-building lifestyle assessments.[105] A number of cities are now requiring or providing incentives for building construction with low embodied carbon.

The World Green Building Council and Green Building Councils partnered to launch the Advancing Net Zero project, with a goal of 100 percent net-zero buildings worldwide by 2050.[106] Since launching the initiative in 2018, the project has more than eighty signatories made up of private- and public-sector actors who have made the net-zero-carbon commitment.[107] The WorldGBC's definition of net zero is "a building that is highly energy efficient and fully powered from on-site and/or off-site renewable energy sources." This is a step in the right direction, but the commitment falls short of eliminating fossil fuels on-site. More recently, WorldGBC released a call-to-action report that issues a vision that all new buildings and renovations will reduce embodied carbon by 40 percent by 2030 and 100 percent of all buildings and renovations will reach net-zero embodied carbon by 2050.[108]

In 2018, the International Living Future Institute released the first worldwide zero-carbon third-party certification standard. The Zero Carbon certification requires that all new construction projects eliminate on-site fossil-fuel combustion and existing buildings offset 100 percent of on-site fossil-fuel combustion.[109] In addition, 100 percent of the energy consumption "must be offset by on- or off-site renewable energy on a net annual basis" and all new projects "must also demonstrate a 10 percent reduction in the embodied carbon of the primary materials of the foundation, structure, and enclosure compared to an equivalent baseline."[110] The Zero Carbon certification, which was introduced in 2018, also applies to residential buildings.

For building retrofits and new construction, ENERGY STAR product certification can identify high-efficiency electric appliances for residential and commercial projects. Many utilities across the United States provide rebates for ENERGY STAR certification products, adding an incentive to building owners to replace older, inefficient equipment. While there are several consumer-facing zero-energy home certification programs and labels,[111] a zero-carbon-home labeling program does not yet exist in the United States.

There is some evidence that green building certification will benefit the owner in terms of higher rental and occupancy rates. A review of available studies suggests that on average, a green-certified building commands an increase in rental income of 4.6 percent, an increase in occupancy rate of 4.3 percent, and an increase in sale price of 14.1 percent.[112] The benefits will vary depending on the market location and saturation of green building offerings.

Implement New Public and Private Policies

The most clear and effective electrification policy would be one that bans the use of natural gas in buildings outright. Several states are putting forth legislation that would prohibit natural gas hookups in new buildings. In July 2019, Berkeley, California announced such a ban and within a year, several more cities in the state joined the list. Dozens of cities outside of California are considering similar bans.[113] Philadelphia and Washington, DC, are evaluating whether the natural gas utilities themselves can be electrified, retiring natural gas pipelines.[114] However, just as there is momentum to electrify buildings there is also resistance mounting, with lawmakers in Arizona, Missouri, Minnesota, Oklahoma, Tennessee, and Mississippi proposing legislation that would prohibit such bans.[115]

Cities around the world are committing to bold climate change targets. Within these densely populated areas, buildings can account for 50 percent or more of GHG emissions.[116] Building electrification must be included in GHG-emission-reduction strategies if we are going to decarbonize by 2050. While much of the focus in future green building planning has been on energy efficiency and renewable energy procurement, there are signs that cities are recognizing the need to move away from fossil fuels completely. According to C40 Cities, a network of ninety-six cities around the world committed to meeting the requirements of the Paris Agreement, twenty-three are working toward 100 percent zero-carbon building goals by 2030.[117]

Recognizing the impact that embedded carbon emissions have on the building carbon footprint, several US state and local governments are stepping forward with policies that consider building materials in their emission-reduction strategies. California's 2017 Buy Clean legislation mandates that all state agencies consider the entire supply chain when evaluating carbon emissions for new construction and infrastructure projects. Washington State is also looking at similar legislation. In Vancouver, a zero-emission building policy puts the city on a path to reducing embodied carbon 40 percent by 2030.

Companies are also announcing corporate policies that address embodied carbon. In 2020, when Microsoft announced its carbon-negative initiative, embodied carbon was listed as an activity subject to fees billed to individual business units. The company created an internal carbon tax that charges each business unit for scope 1, 2, and 3 carbon emissions.[118] The plan further set goals for achieving LEED Platinum and International Living Future Institute's Zero Carbon requirements for retrofitted buildings at Silicon Valley and Puget Sound campuses.[119]

Public-private sector coordination at a global scale could help to accelerate the zero-carbon movement. With this goal in mind, WorldGBC launched its Net Zero Carbon Building Initiative with a call to action to businesses and governments to commit to net-zero buildings by 2030 and zero-carbon operations in all buildings by 2050.[120] By May 2020, twenty-eight cities had signed on to the commitment, including several US cities: Los Angeles; Washington, DC; Seattle; and New York City. Nearly fifty companies have committed as well, including those in the real estate, retail and apparel, and construction industries.[121] Signatories must disclose building energy performance and carbon emissions within two years of signing the commitment. While WorldGBC acknowledges the importance of reducing embodied carbon, it is not included in the commitment. The UN's GlobalABC and WRI's Zero Carbon Buildings for All Initiative share the same vision of zero-carbon building by 2050, working with governments and businesses around the world to share strategies, develop decarbonization policies, and invest in solutions toward this goal.[122]

Incentivize Adoption Using Green Financing

The cost to construct net zero for most building types is often similar to one constructed to code.[123] Yet research on the cost-effectiveness of electrification and zero carbon is limited. Two reports released in 2019 by the Rocky Mountain Institute and Energy and Environmental Economics Inc. evaluated the economics of electric and zero-energy homes and concluded that an all-electric home is likely to cost less than a mixed-fuel home.[124] For commercial buildings, even if electrification comes with a higher initial price tag, a business case can be made to make the investment, especially where renewables are attached. The benefits and savings of electrification and zero-carbon building are still playing out for new construction, and adoption of new technologies in the building industry tends to be slow. Financial incentives, state-level action to eliminate fossil-fueled equipment, and changes to local building codes can accelerate the shift to more sustainable building practices.

Building retrofits are more challenging. For commercial buildings, paybacks for deep energy retrofits average seven to eight years.[125] The standard payback period accepted by most building owners is three to five years.[126] Some building owners have more flexibility when assessing cost-effectiveness. For example, a reasonable payback for federally owned buildings and universities can be as high as ten years.[127] Deep energy retrofits also cause significant disruption to occupants and require skill and expertise given the complexity of equipment and system replacement. Timing of the deep energy retrofit could help to reduce the payback period. Commercial buildings are often updated every ten to fifteen years or sooner due to events triggered by building sale or changes in occupancy. Including energy upgrades as part of a larger upgrade package will reduce costs. Similarly, replacing older inefficient equipment when it fails will result in greater savings and further reduced payback.[128] For residential, homeowners will need to be educated and financially motivated to switch to electric from natural gas products. Incentives and green financing will be critical to decarbonizing the existing building stock and could speed up adoption in new construction.

One way to reduce the cost of electrification is to provide fuel-switching incentives. Several US states and utilities are exploring incentives for fuel-switching. Sacramento Municipal Utility District (SMUD) offers homeowners $4,000 and $2,500 to replace natural gas space and water heating equipment with electric heat pumps, and $500 to replace gas stovetops with electric induction ranges. These fuel-switching rebates are significantly higher than efficiency upgrades. SMUD also offers a $2,500 bonus for all-electric homes.[129] Massachusetts's Energy Efficiency Plan for 2019–2021 provides incentives for customers switching away from fossil fuels to air-source heat pumps or other renewable heating sources.[130] In some cases, barriers need to be removed for fuel-switching to happen. In 2019, California regulators modified the energy efficiency three-prong test, which previously discouraged fuel substitution, to allow for electric appliances to be evaluated on a per measure basis using carbon emissions as a metric.[131]

PACE, or Property Assessed Clean Energy, is an innovative approach to financing energy efficiency and renewable energy projects for residential and commercial buildings. PACE covers the up-front costs for building upgrades, allowing the owner to pay back the loan through a special property assessment. The loan is secured by the property itself and paid as a property tax addition, usually over a period of ten to twenty years.[132] The assessment is attached to the property not the owner and therefore conveys with any property sale. Many mortgage lenders have a problem with PACE because in the case of foreclosure, the loan would be paid off prior to the mortgage.

States enact PACE-enabling legislation while local authorities administrate the program. According to DOE, more than thirty-five states and the District of Columbia have commercial PACE legislation, while residential financing is available in three states.[133] The PACE model directly addresses one of the biggest barriers to building retrofits, the initial cost outlay. Building electrification doesn't appear to qualify as an energy upgrade; however, were the owner to pursue high-efficiency electric equipment replacements the cost would be covered along with the addition of a renewable energy system.

Innovative subscription offerings are also emerging as a solution to reducing initial costs and building operations. Energy-as-a-service is a business model in which customers pay a monthly subscription fee for equipment leased by a service company, avoiding the capital expense. There are several takes on this model, but the energy services agreement, or ESA, holds the most promise for electrification of existing buildings. Companies that provide ESAs own and operate the equipment and charge customers a monthly or quarterly fee based on the energy savings realized over a predetermined period. Companies also provide regular equipment maintenance and building performance monitoring. With an ESA, the combination of utility bill and fee are lower than the utility bill the customer would have paid prior to the upgrades.[134] Mesa Energy and Sparkfund are examples of companies offering ESAs.[135] The focus of current ESA programs is on energy efficiency upgrades; however, Sparkfund is also offering services for electric vehicles and energy storage. Building electrification could be an extension of these companies' product offerings.

One of the biggest challenges faced by any building upgrade is the split-incentive created when the owner takes on the cost of the upgrade but the tenant reaps the benefits. Green leases include clauses that align both the cost and benefit of building upgrades experienced by landlords and tenants. A green lease establishes up front the share of operating costs between landlord and tenant as well as benefits of the improvements, and the framework for meeting shared sustainability goals for the property. If the green lease is a gross lease, the landlord is responsible for utility costs and therefore will be more incentivized to invest in whole-building upgrades. This type of green lease removes the split-incentive, but it doesn't encourage energy conservation on behalf of the tenant, who pays a set monthly rental amount regardless of savings from those upgrades.

In a net lease, the tenant pays the utility bills and therefore is incentivized to make improvements within their own space, but not for the larger building overall. The aim should be to find a way to incentivize both parties. One way to do this is to pass on the energy efficiency upgrades to the tenant through a higher rent while the tenant benefits from lower utility bills as a result of the upgrades. The benefits of green leases can extend beyond annual savings. For example, they can attract new sustainably minded tenants, increase the value of the asset, and strengthen the relationship with existing tenants. A green lease could be used to support renewable energy projects and fuel-switching from gas to electric building equipment if the owner and tenants can agree on the benefits of electrification.

Funding energy efficiency building improvements through green bonds is another way to cover the capital expense of deep energy retrofits. Green bonds are the same as regular bonds except that 95 percent of the funding must be earmarked for projects that will result in environmental and climate benefits. Green bond issuers include financial corporations, nonfinancial corporations, green asset-backed securities, government-backed entities, development banks, and country and local governments.

While bonds have been around for centuries, green bonds are fairly new, with the first being introduced by the World Bank in 2008. According to the Climate Bonds Initiative, the global green bonds market reached $2.6 billion by 2012 and quickly climbed to $41 billion by 2015.[136] Just four years later in 2019, green bond issuance reached $257 billion. The Covid-19 pandemic slowed green bond growth in 2020, but Moody's estimates 2021 issuance to reach $300 billion.[137] Building electrification could be accelerated through green bond issuance. Yet green bonds are still less than 5 percent of the total global bond market.[138] Green bonds in general face several barriers, including a lack of global standardization creating market confusion as to what is "green" and limited data on the pricing benefits of green bonds compared to traditional bonds.[139]

The United States, China, and France represented almost half of the total green bonds issued in 2019.[140] Investors cite greater, more transparent corporate commitments to sustainable strategies and new political and sovereign mandates as reasons why the green bond market has seen more recent growth.[141] Indeed, nonfinancial corporates saw a doubling of issuance in 2019, representing 23 percent of the overall green bond market.[142] Financial corporates and government-backed entities represented 21 percent and 15 percent, respectively.[143] Sovereign green bonds are also experiencing steady growth, according to the Climate Bond Initiative, as countries around the world realize that the green investment needed to reach their climate goals could be achieved using this financial tool. Buildings represented 30 percent of global green bond issuance in 2019.[144] Just three years ago, buildings (and industry) represented a small 2 percent of the green bond market.[145] This is due in part to Fannie Mae, which leads the market in 2019 green bond issuance, with nearly $23 billion issues, 80 percent of which is devoted to building projects.[146]

The Fannie Mae Green Bond is a "fixed-income single asset security backed by one loan and one property, providing the investor insight into both the environmental and financial attributes of the asset."[147] Within its mission to provide affordable housing, Fannie Mae's green bonds support US rental housing retrofits to reduce energy and water consumption, lowering utility bills for tenants and building owners. Through its green bond issuances, Fannie Mae supported projects that reduced GHG carbon emissions by 287,000 pounds and saved families an average of $145 on their annual utility bill.[148] Multifamily properties accessing Fannie Mae green financing must have a nationally recognized green building certification (for example, LEED or ENERGY STAR) and/or make building improvements that reduce energy and/or water consumption.[149]

Today, issuers follow voluntary green bond principles regarding transparency and disclosure set forth by the International Capital Management Association. Efforts are under way to try to standardize frameworks. It's not yet clear whether green bonds pricing will rival that of vanilla bonds. However, issuers are realizing the benefits of green bonds, particularly in attracting new investors. According to the Climate Bonds Initiative, 98 percent of issuers surveyed in 2020 responded that their green bonds attracted new investors. Most of the respondents also said that green bond pricing was equivalent to or less than vanilla offerings.[150] Equivalent risk and yield along with strong demand from a diverse pool of investors could accelerate green bond issuance. Building electrification could benefit if adopted more broadly as an acceptable clean energy measure.

For the buildings sector, sustainable technologies are available and the path to decarbonization is clear. Efforts to reduce scope 2 building emissions, which are the biggest share of emissions, through renewables and grid decarbonization will go a long way to reducing the impact of this sector by 2050. Electrifying new building construction in countries experiencing significant growth will help to curb the projected growth in scope 1 emissions. However, even if every new structure built was electrified starting tomorrow, we would be left with a substantial inventory of older, fossil-fuel-powered buildings, particularly in developed countries. To turn over these existing buildings, green financing for capital investments will be crucial, as will customer and tenant demand for zero-carbon operations. After decades of promoting energy-efficiency in buildings, we are finally seeing a swell of investment in zero-carbon projects. Ultimately, electrification, reduced embodied carbon, and buildings as carbon sinks are relatively new approaches to building decarbonization and need to be ramped up significantly.

CHAPTER 6

THE AGRICULTURE SECTOR

N

O OTHER INDUSTRY is so directly affected by climate change as agriculture. Significant shifts in temperature, weather patterns, water accessibility, and pest populations put stress on agriculture production. There are already signs of this happening in countries such as Australia, where persistent hot and dry conditions have contributed to the deterioration of pasture conditions, rising grain prices, and low water supplies. Record-breaking rains flooded the Queensland region in 2019, leaving five hundred thousand cattle dead in their wake.[1] While other beef-producing countries have seen increases in production over the last five years, data published by the US Department of Agriculture (USDA) estimate a decline in Australian production for 2020 and 2021 as farmers rebuild herds previously lost to a multiyear drought.[2] In a land of extremes, pockets of Australian livestock farming may never recover.

The United States experienced its own record-breaking year in 2019, when one million acres of cropland were damaged in the Midwest after a cyclone storm in the spring.[3] After an extremely wet twelve-month period from May 2018 to May 2019, the USDA reported that farmers were unable to plant on more than nineteen million acres in 2019.[4] According to a study published in the Proceedings of the National Academy of Sciences, for every 1 degree Celsius increase in global mean temperature, global yields of wheat, maize, rice, and soybeans would be reduced by 6.0 percent, 3.2 percent, 7.4 percent, and

3.1 percent, respectively.[5] Some regions could be hit harder than others. For example, the study suggests that in the United States, maize production could be reduced by more than 10 percent with a 1 degree Celsius increase.[6]

Agriculture is on the front line of the climate change battle. It is one of the reasons why we find ourselves racing against the clock to mitigate emissions. The agriculture, forestry, and other land use sector accounts for 24 percent of global GHG emissions, with agriculture representing the majority of them.[7] For this industry, decarbonization includes not only carbon dioxide emissions but reduction of methane (CH_4) and nitrous oxide (N_2O) emissions, which represent 22 percent of global GHGs[8] and 82 percent of total agriculture GHG emissions.[9]

Methane and nitrous oxide are potent GHGs. Global warming potential, which is the energy that a gas will absorb over a hundred-year time frame relative to one ton of CO_2, is 28 for CH_4 and 265 for N_2O.[10] Methane only stays in the atmosphere for ten years but absorbs more energy than CO_2, while N_2O holds less energy but stays in the atmosphere longer than CO_2. This means that CH_4 and N_2O are more potent than CO_2 even though they represent only a quarter of all gas emissions worldwide (CO_2 represents most of the remaining percentage at 76 percent).[11] While much of the public focus has been on CO_2 mitigation, addressing agriculture-driven methane and nitrous oxide emissions is critical to mitigating climate change.

Increasing the challenge of decarbonization is that we need to substantially increase agricultural production to be able to feed a growing global population. In 2020, the world population was estimated to be nearly 7.8 billion people.[12] The UN predicts there will be 8.8 billion people by 2035 and 9.7 billion by 2050.[13] With this growth in population comes an increased demand for food. The UN's Food and Agriculture Organization (FAO) estimates that by 2050, 49 percent more food will need to be produced compared to 2012 global production.[14] The World Bank suggests that global food production will need to grow by 70 percent by 2050.[15] The nonlinear relationship between population and production growth is driven by predictions that developing countries, which will experience greater prosperity and expanded diets over time, will serve as the primary source of the significantly higher rise in demand. How can we scale farming operations to effectively and sustainably meet these growing needs?

Complicating matters, as developing countries grow in wealth, they tend to shift to more protein-rich diets. According to the Organisation for Economic Co-operation and Development's (OECD's) FAO "Agricultural Outlook 2018–2027," rising per capita income in developing countries will drive demand for beef and dairy products.[16] Global expansion of livestock, particularly dairy and meat production, and the feed production to support this growth, leads to greater GHG emissions. This is evidenced by the increase in non-CO_2 emissions (CH_4 and N_2O) of nearly 1 percent each year between 1990 and 2010, according to the IPCC.[17] The IPCC warns that agricultural N_2O emissions could grow between 35 percent and 60 percent by 2030 due to increased fertilizer use and manure production. Livestock-sourced methane could rise 60 percent by 2030 if CH_4 emissions grow in proportion to projected increases in livestock numbers.[18]

Further complicating matters is that food production also has a significant impact on water resources. Agriculture accounts for 70 percent of freshwater withdrawals worldwide.[19] Across the planet, we face regional water shortages that can reduce farming yields and significantly hamper access to clean and potable water. The emerging global water crisis is accelerating as climate change has a negative impact on both water supplies and agriculture yields, putting further pressure on harvesting limited water resources. While we focus on GHG emissions in this chapter, many of the technologies and approaches identified also offer opportunities for reductions in water consumption.

On a positive note, the agriculture sector is somewhat unique in that it includes potential carbon sinks that could remove CO_2, primarily through forest growth. According to FAO, net emissions from deforestation dropped 25 percent between 2000 and 2015.[20] The rate of deforestation has continued to slow; between 2015 and 2020, an estimated ten million hectares were cleared, down from fifteen million between 2000 and 2010.[21] Yet reducing deforestation and the protection, maintenance, and expansion of carbon sinks will be critical to reaching a carbon balance on the planet. We discuss the carbon sink opportunity later in this chapter following the discussion on other decarbonization options.

Agriculture is positioned to have a substantial impact on the speed and trajectory of climate change, either positively or negatively. Best practices and greater efficiencies will help to drive down emissions, but to decarbonize by 2050, we need to think in drastically different ways about how we grow and consume food. Fortunately, there are opportunities in this sector to significantly reduce CH_4 and N_2O emissions. According to FAO, livestock farming, including manure application and management, represents 66 percent of global agriculture emissions. Synthetic fertilizers, namely nitrogen-based, represent another 13 percent of emissions. (A handful of other sources contribute to the remaining 21 percent including rice cultivation, burning crops and savannah, crop residues, and cultivation of organic soils.[22]) If we can address these two biggest culprits—livestock farming and soil management—we will be well along a path toward decarbonizing agriculture. Of course, that is a big "if."

LIVESTOCK: BELCHING AND FARTING ARE NO JOKE

The term *livestock* primarily refers to cattle or dairy cows, chickens, goats, pigs, horses, and sheep. Livestock farming represents 80 percent of agriculture land use, when accounting for pasture grazing and feed production.[23] Animal domestication dates back to early civilization. Cattle in particular were used not only to provide meat but to work on the farm. The principles behind livestock farming didn't change much until the late 1700s, when British agriculturalist Robert Bakewell introduced selective breeding, a discovery that would serve as an important first step toward today's scientific methods for controlling livestock quality and production. In the decades that followed, improved nutrition, disease-control measures, and genetic engineering have allowed livestock farming to keep up with global demand.

By the 1900s, expansion of railways and refrigeration technology in the United States had opened up the distribution of agriculture products, shifting the industry to more centralized production at a commercial scale. This allowed for larger, manufactured meat production, making meat more available across the country. Beef and chicken consumption got a boost mid-century with the introduction of fast-food chains such as McDonald's and Kentucky Fried Chicken.

Yet after peaking in the 1970s, per capita US beef consumption has dropped by one-third, while chicken consumption continues to grow.[24] Despite its more recent decline, beef continues to be a top choice on the American menu and is becoming more popular in developing countries that have a rising middle class and access to new wealth. The rise in chicken demand comes with its own environmental concerns, but with regard to land impact and carbon emissions, beef remains the worst offender. According to the World Resources Institute, beef production is seven times more land- and GHG-intensive than chicken and twenty times more intensive than plant-based proteins.[25]

Methane represents the biggest source of livestock GHG emissions: FAO estimates 50 percent, with N_2O and CO_2 splitting the remaining 50 percent.[26] Manure management and enteric fermentation—primarily, cattle belching—contribute more than half of these emissions.[27] Feed production to support livestock represents 41 percent of the remaining emissions, while energy consumption accounts for a small portion (5 percent).[28] Some of the solutions proposed for livestock management could also have an impact on demand for feed production, potentially reducing emissions in those operations as well.

Several species contribute to livestock methane emissions, but cattle (beef and dairy) represent the largest share, at 60 percent, followed by pigs, chickens, buffalo, small ruminants, and other poultry (Figure 6.1).[29] Beef meat is the second most carbon-intensive (that is, emissions per protein) livestock behind buffalo. The storage of livestock manure emits methane, from anaerobic decomposition of organic matter, and N_2O through nitrification or denitrification.[30] N_2O is also released during manure soil application.

The approach to managing manure on-site depends largely on farm size. Smaller farms tend to collect and spread solid manure daily or weekly, while larger farms typically have sizable lagoons for long-term liquefied manure storage pending application to fields or off-site transport. Emissions tend to be higher from liquid treatment systems.[31] One analysis of dairy farms in Wisconsin showed that large farms deploying liquid storage are two to three times more GHG intensive (CO_2-eq/ton manure) than smaller farms managing solid manure.[32] The methane released during liquid storage represented 70 percent of larger farms' emissions.[33] According to FAO, CO_2-equivalent emissions from manure management have been climbing since 2001 (see Figure 6.2).

Enteric fermentation happens in the ruminant digestive track, where plant

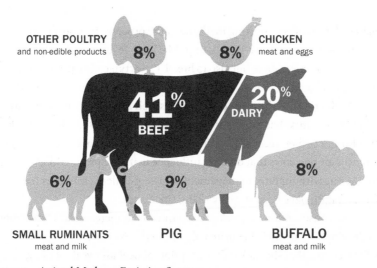

FIGURE 6.1 Animal Methane Emission Sources

Source: FAO, accessed March 11, 2021, "By the Numbers: GHG Emissions by Livestock," fao.org/news/story/en/item/197623/icode

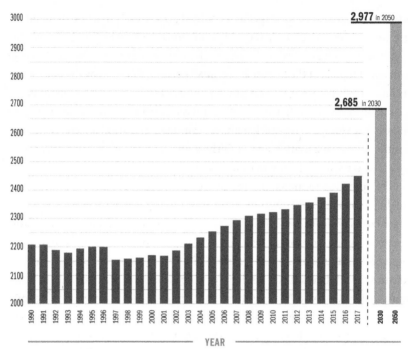

FIGURE 6.2   Global Methane Emissions from Livestock (mega metric tons CO$_2$ equivalent)

Source: FAOSTAT, accessed March 11, 2021, fao.org/faostat/en/#data/GM

material is digested, emitting methane in the process. The most common pathway for methane release is belching. Methane levels are closely tied to feed quality and composition, but also to breed. Cows typically eat a mixture of grass hay, alfalfa hay, and grains, as well as corn and grass silage (fermented pasture grass). The ratio of these food sources, as well as any vitamins and minerals added to the mix, has an impact on digestion, and thus methane production. In addition to diet, recent scientific research suggests that there are genetic differences among cows that directly influence methane production.[34] According to FAO, as with manure management, CO$_2$-equivalent emissions from enteric fermentation have been steadily rising since 2001.

Meat consumption in developing countries has increased at a faster rate than in developed countries due primarily to the rise in incomes and urbanization. USDA claims that the global consumption of beef and veal, poultry, and pork increased 3 percent annually between the mid-1990s and 2015. Growth in developed countries during this same time period was just 0.4 percent.[35] Yet the United

States continues to be the largest producer and consumer of livestock products. According to USDA, the United States, Brazil, the European Union, and China represented a 60 percent share of both production and consumption in 2018.[36]

Looking to 2050, FAO predicts that growth in global meat consumption will slow due to slower projected population growth, more modest growth in per capita meat consumption (particularly in countries that were previously driving growth), the persistence of poverty, and cultural preferences against meat in some developing countries despite projected population increases (for example, India).[37] Dairy, however, holds potential for significant growth in developing countries with per capita consumptions currently well below that in developed countries.[38] For example, FAO predicts that India will be a driver of growth in dairy consumption; today it accounts for 15 percent of world production, and this share could rise to more than 20 percent by 2050.[39]

Africa is positioned to see significant growth in both production and consumption. Large increases in population, which could double by 2050 in some countries, urbanization, income growth, and shifts in diet will drive demand, and thus production.[40] FAO estimates that African demand for meat and milk will increase 261 percent and 399 percent, respectively, by 2050.[41] To grow Africa's agricultural output will require significant investment in infrastructure. According to an analysis by McKinsey and Company, eight times more fertilizer will be needed to support the growth, along with billions of dollars in irrigation, storage, and other infrastructure and government policies that improve distribution and trade.[42] Recognizing the importance of this region in ensuring food security, private- and public-sector investments are flowing into Africa.

Yet many of the African countries face challenges of undernourishment and food insecurity. Further, the impacts of climate change will be most greatly felt in more arid regions. Africa's ability to support increased demand will also depend on land and resource availability. According to the African Development Bank, these resources exist. Specifically, four hundred million hectares of savannah land could hold the key to increasing in-country production and reducing reliance on imports.[43] The Bank's Technologies for African Agricultural Transformation for the Savannahs initiative was developed in 2017 to cultivate just sixteen million hectares of savannah land for maize, soybean, and livestock production.[44] Organizations like FAO are partnering with USAID and several African governments to ensure sustainable development of the livestock market, including support for local communities.

Meat and dairy production and consumption growth rates will vary greatly depending on region, but overall, there will be an absolute global increase by 2050. Carbon emissions are tied to this growth and will continue to rise without innovative mitigation measures. For livestock, the immediate solutions fall into two categories: methane capture or utilization, and feed modification and digestive support. What if one could modify the cow itself or avoid eating it altogether and still get the protein needed for a balanced diet? Radical solutions are emerging, changing the very definition of a domestic cow, and if commercially scaled, these could drastically cut methane emissions around the world. Methane capture could offer a new renewable energy source to utilities, and thus a new revenue stream for farmers. In the following, we explore several emerging approaches toward livestock decarbonization.

Methane Capture and Bioenergy

For centuries, farmers have been storing manure to apply as fertilizer on feed-crop fields. As previously discussed, a significant amount of methane is released during the storage process, particularly in liquid form. According to the EPA, most of the manure emissions come from dairy and swine farms. Anaerobic digesters are closed systems that can be used to capture the biogas, using the methane as an energy source for heat or electricity. Adding other organic wastes, such as food and crop residues, can increase biogas production.[45] The biogas replaces otherwise piped utility-supplied natural gas. While the burning of it releases CO_2, it avoids the methane otherwise emitted from long-term manure storage. The EPA estimates that as much as 85 percent of methane emissions could be eliminated with the use of digesters.[46]

The EPA estimates that biogas recovery systems are viable options at more than 8,000 dairy and hog farms across the United States. However, just over 250 farms are using digesters today, with dairy operations representing the larger share. Most of these facilities are using the biogas for electricity generation or combined heat and power, in which excess heat from the electricity generation is used to heat the digester or adjacent buildings.[47] One of the barriers to broader adoption of digester technologies is cost. The profitability of a farm using a digester depends on its ability to recover initial capital costs and to establish a long-term revenue stream to cover operational costs. Several states have offered incentive programs with varying levels of success.[48]

To address the capital cost barrier, Smithfield Foods, the largest pig and pork producer in the world, partnered with Virginia's Dominion Energy to pilot several biogas recovery and energy distribution projects in Virginia, North Carolina, and Utah in a new venture called Align Renewable Natural Gas. The farmers cap their lagoons and own the anaerobic digesters that then provide the methane gas to Dominion to process and distribute to consumers. In return, the farmers are provided a long-term contract with Dominion that ensures a revenue stream.[49] In October 2019, the partners announced a doubling of their investment in renewable natural gas projects through 2028 and expansion to other US states, including Arizona and California. According to Dominion, this expansion will result in electricity generation equivalent to powering seventy thousand homes.[50]

Feed Additives and Probiotics

Feed additives can reduce the number of microorganisms responsible for methane production. The corn, soybean, and grass typically eaten by cows cause digestion challenges that lead to more emissions. Viable additives and supplements include natural substances, compounds, fats, and oils. In 2020, UC Davis scientists shared results from a study that explored the potential methane reduction from incorporating red seaweed supplements in cattle feed. They found that when red algae (Asparagopsis taxiformis) was added to the feed, even in a small amount (0.5 percent), methane emissions were reduced by as much as 80 percent over a five-month period.[51] Testers of the milk produced from seaweed-fed cows indicated there was no difference in taste in the products.[52] US-based company Ocean Blue Farms, which supported the UC Davis study, has plans to commercialize a red algae feed supplement by the end of 2021.[53] A bonus for the product is that early testing has shown that feed could be reduced by 14 percent without any loss in average daily weight gain, saving farmers money on feed.[54]

Other researchers are working on probiotics to reduce methane. One company, Bezoar Laboratories, is working on a probiotic that, when coupled with nitrate, decreases methane production by 50 percent.[55] The *Paenibacillus fortis* probiotic also increases productivity and reduces pathogens. Bezoar's founder received the Unilever Young Entrepreneurs Award in 2017 for the product.[56] The key to broader adoption of additives and supplements is that they address not just the methane problem but also productivity and the overall health of the cow. In fact, there seems to be a close relationship between these factors. According to FAO, beef and dairy emission intensities are high in low-productivity systems, due in part to low feed digestibility.[57] Healthier, higher-producing dairy cows means a smaller herd is needed to meet demand.

Genetic Breeding

In Canada, scientists are working to improve feed efficiency and reduce methane emissions through selective breeding. In theory, it's not that much different from Bakewell's work in the late 1700s to choose and breed animals that are healthy and productive. Yet this approach to breeding goes even further, down to the cellular level. In 2009, the domestic cattle genome was sequenced,[58] providing scientists and farmers the opportunity to identify the most productive beef and dairy cattle in the herd, and to breed on the basis of desired traits. One of those traits might be lower methane production. Genome Canada is funding an international effort to identify the markers associated with improved feed efficiency and lower methane emissions. Preliminary results from research conducted by the Efficient Dairy Genome Project suggest that breeding cattle with higher feed efficiency and reduced methane emissions can reduce feed costs by $108/year per cow and emissions by 11 to 26 percent.[59] A goal of the project is to develop a global database to validate genomic predictions for feed efficiency and methane emissions.[60]

Other researchers are working to identify organisms found in the rumen (the first of two stomachs where initial digestion takes place with the help of bacteria and microrganisms) that produce methane and isolate the associated microbial genes for selective breeding to reduce emissions.[61] The hope is that through this selective breeding based on genome sequencing, farmers can cultivate more productive, low-GHG herds.[62] The goal of the Canadian genome project is to distribute the "environmentally responsible" genes more broadly, particularly in regions of the world that otherwise would not have access to this kind of research.[63] Global distribution of a patent-free technology would more quickly scale this solution, but even so, selective breeding takes time.

CROPS: ALL ABOUT SOIL MANAGEMENT

Plant cultivation began about ten thousand years ago, when humans left the nomadic hunter-gatherer lifestyle behind for one that provided more stable food sources in animal and crop farming. This is commonly known as the first agricultural revolution. Most researchers agree that agriculture largely originated in the Fertile Crescent, which included modern-day Iraq, Syria, Lebanon, Israel, and Jordan.[64] The second agricultural revolution came in the 1800s, when mechanization of farming and the use of chemical fertilizers gave rise to large commercial farming operations and higher production.[65] Steel plows,

grain elevators, and steam tractors were some of the new technologies introduced during this era, all of which focused on automation and efficiency.[66] The
third revolution came in the 1970s and 1980s with the introduction of genetically modified organisms (GMOs) as a way to increase production.[67] Controversial from the time of their introduction, GMOs dominate some crops such
as soybeans and are used by over seventeen million farmers worldwide.

After centuries of farming that focused on fertilizing and cultivating to
boost crop yields, the industry is beginning to realize the unintended consequences of these activities on soil degradation. According to "Global Opportunity Report 2017," released by the United Nations, about 40 percent of soils
used for agriculture activities around the world are degraded; 70 percent of
topsoil critical to plant growth has vanished.[68] Soil degradation not only has
an impact on field production but also reduces the amount of carbon stored,
which further amplifies climate change. According to FAO, soil degradation has
released seventy-eight billion tons of carbon into the atmosphere.[69] Livestock
overgrazing is responsible for 35 percent of this degradation. Another 30 percent
of topsoil loss is due to agriculture activities, namely cropland mismanage-
ment.[70] Even more alarming are data based on research conducted by the US
DOE's Lawrence Berkeley National Laboratory that suggest that carbon stored
in deeper soil layers may be more sensitive to warming than previously believed.
Calculations show that by 2100, deep-soil emissions could account for as much
as 30 percent of human-caused annual emissions.[71] While much attention has
been on topsoil, it appears that the problem could go much deeper.

This greater recognition of the impacts of modern farming on soil quality is
leading to what many industry experts and policy makers believe is the advent of
a fourth agricultural revolution, one that focuses on sustainable farm management and relies on digital technologies to achieve it.[72] Smart farm technologies
being introduced today aim to maximize yields, while preserving soil health,
and to reduce distribution inefficiencies. These technologies will not only help
ensure that production is able to scale to meet the rising demand for food but
could also drive down GHG emissions in the process.

Soil acts as both a GHG emission source and a sink. In fact, soils hold more
carbon than the atmosphere and all vegetation combined, second only to our
oceans.[73] There are several factors that determine the carbon flux between the
two. Biological drivers of soil emissions include microbial activity, root respira-
tion, and chemical decay processes.[74] Flux rates are dependent on several factors,
but the most influential are humidity, temperature, nutrient availability, and

pH value.[75] These factors can interplay with one another, and they vary widely across the globe. In general, increasing soil temperatures, widely fluctuating moisture levels, and excessive nitrogen fertilizer application result in increased N_2O emissions.[76] As a result, climate region (temperate, Mediterranean, and subtropical), as well as farming practices, greatly influences soil emissions.

N_2O is produced by denitrification (removal of nitrogen) under anaerobic conditions. Soils naturally release N_2O into the atmosphere, but the addition of nitrogen-rich fertilizers greatly increases these emissions. Nitrogen is delivered through synthetic fertilizers, such as urea or anhydrous ammonia, or organic fertilizers, such as manure. Whatever is not used by the plant is devoured by microbes in the soil, combining it with oxygen and releasing N_2O into the atmosphere. Only about half of the nitrogen is taken in by the plant, while the other half is either tied up by microbes or released into the environment.[77] Some research suggests that the N_2O emission rate increases exponentially with increases in fertilizer rate.[78]

According to FAO, global nitrogen-rich fertilizer consumption has significantly increased since 1960 and is expected to continue to rise through 2050 (Figure 6.3).[79] FAO suggests that cultivated land will need to increase by seventy million hectares by 2050 to meet growing population needs.[80] Efforts to improve yields, which increases production per hectare of land and reduces the amount of land needed to feed a growing population, may require higher rates of fertilizer. Nitrogen fertilizer was responsible for 40 percent of per capita food production increases during the second half of the twentieth century.[81] In the early 1960s, twenty million tons of nutrients (including nitrogen, potassium, and phosphorous) were used for crop cultivation. By 2005, this number had reached sixty-six million tons.[82]

Complicating matters are relative differences in population growth dynamics in regions of the world. World per capita food consumption has increased over the last fifty years, from 2,358 kcal/person/day in the mid 1960s to 2,940 kcal/person/day in 2015.[83] While this is well within global nutritional guidelines, there continues to be global imbalance. Just over one million people living in Sub-Saharan Africa average less than 2,500 kcal/person/day as compared to industrialized countries averaging 3,440 kcal/person/day.[84] This is expected to change as developing countries expand farming operations and, as a result, grow to represent 75 percent of fertilizer consumption by 2050.[85] The challenge ahead will be reducing the carbon footprint of farming while finding ways to more efficiently distribute food to meet the demands of expanding developing countries.

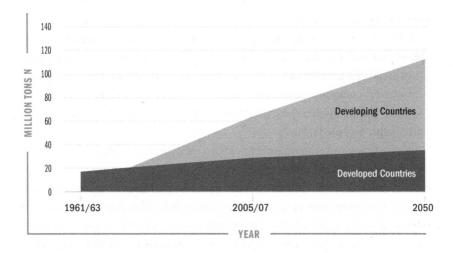

FIGURE 6.3   Global Fertilizer Consumption: Historical and Projected
Source: N. Alexandratos and J. Bruinsma, "World Agriculture Towards 2030/2050: The 2012 Revision, Table 4.15," ESA working paper No. 12-03, UN Food and Agriculture Organization, http://www.fao.org/3/a-ap106e.pdf

Opportunities to reduce soil N_2O emissions lie in the timing, rate, and placement of nitrogen fertilizers. The sharing of technologies and best practices by developed countries to reduce the nitrogen fertilizer use with farmers in developing economies would go a long way to reducing the emissions tied to cropland expansion. New technologies and practices, such as digital or precision farming and gene editing, can provide even greater opportunities. Let's take a look at the technologies and best practices that have the best potential for significant decarbonization of farming.

Regenerative Agriculture

Regenerative agriculture is a holistic approach to farming, incorporating best practices that seek to enrich soils, improve watersheds, increase biodiversity, and support local farming communities. Increasing carbon stored in soils has the added benefit of higher yields, and many best practices cost little for the farmer to implement.[86] Managing the nutrients put into the soil, both in timing and substance, can have a significant impact on soil emissions. Of course, the effectiveness of these practices is highly dependent on soil and climatic conditions, which vary depending on region.

Conservation tillage refers to no-till or reduced-till practices that leave residue from last year's crop on top of the soil instead of being plowed under by tractors. Traditionally farmers plowed fields for weed control and to prepare soils for the next planting. Disrupting the soil releases carbon into the atmosphere. Advancements in weed control and planting equipment have provided farmers the opportunity to use no-till and reduced-till approaches, conserving topsoil, improving soil health, and reducing carbon emissions in the process.[87] However, these emission reductions won't be realized unless these practices are paired with organic farming.

Cover crops and crop rotation have been used for thousands of years. Cover crops—those planted temporarily between main cash crop plantings—can extract excess nitrogen not used by the previous plants and help to sequester carbon. Retaining cover crop residue on fields can further increase the amount of carbon stored in the soil. Switching from a monoculture to polyculture rotation, or the planting of many different crops at the same time, can also increase carbon storage.[88]

Nutrient management is a particularly impactful practice. Effective fertilizer application follows what's known in the industry as the 4 Rs: right source, right rate, right time, and right place. Fertilizer formulations can have a significant impact on N_2O emissions. One example is corn-soybean rotations, from which emissions can be between two and four times higher using anhydrous ammonia than urea ammonium nitrate.[89] Additives can also reduce N_2O emissions—nitrification inhibitors can delay microbes' transformation of ammonium to nitrate closer to the time that plants are able to use it.[90] Slow-release formulations such as polymer coatings might also reduce emissions.[91] More field studies are needed to measure the direct benefits of these approaches on reducing N_2O emissions. Determining the rate in which the fertilizer is applied so that it meets the needs of the plant and reducing the amount of available nitrogen in the soil will reduce N_2O emissions. Timing fertilizer application to the needs of the plant throughout the growing cycle will have an impact on emissions. For example, applying it a few weeks after—instead of during or prior to—planting increases the likelihood of the nitrogen being picked up by the crop.[92] Finally, application close to the plant roots can ensure uptake.

Smart or Precision Farming

Introduced in the early 1800s, the *Farmers' Almanac* was a farmer's best source of predictive weather data. Today the almanac is more novelty than guide, as farmers have access to more precise, regional short-term forecasts and predictive modeling tools. Climate-smart agriculture will rely on the farmer's ability to more precisely manage the health of crops with the help of data, in addition to monitoring weather conditions. By more precisely monitoring and addressing plant and soil health, farmers can reduce the number of inputs needed to produce food. The big-data opportunity is opening the door to technology companies that are investing in agriculture-specific digital solutions.

Sensors put directly in the soil can be effective at measuring soil health, informing the farmer of variability and problems. The sensors provide a soil map, which allows farmers to manage smaller tracts and pinpoint concerns. Once a problem is identified, soil samples are sent to a laboratory for more in-depth testing. However, there are some real-time solutions being introduced to the market by companies such as AgroCares, which offers a handheld scanner that monitors soil fertility, providing data on important nutrients such as pH, nitrogen, and phosphorous.[93] Sensors can also monitor soil moisture, which allows the farmer to more efficiently irrigate different parts of the field depending on need. Monitoring and micromanaging soil nutrients and moisture across the field will result in a more productive and sustainable operation.

Drones are also being deployed to monitor crops and provide insight into plant and soil health, readiness for harvest, potential diseases, and pest infestations in real time. Farmers can more quickly and accurately assess every inch of their fields and stay ahead of problems that may have an impact on production. In addition to data collection, some drones are equipped with the ability to spray crops. Able to scan the ground in flight, the drones hover at an ideal height, modulating spray as needed and avoiding drift, which results in less water and fertilizer or herbicides being used and faster spray times.[94] Yet there are some challenges with drone deployment. Drones that come equipped with the image sensors and software needed for agriculture operations can cost tens of thousands of dollars, although one would expect that cost to decline with widespread adoption. FAA and local laws must also be met to operate a drone.[95]

Access to data is critical to climate-smart farming, but the volume of this data can be overwhelming to the farmer. Artificial intelligence can take large datasets and quickly perform analyses, suggesting a course of action based on predictive modeling that the farmer can then evaluate in real time. Per industry discussions, it is not quite ready for agriculture primarily because of the lack of consistency and comparability across data platforms. Managing and compiling many different types of data inputs in order to make farm-level decisions adds to the complexity. Collaboration between companies racing to provide data solutions, and even the creation of open-source software, will facilitate adoption of AI tools.

The success or failure of these digital solutions will depend first and foremost on whether they are easy to implement and understand, and whether they meet farmers' basic needs in terms of production and profit.

Gene Editing of Crops

Traditional plant breeding has been used for thousands of years to create more productive and resilient crops. In the past century, researchers have continued to manipulate plant genetics to improve productivity. Perhaps the most successful and widely implemented is hybrid rice. Discovered by Chinese scientists in the 1970s, hybrid rice is the result of cross-pollination between rice varieties to achieve fertilization. Hybrid rice has helped to increase productivity and feed millions of people around the world. For example, in Nepal, where local rice yield was between 2.5 and 3.5 metric tons per hectare in 2001, hybrid rice raised this yield to 7.2 tons by 2014.[96] Hybrid rice is helping to feed a growing Chinese population, which accounts for 21 percent of the world's population, using only 7 percent of arable land.[97]

More recently direct gene editing has emerged as a promising approach to ensure global food security and reduce the environmental impacts of farming. Gene editing tools like CRISPR-Cas 9 have emerged as powerful plant-breeding innovations that provide an opportunity to speed up the process and time to discovery. Gene editing is when a scientist makes a small change in the native DNA of a plant (for example, deleting or replacing) to alter a gene expression. It accelerates what could happen naturally but would take years of selective breeding to achieve.

Scientists are targeting a number of opportunities to use gene editing to help decarbonize crops. Increased yields, long a target of selective breeding efforts, also help to avoid acreage expansion and the emissions that come with land conversion. Crop resilience remains a priority and will increasingly be necessary given the potential for significant losses due to pests and water shortages as temperatures rise. There are even opportunities to genetically edit crops to help mitigate N_2O emissions.

Scientists also are researching ways to design crops to make their own nitrogen, eliminating the need for nitrogen fertilizer. Legumes such as soybeans and peas have long been revered for their natural ability to fix nitrogen through a symbiotic relationship with rhizobia bacteria. Fixation is the process in which bacteria turn N_2, an abundant gas in the atmosphere, into the more usable ammonia form, NH_3. The bacteria invade the root system and the plant provides nutrients that support the growth of nodules. Once matured, the nodules fix nitrogen, which is then supplied to the plant.[98] A limited amount of nitrogen fertilizer may be needed in the early growing period, but once established, the nodules are able to fix most of the plant's nitrogen needs depending on the type of legume.

Some scientists and innovators are pushing even further to see if commodity crops like corn, wheat, and rice could be turned into nitrogen fixers. The gene editing answer may not be in the plant itself, but rather in bacteria. One company, Pivot Bio, found that nitrogen-fixing bacteria existed on corn roots, but had gone dormant. In 2018, the company launched the first microbial nitrogen-fixing solution into the US market. The product, which is essentially a liquid probiotic, adheres to the roots of the corn plant feeding it nitrogen directly. In this case, the microbial is gene-edited, not the corn plant. It doesn't completely replace the need for fertilizer, but greatly reduces the amount needed.[99] Pivot Bio is backed by large investors, including Bill Gates's Breakthrough Energy Ventures. In 2020, Pivot Bio closed $100 million in funding, allowing the company to scale production to a global scale.[100] The company claims that the production of the Pivot Bio-PROVENTM product eliminates 99 percent of the GHG emissions otherwise produced by synthetic fertilizers.[101]

Of course, when some people hear the words "gene editing" they think of genetically modified organisms. GMOs remain controversial. Creating GMOs involves the introduction of genes from other organisms that wouldn't happen in nature, for example, introducing soil bacteria into corn to improve insect resistance. While traditional GMOs are a type of gene editing, there are new ways to edit plants without introducing foreign DNA. However, gene editing will need to overcome negative perception surrounding genetic modification including regulatory barriers that exist in parts of the world if it is to be a truly disruptive technology in agriculture.

Indoor Vertical Farming

Indoor vertical farms provide operators greater control over climate conditions, allowing for consistent, year-round harvests. Plants are stacked in towers, maximizing the yield per square footage of space. A combination of natural and artificial light is used to achieve the perfect level of light needed for growth. Vertical farms are protected from adverse weather conditions and pests within the building structure. This allows for farming without harmful pesticides. Water consumption is greatly reduced—some estimate as much as 95 percent compared to conventional outdoor farms[102]—as a result of capturing the moisture transpired by the plants and returning it to the system.

There are three types of growing systems: hydroponics, in which water serves as the medium—often with the addition of soil-free options such as peat moss and coconut husks to provide structure; aquaponics, which is similar to hydroponics but with the addition of fish that provide nutrient-rich water to the plants; and aeroponics, in which roots are suspended in the air and water mist and nutrients are applied directly.[103] Today, hydroponic systems are the least expensive and the most often deployed across all indoor farming operations.

The crops most suitable for vertical farming are quick to turn—that is, they have a short time period from seed to maturity and market. These include lettuces, mustard and collard greens, basil, and mint.[104] In a 2017 Agrilyst survey, growers reported that lettuces and microgreens offer the highest profit margins—as much as 40 percent—compared to other indoor-grown edible crops.[105] One important advantage of indoor farming is food safety. Growers can control every input into the growing process, including filtering the water used to irrigate the plants, which is often a source of E. coli breakouts across conventional lettuce farming.

Given their flexible indoor design, many vertical farms are being built in urban areas, which brings food closer to consumers, reducing transportation costs and associated CO_2 emissions from fossil-fueled transport. While there are some concerns around increased electricity use—energy is the largest operating cost with the lighting system, representing as much as 70 percent of the total[106]—growers are turning to more efficient LEDs to reduce lighting loads. As we have discussed in previous chapters, such electrification can be attractive if we are able to switch to zero-emitting sources of electricity such as renewables.

Several factors are driving the growth of vertical farming, including global urbanization and consumer interest in locally sourced foods; extreme weather events and soil depletion; and demand for self-sufficiency, particularly in regions that do not have access to fertile land.[107] Yet even with this expected growth, vertical farming will likely represent only a small portion of overall farming operations. Globally, vertical farms are expected to grow to twenty-two million square feet (500 acres) by 2023.[108] Traditional outdoor farmland covers about 2.3 billion acres worldwide.[109]

Of course, acreage isn't quite the right metric for comparing vertical farms with outdoor farming, as the former can produce more food using less space. In some cases, yield estimates for indoor vertical farms can be thirty times that of conventional farming.[110] According to Plenty, a vertical farm company, a 2-acre indoor vertical farm can produce as much food as a 720-acre "flat farm."[111] Aero Farms, another vertical farm company, claims that their farms are 390 times more productive per square foot compared to traditional agriculture.[112]

Even so, several challenges threaten the accelerated adoption of vertical farms. One barrier is the large capital expense needed to build the vertical farm. Many of these farms are positioned for urban markets, and land and construction costs within cities can be steep. Profitability has been hard to prove over the years, with many vertical farms going out of business. Yet the interest by investors is growing—$60 million in investments seen in 2015–2016 exploded to $414 million by 2017–2018.[113] Investment is coming largely from socially responsible funds looking to benefit from the local-farm-to-table movement and invest in companies that offer sustainable practices and clean technologies.

Another significant cost is labor. According to one survey, larger vertical farms (greater than ten thousand square feet) employ 51 workers on average, which equates to 2.5 workers per acre cultivated.[114] In comparison, conventional farms in the United States employ less than 1 worker per acre farmed.[115] Beanstalk Farms in Virginia is using machinery to automate more mundane tasks, reducing labor costs while offering the additional benefits of consistent high-quality and safe produce due to less handling of the crops throughout the growing cycle.

Initial growth will likely be concentrated in urban centers, providing a more sustainable substitute farming source for those populations, avoiding further farmland expansion, and substituting a small portion of traditional farming. The best opportunity will be in the organic market, where consumers have demonstrated a willingness to pay for sustainably sourced and grown greens. However, until the price of indoor vertical farmed greens matches that of organic greens there will be stiff competition in that space. In 2020, the market price for indoor vertical farmed greens in the United States was $33/kg of leafy greens compared to $23/kg for organic greens.[116] Continued investments in the technologies and automated systems should continue to drive costs down.

Extending the technology to crops like corn, rice, and wheat will be a bigger challenge and is not currently the goal of market entrants. These crops are the primary drivers of our global food supply. For indoor vertical farming to serve as a key driver of agriculture decarbonization, these crops are critical. However, given the current cost structure of vertical farming and the sheer volume of these crops needed to be grown, it appears unlikely that vertical farming will be a solution broadly.

WILDCARD DISRUPTOR: CLEAN MEAT

Clean meat, in-vitro meat, cell-based meat, cultured meat—these are all identifiers being used by the food industry for a new alternative to conventional meat products. Clean meat is grown in a laboratory and is derived from a sample of animal cells that are replicated in a culture outside of the animal. In addition to zeroing out methane emissions from enteric fermentation and manure, moving meat production from pasture to laboratory opens land for other types of farming or reforestation and quells concerns around animal welfare and antibiotic use. Perhaps not surprisingly, PETA (People for the Ethical Treatment of Animals) has indicated support of clean meat.[117] The laboratory process also offers faster production times compared to the time it takes to breed and grow animals for slaughter.

The clean meat production process, while complex, leverages knowledge gained from years of research in the medical field. However, translating technologies used for medical processes to support clean meat is a significant challenge. There are several steps to producing clean meat: establishing cell lines, growing cells in media, scaffolding to differentiate cell types and encourage an organized pattern of growth, and scaling growth in bioreactors.[118] Today, each of these stages requires significant and expensive research and development.

There are major challenges ahead, including price point and consumer acceptance. The first clean meat hamburger, introduced in 2013 by Dr. Mark Post of Maastricht University, came with a $330,000 research price tag.[119] While "alternative meat" products have been in supermarkets for years, these have focused exclusively on using plant substitutes. The adventurous, sustainably minded foodie might embrace clean meat, but the general population will likely be wary of food grown in a laboratory. As clean meat commercializes and scales, prices for product offerings should become more palatable to the average consumer. During an industry panel at the Animal AgTech Innovation Summit in March 2019, half of the industry representatives agreed that clean meat will reach cost parity with traditional beef within the next ten years. Consumer perception about lab-grown meat may be the bigger barrier to broader adoption.

One of the primary concerns of consumers is the belief that laboratory-grown meat is not "natural."[120] A study conducted by Faunalytics in January 2018 found that 66 percent of consumers would try clean meat, with 40 percent willing to pay a premium for it, but only when presented with education and positive messaging around clean meat.[121] Results from the study suggest that focusing on portraying clean meat as natural may be a lost cause, and messages that focus on taste, animal welfare, and environmental benefits may do more to convince consumers.[122]

There is a lot of excitement today around clean meat. We are witnessing a growing number of start-ups in the meat industry, all of which are working to drive prices down and convince consumers that clean meat is just as good as, if not better than, conventional meat. Products range from beef to chicken to fish. Start-ups in the United States alone include Memphis Meats, Finless Foods, Wild Type, BlueNalu, Mission Barns, New Age Meats, and Just Inc. Even incumbent meat companies are entering the game. In January 2018, Tyson Foods announced its investment in Memphis Meats.[123] These new ventures have an opportunity to capitalize on the success of alternative protein meat companies that have worked to change the way consumers view staples like beef burgers.

While customer acceptance will indeed be critical to the acceptance of clean meat, there are some regulatory hurdles as well. In December 2020, Singapore was the first country to approve the sale of clean meat within the country.[124] In the United States, the US Department of Health and Human Services Food and Drug Administration and the US Department of Agriculture Food Safety and Inspection Service entered into an agreement in 2019 regarding oversight of the production of cell-based meat. The USDA is currently working to develop appropriate labeling for clean meat.

THE UPSHOT: AGRICULTURE DECARBONIZATION IS HIGHLY UNLIKELY BY 2050

Agriculture is a critical and complex sector when it comes to decarbonization by 2050. At roughly a quarter of all global greenhouse gas emissions, the sector must see significant reductions in order to achieve the Paris Accord targets. This will not be easy—demand for food will only increase as the worldwide population grows and demand for protein-rich foods by developing countries increase.

Unlike in the transportation and energy sectors, there are no obvious emerging technologies, such as electric vehicles and renewable energy, that seem poised to radically disrupt the status quo. Rather, a sustainable transformation will likely require a combination of the diffusion of best practices, changes in consumer preferences, and the emergence of a portfolio of novel solutions that leverage technology to lower the agricultural carbon footprint. All of this will have to happen in a global industry made up of millions of enterprises, from large multinationals to small family farmers.

A viable path to 2050 seems unlikely, yet no other sector is as critical to human survival as agriculture. Decarbonization will likely necessitate a world-wide effort led by individual nation-states to create significant incentives and programs to dramatically change agricultural practices at the local level. Such a wholesale change seems daunting and unrealistic within this time frame. Despite the exciting efforts in the biotech and digital agtech segments, the prospects for a technological silver bullet seem very dim indeed.

We choose optimism, however. Agriculture is one of the few sectors with a high potential to serve as a carbon sink. Improved land-management practices and the conversion of lands to forests and other carbon sinks could greatly offset agricultural emissions. Yet all available levers must be pursued in order to achieve decarbonization by 2050.

HOW CAN WE DECARBONIZE AGRICULTURE BY 2050?

For decarbonization to happen in the agriculture industry, levers need to be pulled throughout the entire food chain: production, distribution, and con-sumption. There is no silver-bullet technology, and the answer will likely be a mix of best practices, dietary shifts, and smart farming. It will also likely be regional, with different approaches identified on the basis of country, farm size, and commodity.

The low-hanging fruit is education, yet even this is no small task given how diffuse the agriculture marketplace. According to FAO, 90 percent of farms around the world are managed by one person or a family, and these farms produce 80 percent of agricultural output.[125] Reaching these farmers will be critical to decarbonizing the industry. Agriculture extension organizations take information gained from science and research out to rural areas to edu-cate farmers on the latest best practices and technology opportunities. These extensions are in place in both developed and developing countries, but there is often distrust in the information once it reaches the small farmer, particularly in developing countries.

Organizations such as FAO and WRI are working to put systems in place to support small farmers in these countries and build trust in science.

Private-sector initiatives, like that being spearheaded by the Gates Foundation, are also working to educate small farmers in developing countries. Major food companies are working in their own supply chains to educate their suppliers. The spread of mobile phones into rural areas is assisting with the dissemination of information to these farmers. However, Pew Research Center reported that only 78 percent (median) of people living in emerging economies own a mobile phone and 45 percent own a smartphone; this is compared to 94 percent and 76 percent respectively in developed economies.[126] Further, subscriptions are concentrated more in urban areas and less where farming takes place.[127]

To meet our 2050 goal, education must be coupled with adoption of new technologies and changes in consumer demand. What are some of the other levers that can be pulled to accelerate this shift?

Increase Consumer Demand for Sustainable Alternatives

In this industry, the consumer drives change. There is a growing interest within more developed, industrialized food markets in local production and greater transparency into how food is sourced. Consumers are increasingly interested in the health of food: specifically, how it's managed and produced. According to the National Restaurant Association's "What's Hot in 2019" survey of more than six hundred chefs across the United States, top food trends included zero-waste cooking, locally sourced ingredients, and veggie-centric or vegetable-forward cuisine.[128] In 2020, plant-based proteins were listed as the second hottest trend behind eco-friendly packaging.[129] The Association's report suggests that the results "indicate that Americans are still hungry for healthy food, but they're also interested in more options, new alternatives, and going beyond simply healthy into sustainable options that are good for everyone and the environment."[130]

There are many examples in which consumer interest has greatly influenced not just what companies produce but how they produce food. The rise in consumer concerns related to animal welfare and the use of antibiotics caused a seismic shift by big companies away from broader herd management and treatment toward more predictive medicine on an individual animal basis, with the help of artificial intelligence and access to real-time data. Consumer interest has driven companies such as Purdue to move toward 100 percent antibiotic-free production, and it will continue to push major brands to explore more sustainable alternatives to mainstream products.

In the United States, we have seen a sizeable shift away from dairy consumption to alternatives such as soy, almond, and coconut, due largely to consumer belief that plant-based products are healthier and better for the environment.[131] Overall milk consumption declined by 22 percent from 2000 to 2016, and alternative milks (plant-based) are predicted to represent 40 percent of US milk sales by 2021.[132] However, as mentioned earlier, there will be a significant increase in milk consumption in developing countries that could more than balance out any declines seen in more developed countries.

Plant-based burgers have been available in stores for years, but they have been largely viewed as strictly a vegan alternative. Environmentally conscious flexitarians, or consumers who largely eat a vegetarian diet but consume meat occasionally, are looking for alternatives, but don't want to give up taste. Companies such as Impossible Foods and Beyond Burger have introduced plant-based alternatives that serve as substitutes for meat lovers, as opposed to speaking to the vegan population, competing with conventional beef patties on texture and taste. In the United States, their products have been picked up by national restaurant, quick-service, and grocery chains, more quickly expanding product reach across the country. While the two companies are becoming household names, according to the Good Food Institute there are more than 150 plant-based companies in the United States.[133]

Today, plant-based meat represents only 1 percent of total meat sales.[134] However, plant-based sales are expected to grow from $4.6 billion in 2018 to $85 billion by 2030.[135] Perhaps even more telling of the potential threat to the meat industry is that nine out of the ten largest US meat companies have launched, bought, or collaborated on a plant-based brand.[136] Ultimately, taste will drive greater acceptance of alternative proteins. If producers can get the balance of taste and price point right then we should see greater uptake in the United States and other developed markets.

Consumer demand for sustainably sourced wood products can help to reduce deforestation and encourage growth of new forests and carbon sinks. International labeling programs such as the Forest Stewardship Council and the Program for Endorsement of Forest Certification certify products that are produced from responsibly managed forests. These third-party organizations offer searchable databases of products and companies, and major retailers like The Home Depot carry certified products.

For these alternatives to be successful in replacing traditional agriculture products they must offer consumers the same taste, performance, and price point. Until this happens, they will continue to be niche. Standardized labeling will help consumers to identify sustainable products and educate them on their benefits. Attention must also be paid to the potential for non-GHG environmental impacts that could come with the production of alternatives. For example, almond milk has been criticized for its significant water consumption during production.

Reduce Food Loss and Waste

According to FAO, one-third of the food produced annually for human consumption is lost or wasted, which equates to 1.8 billion tons of food (Figure 6.4).[137] FAO estimates that food waste represents 8 percent of global GHG emissions.[138] If food waste were a country, it would be the third-largest emitter.[139] Where this loss or waste happens along the supply chain depends primarily on the global region.

In developing countries, loss happens at the harvesting, storage, and cooling stages due to financial, managerial, and technical barriers.[140] Some estimates suggest that only 10 percent of perishable food is refrigerated.[141] Cold chain (that is, refrigerated supply chain) storage and transportation could greatly reduce food waste in developing countries. One example is India, which represents 28 percent of banana production, but exports less than 1 percent due to an incomplete cold chain system.[142] Smaller-scale, low-cost technologies that can be deployed in rural areas and policies that help to support their adoption could reduce carbon emissions otherwise attributed to overproduction of food to account for losses.

In developed countries, where infrastructure is in place to support the supply chain, waste occurs at the retail and consumer stages. In the United States, ReFED estimates that fifty-two million tons of food produced each year is sent to landfills. A lot of attention has been paid to efforts to save "ugly" food, attracting new ventures that buy imperfect fruits and vegetables from farmers and distribute directly to consumers. Yet 85 percent of the waste happens at

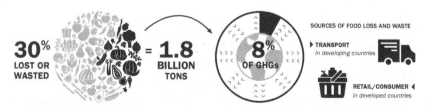

FIGURE 6.4   Food Waste in Developed and Developing Economies

these later stages.[143] ReFED evaluated twenty-seven waste reduction actions that offer the potential to reduce eighteen million tons of GHG emissions annually in the United States.[144] The three actions identified as the biggest contributors to this reduction if implemented are centralized composting, waste tracking and analytics, and consumer education campaigns.[145]

Composting turns organic waste into humus, which can then be used to support healthy and fertile soil. Central composting facilities could be regionally located, working with multiple smaller community operations and providing the benefit of economies of scale, reducing the cost of the organic fertilizer that is then sold to the community. However, there are challenges. The capital costs for the facility and equipment can be prohibitive, low-cost synthetic fertilizers continue to benefit from cheap oil and industrial production, and food wastes need other carbon-rich sources to balance the nitrogen-rich compost.

Restaurants and retailers largely aren't aware of the amount of waste they are generating on-site. Auditing waste streams is the first step to identifying reduction opportunities. Solutions may include adjusting inventories, tracking sell-by dates, donating to food banks or livestock farms, and composting. All these solutions carry their own carbon-reduction potential. Using software solutions to track food waste can be daunting and will require time and resources to implement.[146]

As with many environmental issues, consumers understand the food waste problem, but do not see themselves as part of the solution. According to the United Nations, households represented 61 percent of food waste globally in 2019.[147] Interestingly, consumer education was also identified by ReFED as the top action with the most financial benefits to society, or economic value per ton.[148] The challenge lies in the fact that food is relatively cheap in the United States and that behavior is hard to change unless the change is emotionally or financially motivated. National and local consumer education campaigns that engage public and private industry stakeholders, with messaging that touches on those issues most important to the average American, are critical.[149]

Increase Public-Sector Investment and Incentives

For decades, US farmers have relied on the Farm Bill to support them through tough growing seasons and to help stimulate demand for domestic crops. The bill was first drafted in 1933, at the time of the Great Depression, to address farmer needs and widespread poverty in the United States.[150] Farmers needed to produce to make a living while demand for their goods was declining. The federal government paid farmers to slow productions and bought surplus goods to help feed hungry people. Every five years, the Farm Bill is reviewed by the federal government to ensure it adequately addresses the needs of farmers and Americans. To date, most of the bill spending has gone to nutrition, namely the Supplemental Nutrition Assistance Program (SNAP).[151] Other areas addressed include commodity crop revenue insurance, international trade support, guaranteed credit and loans, rural development, and natural disaster crop insurance.[152]

The most recent Farm Bill was signed into law on December 20, 2018, and it will expire in 2023. There are several parts of the bill that address soil and forest conservation, and more climate-friendly farming practices in general. For example, incentives are provided for best practices such as cover crops, crop rotation, and advanced grazing management, as well as comprehensive conservation planning.[153] There are also new research priorities around soil health and authorization of policies that support adapted seed varieties to navigate the effects of climate change.[154]

While the inclusion of conservation-focused incentives in the Farm Bill is promising, the fact is that US public funding for agriculture R&D has trended downward since 1970. Fortunately, private funding seems to be picking up where public investment has left off. According to the USDA, public-sector funding of agriculture R&D began declining in 2003, and for the first time, private-sector investments surpassed those from government sources.[155] By 2013, federal and state government funding represented 23 percent of total US agriculture R&D investments, while the private sector and other nongovernmental sources (such as foundations and farmer organizations) represented 76 percent.[156]

Elsewhere in the world, public funding for agriculture R&D has seen an increase, led by China, where government investment in R&D increased almost eightfold between 1990 and 2013.[157] The share of private-sector R&D investment also increased during this period, from 3 percent in 1995 to 16 percent in 2006 of total country expenditures on agriculture.[158] In 2010, Chinese total R&D in agriculture surpassed that of the United States.[159] Between 2013 and 2016, total venture capital in China increased from $3 billion to $34 billion.[160] Investments in agrifood start-ups increased by 222 percent between 2017 and 2018.[161] For China, a country with the largest population in the world, the driving force for investing is food security. With that in mind, China is also investing heavily in the modernization of African farming. China's primary interest is in trade between the two economies—agricultural product trade increased from

$650 million in 2000 to $6.92 billion in 2018—however, China is also investing in the African knowledge base, educating nearly ten thousand officials, farmers, students, and technicians each year.[162]

Conservation programs are also being implemented in other parts of the world. The European Union requires member states to allocate 30 percent of income support to greening activities, providing direct payment to farmers that adopt best practices that preserve natural resources.[163] In 2020, the EU Commissioner announced the pursuit of the Farm Carbon Forest Initiative, which would reward farmers and forest managers for practices that sequestered carbon.[164]

Government policy can serve as a barrier to new technologies and practices. For example, plant gene editing requires no additional regulatory approvals if scientists stay within breed. It's a different story for livestock, which is regulated like a pharmaceutical drug. While countries such as Brazil and Argentina allow gene editing of animals within the same genetic code, similar to plants, the European Union and the United States treat gene editing like a GMO, requiring additional approvals. Yet the very definition of gene editing is different from that of a GMO, with the former referring to edits made within the same genome and the latter defined as introducing foreign DNA into the sequence.

Even within the seemingly more supportive plant gene-editing world, there are differences in opinions about their benefits. For example, the genetically edited hybrid Golden Rice (engineered to be high in beta-carotene) was introduced in 1999 as a solution to countries with widespread Vitamin A deficiencies. Nearly twenty years later, it was approved for consumption in the United States, Canada, New Zealand, and Australia and only recently approved in the Philippines, a country suffering from Vitamin A deficiencies, the delay in all because of general GMO concerns.[165] Regulations for gene-editing activities are crucial to ensuring food safety, but movement toward internationally recognized standards and research that protect public health while allowing for innovation and scientific advances could accelerate the shift to more climate-friendly and resilient food sources.

Leverage the Supply Chain

For many food companies, the majority of carbon emissions comes from their supply chains, otherwise known as scope 3 emissions. Influencing and tracking those emissions can prove difficult for even the biggest brands accustomed to wielding their purchasing power. These companies are in the best position to influence change in these channels, but many are not measuring or disclosing supply chain emissions. According to Ceres, a nonprofit organization that works to build the business case for sustainability, of the fifty top food and beverage companies that sell consumer goods in the United States and Canada, only fifteen are reporting emissions from upstream agriculture.[166] For those companies, scope 3 emissions accounted for a surprising 86 percent of total company-reported emissions.[167]

Emission accounting protocols and tools are critical to company efforts to track GHGs and identify opportunities for reduction throughout the supply chain. Global organizations like Ceres are developing resources such as standards, methodologies, and calculators for evaluating emissions from upstream agriculture operations and land-use change activities.[168] Standardizing methodologies and protocols can help suppliers to consistently report performance across multiple customers.

Even when emission sources can be identified and measured, influencing multiple suppliers and distributors—particularly in other countries, each with their own regulatory requirements—can be challenging. To give a sense of the size of such a challenge, Unilever mapped and released information on the 1,500 mills and 150 palm oil facilities that provide palm oil to their suppliers, most of which are located in Southeast Asia and South America.[169] The increasing popularity of palm oil—almost 50 percent of packaged products for sale at supermarkets use it—is blamed for deforestation increases in countries with high species diversity and dense forests.[170] To work with these international governments to achieve meaningful action requires in-country expertise and established relationships.

Some corporations are partnering with ag-science companies that have farmer networks already established to source sustainably grown inputs. In 2019, Anheuser-Busch and Indigo Agriculture announced a partnership to supply the beer company with 2.2 million bushels of Indigo Rice. According to Indigo, growers contracting with Indigo to produce rice for Anheuser-Busch will reduce water and nitrogen use by 10 percent, which will result in a 10 percent reduction in GHG emissions.[171]

These company-led commitments are encouraging, but to shift supply chains, there is strength in numbers. Multibrand partnerships with nonprofits and other stakeholders have proven effective at influencing change within a given input supply chain. Palm oil serves as a good example: the nonprofit Roundtable on Sustainable Palm Oil (RSPO) brought together producers, consumer goods companies, retailers, traders, and NGOs to develop internationally recognized standards for sustainable palm oil. RSPO member companies also commit to implementing the standards. Some of these companies are sourcing 100 percent sustainable palm oil, including Walmart, Unilever, McDonald's, General Mills, Hershey, Mars, and Kraft Heinz.[172] According to RSPO, 19 percent of the palm oil produced globally has been RSPO-certified.[173]

Another example of multistakeholder engagement is the Soil Carbon Initiative, a partnership between nonprofits Carbon Underground and Green America and corporate advocates Ben and Jerry's, DanoneWave, Annie's, and Megafood to develop a global standard for food grown from regenerative farming.[174] Multistakeholder partnerships like these can help to accelerate the creation and adoption of the global standards needed to more quickly decarbonize food supply chains.

Increase Carbon Sinks

Carbon sequestration currently offsets about 20 percent of global agriculture emissions. Increasing our carbon sinks while working to mitigate agriculture emissions could lead to a significant reduction in our global carbon footprint. The good news is that options are already at our disposal, many of which are being implemented in developed countries. According to the Nature Conservancy, nature-based solutions are readily available and can get us a third of the way to Paris Agreement targets by 2030, with a tenth of that attributed to US action.[175] Mitigation pathways range from reforestation, forest management, and fire management to grazing optimization, cover crops, and alley cropping (the planting of trees alongside rows of crops).[176] Many of these pathways would require low cost to implement.

However, forests, once considered the biggest carbon sink opportunity and hope for carbon balance, could actually contribute to climate change if atmospheric warming continues. A study published by Harvard suggests that at some point, forests may emit more carbon than they sequester. Scientists warmed forest soils over the span of twenty years and measured not just one pulse of CO_2 but subsequent releases that suggested an evolution of the microbes exposed to the warming temperatures, accelerating the rate of emissions.[177] Another study suggests that the world's tropical forests are acting as a net source of CO_2 (instead of sink) due less to deforestation and more to reductions in carbon density within standing forests from degradation or disturbance—scientists in that study calculated almost 70 percent of losses attributed to existing forests.[178]

Our best hope at mitigating GHG emissions might be through growth of new forests. A study released by the Birmingham Institute of Forest Research suggests that younger forests may better sequester carbon than old-growth forests such as tropical rainforests. Researchers found that more than half of the global carbon sink represented by forests is found in middle- and high-latitude forests less than 140 years old.[179] One theory is that reforested land is open and sunny, allowing newly planted fast-growing species to sequester carbon and incorporate it into their biomass quickly, while old-growth trees must compete for resources with neighboring trees in close proximity.[180]

Another hopeful emerging carbon sequester is hemp. An inherently resilient and sustainable crop, hemp is low maintenance—requiring less water, pesticides, and fertilizer than corn—and offers a list of uses from livestock feed to textiles. Hemp grows vigorously, can be grown in fields otherwise retired from farming, and can also be used as a cover crop with the benefit of replenishing soils. According to some estimates, hemp can sequester 1.63 tons of CO_2 per ton grown.[181] Changes in federal regulations over the last few years have paved the way for hemp cultivation in the United States. Hemp was banned in the 1950s due to concerns around marijuana, but the 2014 Farm Bill opened the door for it through the allowance of state-controlled pilots. A year later, 1,500 acres of hemp had been planted.[182] The 2018 Farm Bill officially lifted the ban on hemp, and by 2019, land area devoted to growing hemp jumped to 146,000 acres in thirty-seven states.[183]

We are in the early stages of researching and truly understanding the benefits of land-use change and the long-term effects of warming on these sinks. The carbon sequestered will be a finite amount, and any work to expand carbon sinks must be coupled with continued declines in deforestation and reductions in emissions from agriculture operations.

Create a Market for Carbon

For agriculture, there is value in carbon sequestration in terms of soil productivity, but in addition to higher yields, what if farmers were also paid for the carbon? The idea of "carbon farming" is getting some attention, particularly in cap-and-trade markets. In 2015, the California Air Resources Board approved the inclusion of rice farmers in the statewide cap-and-trade market, allowing for the generation and sale of carbon offsets based on a protocol of land-management best practices.[184]

Before any trading could begin, the carbon-reduction methodology had to be approved by the American Carbon Registry—a nonprofit that sets standards for carbon offsets—and the State of California. For rice, best practices around water management and drainage can result in reduced methane emissions.[185] In 2017, Microsoft purchased the first-ever carbon credits from US rice farmers.[186] Other companies are following suit. More recently, Indigo Ag shared a diverse list of companies that committed to buying its carbon credits at $20/ton of CO_2 equivalent sequestered during the 2020 growing season using protocols from Climate Action Reserve and Verra. Companies included Barclays, JP Morgan Chase, IBM, and New Belgium Brewing.[187]

Additional protocols are being developed, led by nonprofits like the Environmental Defense Fund. In 2019, the American Carbon Registry approved a grassland management protocol. Research suggests that grasslands may be better carbon sinks than forests, able to retain carbon even during wildfire events.[188] Yet 1.6 million acres of grasslands aged twenty years or older were converted to croplands between 2008 and 2012.[189] In 2018, more than 500,000 acres of grassland were lost across the US Northern Great Plains.[190]

Although many countries have developed carbon-trading schemes, agriculture is not often listed as a participating industry. This is an area of great promise and opportunity, yet much work needs to be done to establish protocols and build the necessary infrastructure to support such a program. What is clear is that if we are to have any hope in decarbonizing the agriculture sector, we need a comprehensive multipronged approach developed specifically for the sector and to recognize the vast differences across the globe in agriculture practices and challenges.

CHAPTER 7

THE PATH FORWARD

WHAT DOES THE FUTURE HOLD FOR US? Will we be able to achieve decarbonization of the global economy by 2050 and avoid the worst impacts from climate change? There is much about which to be hopeful. Disruptive sustainable technologies such as electric vehicles and renewable energy are making incredible progress both technologically and in the marketplace. In a diverse set of industries, intrepid entrepreneurs and established innovators are working on new, potentially disruptive sustainable technologies, from precision agriculture to green cement to clean meat.

Yet these disruptions are neither guaranteed nor sufficient to achieve the 2050 target. Decarbonization requires disruption across all the sectors outlined in this book—energy, transportation, industrials, buildings, agriculture. What is clear is that we will not achieve decarbonization by 2050, or perhaps ever, on our current trajectory, technologically or otherwise. We will need a concerted effort from numerous stakeholders to shape the institutional envelope around which business and markets function. We need a comprehensive and global technology policy that explicitly cultivates the conditions under which sustainable technologies can transform the status quo.

What would such a broad-based technology policy look like? Any plan should achieve decarbonization in the most efficient and least expensive way feasible. The plan should recognize both the limits of market economies and the opportunities they create. We should be wary of various calls to national-ize industries so as to force them to adopt climate-friendly technologies. We clearly need more innovation, and markets have proven incredibly potent in generating "gales of creative destruction," to borrow from Austrian economist Joseph Schumpeter. When technologies become preferred on the existing basis of merit, say delivering solid value at low cost, the market can quickly facilitate their diffusion.

Some have argued that what we really need are changes in people's con-sumption patterns—a grand awakening in which all people place great value on sustainable goods and services. No doubt, such an awakening would be transformational. We are cautious, though, of the feasibility of the wholesale changes in behavior that would be necessary to lead to decarbonization by 2050. We absolutely believe that efforts can be undertaken to increase the relative value of sustainable solutions versus others in the eyes of consumers. However, these behavioral "nudges," as they are often called, are only one lever that needs to be part of a broader technology policy to drive massive disruption toward sustainable technologies.

We already know what such a disruption will likely look like (see Figure 7.1): (1) a reconfigured electrical generation portfolio featuring wind, solar, hydro, and nuclear power distributed across millions of generators, including homeowners, traded via a smart grid and with massive storage capacity; (2) electrification of all vehicles on the road either via batteries or fuel cells with bio-fuel or hydrogen solutions for challenging transportation needs like airplanes and shipping; (3) electrification of heating and cooking needs in buildings; (4) electrification of industrial processes when possible, new green technolo-gies in some problematic sectors like cement and petrochemicals, and carbon capture utilization and storage as a last resort; and (5) a massive effort to green agriculture, including precision farming, developing protein alternatives, and growing of carbon sinks.

How can we bring about all these changes in so many different sectors across the globe within thirty years? First, we must observe that individual national efforts are insufficient. We need a coordinated, international approach. Not to say that every country needs to be a leader. One of the great advantages of an innovation approach to the problem of climate change is that technologies that become preferable absent price supports, say, for example, low-cost electric vehicles, should continue to diffuse even in the absence of policy interventions in a particular country or region. Thus efforts by a small number of countries

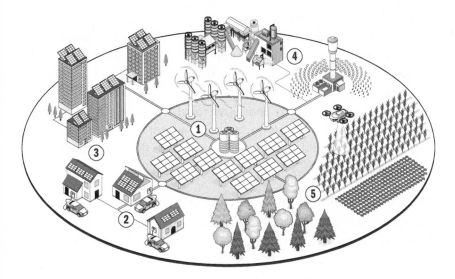

(1) **A reconfigured electrical generation portfolio** featuring wind, solar, and storage capacity

(2) **Electrification of all vehicles on the road** either via batteries or fuel cells with biofuel solutions for challenging transportation needs like airplanes and shipping

(3) **Electrification of all buildings** including heating and cooking processes

(4) **Electrification of industrial processes** supported by renewables when possible, new green technologies in some problematic sectors like cement and petrochemicals, and carbon capture and storage as a last resort

(5) **A massive effort to green agriculture** including precision farming, developing protein alternatives, and growing of carbon sinks

FIGURE 7.1   Decarbonization by 2050

to advance a sustainable technology could potentially diffuse that technology around the world if the economics become favorable.

Second, a comprehensive technology policy should recognize the important differences between sectors. A promising lever for one sector may be less so for another. For example, electrification of vehicles is occurring. The technology is available on the market and has been experiencing exponential growth. We are in the midst of a major disruption. Worrying about fuel economy standards in 2030 is likely pointless at this time. By 2030, CAFE standards will be moot if current trends continue. Rather, policy makers would be well served to focus on building out charging infrastructure. A policy to fund infrastructure could be catalytic.

Contrast this with green cement, which remains a nascent technology. Right now, green cement is not commercially viable compared to existing Portland cement. Subsidizing R&D may be the most impactful lever to pull at this time. The goal is to spur innovation that will hopefully drive down the cost of green cement, making it preferable in the marketplace. Or perhaps there need to be efforts to help underwrite the risk of scaling green cement production that may lower costs through economies of scale. Either way, our technology policy should advance specific proposals that meet the unique needs of each sector.

TOWARD A COMPREHENSIVE TECHNOLOGY POLICY

In 2018, the University of Virginia's Batten Institute convened the Jefferson Innovation Summit to catalyze innovation and entrepreneurship to address climate change in the United States. Fifty delegates—policy makers, academics, entrepreneurs, elected officials, CEOs, nonprofit leaders, investors—convened in Washington, DC, to workshop a policy playbook for climate change, with a particular emphasis on catalyzing disruptive, sustainable innovations. What emerged were six key strategic initiatives (see Figure 7.2): (1) launch a national "moonshot" on clean technology, (2) create a national cleantech bank, (3) energize next-generation technology development, (4), build the utility of the future, (5) declare a "new deal" for clean technology, and (6) educate the public on clean technology.

Collectively, the initiatives were based on the life-cycle dynamics of successful innovations, starting with the creation moment when research and development provide the fountainhead of new ideas (see action 1), moving through investment and commercialization (see actions 2 and 3), supporting the broader infrastructure that allows innovations to flourish (see actions 4 and 5), and culminating in broad consumer and citizen awareness of the value of new emergent technologies (see action 6).

Central to the recommended initiatives was a recognition of the political challenges in advancing climate change legislation in the United States. While the criticality and scale of climate change action are debated throughout the world, the US is somewhat unique in having prominent politicians question the basic science and existence of climate change.[1] Thus the Jefferson Innovation Summit playbook tried to balance the need for driving sustainable solutions while simultaneously creating jobs and driving economic development, especially in regions that stand to be losers in a shift toward a decarbonized

1. Launch a National "Moonshot" on Clean Technology	Set aggressive goals and put money and collective brain power into technology development. Establish an ambitious and inspirational vision for our clean technology future and a specific goal for achieving it. To meet such a goal, make significant R&D investment in clean technologies in order to move them from emerging to dominant technologies that will outcompete incumbent technologies in price and performance.	
2. Create a National Cleantech Bank	Expand lending opportunities for clean energy technologies and projects that are high-risk investments requiring significant and patient capital. For example, create a quasi-public national bank that would fund loans, loan guarantees, debt securitization, insurance, and other forms of risk management to state, municipal, and regional green banks.	
3. Energize Next-Generation Technology Development	Allow novel ideas to grow and flourish especially in communities that lack access to the knowledge, mentoring, and capital needed to scale great ideas. Identify under-served regions where incubator or accelerator programs either don't yet exist or don't meet current needs. Create local programs to recruit cohorts that offer solutions for mitigating climate change, but don't have access to capital.	
4. Build the Utility of the Future	Build a smarter, more flexible electric grid that can handle distributed generation. Innovate both underlying technology and the utility business model. Regulatory incentives need to focus on consumer choice and education, integration of distributed energy resources behind the meter, enhanced planning, peak demand reduction, increased reliability and access, and support of cleantech innovation. Utilities need to be provided the space to innovate and the freedom to fail.	
5. Declare a "New Deal" for Clean Technology	Create incentives for public and private investment in the training and reskilling of the workforce in communities disrupted by technology transitions. Conduct a comprehensive analysis to identify regions that have experienced significant job loss due to declining fossil fuel industries and evaluate the region's ability to host clean technology research, manufacturing, construction projects and/or support services.	
6. Educate the Public on Clean Technology	Develop a series of pilot public education campaigns in strategically selected regions to craft messages on climate change. Create a national consortium, funded by private companies and non-profits, to oversee the regional pilots, convening members to discuss the findings and develop a national public education campaign. A national theme might be something like "join us in creating the industry of the future."	

FIGURE 7.2   Policy Actions from the 2018 Jefferson Innovation Summit

economy, such as the coal-rich states in the central Appalachian Mountains region of the US.

Purposively excluded from the playbook was an explicit call to put a price on carbon dioxide and other greenhouse gas emissions. There was wide agreement at the Summit that such a price would be extremely valuable in efforts to decarbonize the economy. In the words of the playbook, pricing carbon was excluded "given our desire to recommend novel approaches that break the current political stalemate."[2] With that said, most economists and policy makers agree that placing a price on greenhouse gas emissions, either in the form of a carbon tax or as part of a cap-and-trade mechanism, is one of the most important and impactful levers for reducing emissions.

In the United States, efforts to create a politically acceptable carbon price have gained momentum in recent years. The Energy Innovation and Carbon Dividend Act of 2019 (H.R. 763) proposed a "a fee on the carbon content of fuels, including crude oil, natural gas, coal, or any other product derived from those fuels that will be used so as to emit greenhouse gases into the atmosphere." Hailed as a bipartisan climate solution, the bill calls for an escalating fee over time and the creation of a "Carbon Dividend Trust Fund" from which dividend payments would be made to US citizens and lawful residents. In a nod to conservative legislators, the bill includes a border carbon adjustment for imported goods and a pause in the EPA's authority to regulate CO_2 emissions.[3]

Critical to any legislation is that it sets a price that is economically meaningful—one that either has an impact on the consumption patterns of consumers or incentivizes suppliers to seek alternative decarbonized solutions. Also of importance is whether it creates incentives for developing carbon sinks and carbon capture and storage. An impactful carbon-pricing mechanism would provide incentives to grow forests or sequester greenhouse gas emissions. Last, a carbon price would be best if coordinated across national markets. For example, Nobel Prize–winning economist William Nordhaus has argued that future international climate negotiations should focus on agreeing to a target international carbon price.[4]

While we recognize the desirability of a general carbon price and support legislation and international negotiations designed to create such a mechanism, we focus our attention on policies designed to develop and nurture sustainable technologies that may disrupt current greenhouse-gas-emitting alternatives. To be clear, as we've discussed throughout the book, pricing carbon should be a critical lever to such a technology policy. Rather than debate the merits of a broad carbon price, which we wholeheartedly support, we simply choose to consider targeted approaches to pricing carbon for particularly vexing technologies and sectors.

Building off the themes of the Jefferson Innovation Summit Policy Playbook, we advance a comprehensive technology policy (see Figure 7.3 for a summary). Like the playbook, we consider the political reality of the various proposals and try to balance decarbonization needs with economic development and community welfare considerations. Unlike the playbook, we adopt an explicit sector-based strategy and consider how such a policy could play out on a global scale. Thus we advance strategies for each of the five major sectors discussed in the book: energy, transportation, industrials, buildings, and agriculture.

Critical to our recommended policy portfolio is a recognition of the exploratory nature of innovation. Innovation requires exploring novel pathways, many of which will lead to dead ends. In the mantra of Silicon Valley, successful innovators experiment constantly, fail fast, and quickly pivot to new solutions. Thus our technology policy needs to provide enough leeway to discover and develop novel technologies while simultaneously trying to direct those innovative efforts toward sustainable solutions. In this way, our proposed technology policy is about increasing both the rate and *direction* of innovative activity.

As Mariana Mazzucato outlines in her book *The Entrepreneurial State*, while many bemoan the state "picking winners and losers," the fact is that many major technological innovations were consciously fostered by state enterprises that invested in early-stage research and development to a particular end.[5] From the semiconductor to nuclear power to the Internet to GPS, the state played an active and directive role in the trajectory of innovation. We believe that a similar grand challenge approach is required here. The key is to direct innovative activity while leaving wide enough guardrails to allow for experimentation and exploration of novel solutions.

THE ENERGY SECTOR

With respect to electricity generation, we are seeing the beginning of a potential transition to zero-carbon-emitting sources, most prominently wind and solar. All else being equal, renewables should become more attractive as they move down the learning curve and production expands, capturing economies of scale. Other than small pockets of consumer demand for clean energy, meaning that people are willing to pay a premium for green electricity, electricity is a commodity product for which utilities favor generators who can provide

PRIMARY PILLARS	POTENTIAL LEVERS

Energy

1. Lower the cost of renewables relative to fossil fuels	• Continue renewable subsidies (e.g. tax breaks) • Remove fossil fuel subsidies • Price GHG emissions (e.g. carbon tax, cap-trade) • Adopt RPS's and other regulations • Regulate fracking emissions • Eliminate trade barriers for solar panels, materials • Ease siting restrictions, subsidize communities • Leverage green banks to finance renewable buildout
2. Modernize grid infrastructure	• Invest in batteries and other forms of storage • Invest in smart grid technology and infrastructure • Sponsor infrastructure programs targeting displaced workers
3. Energize next-generation technology development	• Invest in a "moonshot" development program • Increase funding for R&D through agencies like ARPA-E, NSF • Coordinate and catalyze private funding sources • Target early-stage investment in underserved regions

Transportation

1. Encourage faster turnover towards zero-emission vehicles	• Continue EV subsidies (e.g. tax breaks) • Price GHG emissions (e.g. carbon tax, cap-trade) • Subsidize "early retirement" of ICE's
2. Increase investment in charging and hydrogen fueling infrastructure	• Increase government funding • Form industry consortium
3. Energize next-generation technology development	• Invest in a battery research "moonshot" • Create moonshots for air travel and shipping

Industrials

1. Accelerate the electrification of industrial production	• Underwrite capital investment to electrify • Price GHG emissions (e.g. carbon tax, cap-trade) • Provide tax incentives and other subsidies to electrify
2. Energize next-generation technology development	• Target "moonshots" by sector • Increase government funding of R&D
3. Encourage substitution when necessary	• Spur labeling initiatives to nudge downstream customers

FIGURE 7.3 Summary of Sector-Based Technology Policy

PRIMARY PILLARS	POTENTIAL LEVERS

Buildings

1. Incentivize electrification	• Modify building codes to encourage electrification • Promote voluntary programs such as LEED • Provide tax incentives and other subsidies to electrify • Leverage green banks and other financial instruments
2. Adopt behavioral nudges	• Provide means for people to compare their power usage
3. Build carbon sinks	• Invest in a "moonshot" development program • Increase funding for R&D through agencies like ARPA-E, NSF • Coordinate and catalyze private funding sources • Target early-stage investment in underserved regions

Agricultural

1. Invest in education and infrastructure	• Diffuse best practices • Increase public subsidies for better farming • Leverage global supply chain to drive change • Invest in cold storage infrastructure • Subsidize capital investments
2. Encourage farmers to switch from unsustainable practices	• Provide susbsidies for switch to sustainable practices • Regulate use of unsustainable practices • Leverage downstream companies to green supply chains
3. Encourage consumers to switch to climate-friendly alternatives	• Price GHG emissions (e.g. a "cow" tax) • Regulate livestock consumption • Label products to clearly communicate their climate impact • Adopt public ad campaigns to encourage substitutes
4. Create carbon sinks	• Subsidize forest growth • Price CO_2 sinks (e.g. through cap-trade)

reliable, cheap electricity. As costs come down, the potential for a transition to renewables becomes ever more likely.

With that said, whether such a transition will be realized depends on two critical factors. First is whether the price of these sources continues to decline relative to fossil-fuel alternatives. Second is whether the electrical grid can be modernized to deal with the intermittency of renewables and to capitalize on the potential of widely distributed generation, such as rooftop solar. With this in mind, in Chapter 2 we discussed a number of potential levers to help decarbonize the energy sector: price carbon, raise the price of natural gas, regulate utilities, extend tax incentives, invest in storage, modernize the grid, secure abundant supply, and innovate renewables. To simplify our recommended technology policy, we propose the following integrated three-step approach: (1) lower the cost of renewables relative to fossil fuels (2) modernize grid infrastructure, and (3) energize the development of next-generation technologies.

The transition to renewables can be accelerated by any means that *lowers the cost of renewables relative to fossil fuels, especially in the short run.* A carbon tax, regulatory limits on greenhouse gas emissions, increasing the regulation of fracking, and removing subsidies for fossil fuels all will raise the cost for fossil fuels relative to renewables. Similarly, for renewables, tax incentives, feed-in tariffs, eliminating trade barriers such as tariffs, and easing siting restrictions on building new capacity should have a similar impact by lowering the costs of renewables relative to fossil fuels. In all cases, the hope is that such market interventions will only need to be temporary as continued investment in renewables drives down their costs to a point at which they are universally favored over fossil-fuel alternatives.

Ultimately, we recommend a portfolio approach that will likely vary by region and by nation. The regional supply and demand for fossil fuels such as coal and natural gas will have an impact on their price and influence their relative advantage. Thus some nations with abundant coal supplies, such as China, would need to adopt more aggressive measures than other, coal-scarce countries. On the other hand, some countries have attractive wind and sun conditions that make renewables more efficient and may need fewer incentives to drive adoption.

Equally important, the governance of electrical generators varies across the world. In many nations, the electrical sector is a state-owned enterprise. In others, private industry is granted a quasi-monopoly over generation and distribution. Still others have deregulated electrical markets, allowing some degree of competition in generation. In the United States alone, the governance of electrical generation varies by state and region. While economists often debate the first-best, most efficient mechanism for reducing emissions, policy makers need to factor in political realities and pursue second-best but realistic options when required. International agreements should thus allow for local policy flexibility while encouraging pursuit of the common policy goal of decarbonizing all electrical generation by 2050.

Critical to efforts to transform electrical generation is financing the development of new-generation capacity. One of the promises of renewables is that the cost is predominantly a fixed cost occurred during construction with little variable cost to operate. Thus, once operational, they are much cheaper to run and have inherently lower financial risk as compared with natural gas and coal generation, which are tied to the fluctuating prices of fossil-fuel feedstocks. Thus one way to improve the financial attractiveness of renewables vis-à-vis fossil-fuel generation is to help lower the capital costs of building out capacity.

Publicly financed "green banks" have been proposed as one such vehicle for accelerating capital investment. Green banks fund loans, provide loan guarantees, securitize debt, subsidize insurance, and generally help manage risk. While many large private financial institutions are interested in serving this role, the scale of clean technology projects often discourages them from doing so. Green banks help "de-risk" these capital investments by partnering with private financial institutions while insuring against the potential financial downsides of pursuing a project. Such creative financing mechanisms will likely be necessary to put to work enough capital to build out net-zero-emission electrical generation across the world by 2050.

Such a goal will not be achieved, of course, without a concerted effort to address intermittency; otherwise we will never achieve significant penetration of renewables. Thus the second pillar of our approach: *modernize grid infrastructure.* There are three key components of this approach. First, there needs to be significant investment in storage capacity to provide electricity when the wind is not blowing or the sun is not shining. Batteries may ultimately be the critical lynchpin in decarbonizing electrical generation. Utilities need to invest in and create incentives for a massive buildout of storage capacity.

Second, there needs to be a buildout of smart electrical grids that allow for the pricing and trading of electricity from highly distributed sources. One of the grand promises of renewables, especially solar, is the possibility of commercial and residential buildings becoming electrical generators. A smart grid holds promise to catalyze the creation of millions of point sources for generation that create efficiencies and help address intermittency. In many parts of the world, this will need to be coupled with investment in high-capacity power lines to connect locations best suited for wind and solar generation with major centers of demand, such as cities.

We recognize that buildout of significant storage and smart grids is a tall order. Some models of deep decarbonization in electrical generation conclude that the only economical solution to the intermittency challenge will be carbon capture utilization and storage in combination with fossil-fuel-powered generators, such as natural gas plants, that can provide the requisite baseload supply on the grid. To be clear, incentivizing the adoption of CCUS will require state intervention, such as regulation or a carbon tax, and will need to be done on a global basis wherever fossil fuels remain a part of the generation portfolio.

This leads to our third component of a modernized grid infrastructure: we must capitalize on the fact that technologies continue to develop and with them the potential for other game-changing innovations. Thirty years is a long enough period for radical new technologies to emerge to further disrupt our energy production. Battery technology, as mentioned earlier, is critical to the success of renewables. Wildcard technologies such as modular nuclear and wave generators need to be explored more fully. Solar and wind have great potential for further development. Solar photovoltaic cells (PVCs), in particular, have attributes similar to microprocessors that could lead to substantial improvements if people continue to invest. As with microprocessors and Moore's Law, could there be a doubling of capacity at regular intervals over an extended period?

Thus our third pillar is to *energize next-generation technology development*. Borrowing from the Jefferson Innovation Summit (and former US President Kennedy, for that matter), we recommend a "moonshot" development program. To quote the policy playbook: "Like the moon landing, [climate change] can only be solved by setting aggressive goals and putting money and collective brain power into technology development." The moonshot should be a concerted public and private effort. The US federal government, or the governments of other advanced economies such as Japan and the European Union, should play a significant role in investing in the earliest phases of technology development, given that the inherent risks often dissuade such private-sector actors as entrepreneurs and venture capitalists from exploring.[6] Using either direct funding for R&D through agencies like NASA and DARPA-E or subsidies to universities and other research labs through programs like the National Science

Foundation, the US federal government could provide a catalyst for the most unproven but promising technologies.

The private sector becomes critical as we move up the technology S-curve taking emergent technologies and learning how to commercialize and scale them. Private financiers, such as venture capitalists, play a critical role in funding entrepreneurs and innovators at the earliest stages. Other public and private actors can help support as well. On the public side, programs like the US Small Business Innovation Research grants can provide additional capital for financing innovation. On the private side, organizations like Bill Gates's Breakthrough Energy Ventures provide patient capital to cleantech ventures. A moonshot development program should help coordinate and catalyze these public and private efforts.

One of the beauties of the moonshot approach is that it does not require effort by every nation. A handful of nations and companies competing to innovate the next-generation disruptive technologies could be sufficient to drive significant changes to the grid globally. Driving up the efficiency and down the costs of solar PVC panels or wind turbines through novel advancements in one country would likely quickly diffuse to others. Nation-states will have private incentives to pursue moonshots to advance their economies, create jobs, and position themselves on the vanguard of emerging industry sectors. A little healthy competition between nations to generate next-generation clean technology should be encouraged.

Last, we must appreciate that the disruption of electrical generation creates winners and losers. Solar and wind are radically different from fossil fuels. While the sun and wind provide a free input stock for renewable energy generation, coal-fired and natural-gas powerplants are supplied by two large established industries, respectively. They have much to lose in a decarbonized electrical generation sector. Furthermore, the history of technology disruptions raises serious questions about whether coal and natural-gas companies will survive such a transition (see, for example, the New England whaling industry). While some large oil and gas companies have been investing in renewables, there is nothing inherent in their capabilities that translates to renewables, save for biofuels, perhaps. If history is a guide, far more likely these companies will go out of business as demand for their products dries up.

As a result, coal and natural gas companies have every incentive to resist a transition to a clean energy future. They have invested, and will likely continue to, in "non-market" strategies to influence the political process—on local, national, and international levels—to undermine efforts to bring about policies that seek to accelerate the diffusion of renewables. In the United States, some have resorted to sponsoring "Astroturf" campaigns—artificial grass-roots efforts—to raise local concerns about the building of solar fields in communities.[7]

To address these political considerations, we evoke two additional policies from the Jefferson Innovation Summit Playbook. First, moonshot programs should explicitly target early-stage investment programs in underserved regions, especially those that stand to lose jobs during a transition. This could take the form of incubators and accelerators or job training programs. Second, moonshot programs should declare a "New Deal" for clean technology, targeting displaced workers. We use the term in the narrow sense, referring to the originally FDR-led New Deal during the Great Depression in the United States, as opposed to the more expansive use of the term by some liberal politicians in the US and Europe. Such a New Deal could provide federal funds to directly sponsor major infrastructure projects or to create corporate tax credits or other incentives to encourage clean technology companies to establish operations in severely affected regions and invest in local workforce training.

THE TRANSPORTATION SECTOR

If we can decarbonize electrical generation, our overall decarbonization challenge greatly simplifies. The main goal for many industries and sectors would be to electrify. Nowhere is this more evident than in the transportation sector. The electrification of automobiles and other transportation vehicles, by use of either batteries or hydrogen fuel cells, promises to decarbonize the sector if the electricity used to charge batteries or create hydrogen is powered by decarbonized sources. Fortunately, a transformation toward electrification in vehicles is well upon us.

However, the likelihood and speed of total electrification is still very much up in the air. As of 2020, the cost of a battery-powered electric automobile tended to be higher than a comparable-quality traditional gasoline-powered vehicle. Yet the cost of batteries continues to decline, and there is promise that electric vehicles may be of lower cost than ICEs within the decade if not sooner. Continuing that path will be critical to transformation. Equally important will be how quickly we can turn over the existing stock of ICE cars and trucks to electrics. Finally, we will have to make concerted efforts to transform more challenging technologies such as airplanes and ships.

To help facilitate and expedite the transformation to electric vehicles, many have called for putting a price on gasoline emissions. Once again, we are supportive of such efforts, but we worry that their impact may be muted. Recognize that interventions to raise the price of gasoline, such as a gas tax, have an impact on the life-time cost of traditional automobiles but have little impact on the purchase price. While some buyers—for example, fleet purchasers such as logistic companies and car rental agencies—pay attention to such costs, evidence on the sensitivity of individual consumers to the cost of ownership is less clear.[8] This may be a good thing, as the world may very well be entering into a period of sustained low prices for gasoline, especially as the electrification of vehicles decreases worldwide demand for oil.

Thus the first pillar of our technology policy toward decarbonization of transportation is to incentivize adoption of new electric vehicles and thus *encourage faster turnover toward zero-emission vehicles*. Tax incentives to consumers for the purchase of zero-emission vehicles are promising, especially in the short run. One could imagine similar tax breaks for manufacturers that subsidize the price of their electric vehicles. These ultimately lower the purchase price of electric vehicles versus traditional automobiles and spur more demand. This is especially valuable in the current early stage of diffusion. As electric vehicles overtake existing ICE sales, those tax incentives could be retired. More important, policy makers should consider ways to encourage the retirement of existing ICE vehicles. A mix of carrots, such as tax incentives for retirement, and sticks, fees for operating an ICE vehicle, could be adopted to encourage faster turnover.

A second pillar of our approach to decarbonize transportation is to *increase investment in charging and hydrogen-fueling infrastructure*. Some of this investment is being led by private companies such as Tesla. While helpful, such efforts raise the risk of creating multiple, noncompatible infrastructures. We advocate for nations to consider a mix of public and private investment to address their infrastructure needs. In the United States, for example, analysts estimate that about $940 million is needed to provide a robust charging infrastructure in the hundred most populous metropolitan areas.[9] Equally important, efforts should be undertaken, preferably internationally, to drive standardization of charging infrastructure so that all new electric vehicles can use a common charging station.

Last, as with electricity generation, we strongly endorse, as a third pillar to decarbonizing transportation, a "moonshot" development program to *energize next-generation technology development.* In many ways, this is one and the same initiative, since battery and hydrogen fuel cells are important as storage devices to deal with intermittency from renewables on the electrical grid and to power transportation vehicles. While batteries have a clear lead in electrifying automobiles, we should continue to explore alternatives such as hydrogen fuel cells. Once again, thirty years is a long enough period for radical new technologies to emerge. We need to continue to leave room for experimentation and pursuit of alternative technology paths.

This is especially true for the more problematic subsectors of transportation—airplanes and ships. We advance that specific public-private partnerships be formed to push toward decarbonization of these sectors. There should be significant federal funding for basic research and development of novel technological solutions. Furthermore, collaborative coalitions between government, airplane manufacturers, and the airlines should be formed to expedite adoption of advances as they occur. Given the relative consolidated nature of these subsectors, international coalitions between the major economies and major corporate players are possible and should be pursued.

THE INDUSTRIALS SECTOR

As with transportation, the most obvious path to decarbonizing the industrials sector is to electrify manufacturing processes as much as possible and to use renewable energy and other non-carbon-emitting power sources to produce the needed electricity. For many companies, electrification is relatively straightforward. Some have taken the lead in pushing for the use of renewables to produce electricity, either behind the meter or in partnership with electric utilities. Technology companies, especially those operating large cloud computer operations such as Microsoft and Amazon, have been particularly aggressive in pushing for renewable energy.[10]

As a matter of policy, efforts should be undertaken to *accelerate the electrification of industrial production* and the generation of decarbonized electricity. These could take a number of different forms. Financial incentives to electrify or punishments for failure to do so could be provided by government regulators. Favorable debt financing of capital projects to convert existing fossil-fuel infrastructure to electrification could be underwritten by the federal government.

Putting a price on carbon would raise the costs of having scope 1 emissions and motivate companies to electrify.

As discussed in Chapter 4, in some subsectors of industrials, electrification is not possible or economical given existing technologies. We advance that for each of these sectors, targeted policies be adopted to try to address their specific technology challenges. In steel, a viable electrification path exists with mini-mills and electric arc furnaces. The challenge is in making the transition away from basic oxygen furnaces, especially in China, the dominant steel producer. It is unlikely that mini-mills could provide all the steel production currently demanded. In cement and petrochemicals, the challenges are even more complicated. There need to be economically viable alternatives to Portland cement and traditional plastics, respectively.

Research and development in alternatives are critical. The second pillar therefore is to *energize next-generation technology development*. For the more challenging subsectors of industrials, we recommend a targeted "moonshot" approach, similar to those suggested for energy and transportation. International coalitions of public officials and private corporations should be tasked with developing targets and roadmaps. Government funding of basic research should be increased, as should investments in proof-of-concept projects and commercialization efforts. It will be important to encourage experimentation while pursuing aggressive targets for decarbonizing each challenging subsector.

A final pillar in efforts to decarbonize industrials should be to *encourage substitution when necessary* for those products and subsectors that are particularly difficult to decarbonize. Petrochemicals, in particular, seem to present opportunities for less-carbon-intensive substitutes. Interventions may include behavioral nudges to encourage consumers to substitute with less-carbon-intensive products. For example, international product label standards could be established by coalitions of public and private entities. Downstream companies, such as retailers, may play a particularly critical role in driving changes up the supply chain.

A final resort would be the need to incentivize carbon capture utilization and storage to achieve full decarbonization of industrials, especially in difficult subsectors like cement and steel. This may be achieved through putting a price on emissions, either through carbon taxes or a cap-and-trade system, or by directly requiring CCUS through regulation.

THE BUILDINGS SECTOR

The buildings sector shares the same refrain with transportation and industrials: to decarbonize, we should push to electrify heating and cooking and make sure the electricity needed to electrify is powered by renewables or other zero-emitting sources. The good news is that the technologies needed for electrification are already widespread and economical in many instances. The primary challenge is converting existing fossil-fuel-dependent infrastructure with electric alternatives. The challenge is compounded by the decades-long life cycles of our built environment that create resistance to change.

For policy makers, a mix of carrots and sticks will likely be necessary. As with other sectors, one pillar would be to *incentivize electrification*, through a portfolio approach with policy instruments adopted to meet regional conditions. One obvious lever is building codes that require, or at least favor, electrification. Similarly, voluntary programs such as LEED certification could provide incentives to adopt electrification over carbon-emitting products. Tax incentives and other subsidies could further motivate the adoption of electrical solutions. In all these cases, incentives could be structured to motivate retrofitting of existing fossil-fuel-dependent infrastructure with electrical alternatives. One could also imagine debt-financing mechanisms to help reduce the costs to making retrofit capital expenditures. Similar to the green banks concept discussed earlier, both public and private entities could help lower the cost and risk of making major building improvement expenditures.

Another tool that could be deployed would be to *adopt behavioral nudges* to encourage electrification and energy efficiency. Information systems that compare a building's carbon footprint relative to others has proven an effective means to get building owners to consider energy efficiency and decarbonization investments. Opower, now part of Oracle Corporation, has created such systems to allow individual homeowners to compare their carbon emissions and energy usage with neighbors. The digitization of the home, including HVAC control systems like Nest from Google, is creating opportunities for owners to more fully appreciate their impact and to motivate change.

Last, efforts to *design buildings to be carbon sinks* should be encouraged and incentivized. These carbon sinks could help offset persistent fossil-fuel technology, such as the use of gas to cook. In the best-case scenario, the built environment could become a net-negative sector, offsetting emissions from other major sectors. Fortunately, there are many opportunities to create building carbon sinks, including the use of structural timber, adoption of carbon-absorbing cement, building of green roofs, and the installation of solar panels. As with electrification, a mix of policy levers crafted for regional conditions could be deployed to encourage the building of carbon sinks.

THE AGRICULTURE SECTOR

Agriculture, our last major sector, is arguably the most challenging sector to decarbonize. The decentralized nature of farming, with millions of diverse farms spread around the world, makes a technological fix highly unlikely. The challenge is largely about diffusing existing practices that minimize fertilizer use and increase the efficiency of the food production and supply chain. Ultimately, food production needs to be expanded to meet a growing global population while simultaneously increasing yields to a point that the amount of land dedicated to agriculture is reduced. Freeing up farmland is critical in creating carbon sinks, such as repatriating croplands for forests, to offset difficult-to-eliminate greenhouse gas emissions for this and other sectors.

The first pillar on our recommended approach is to *invest in education and infrastructure.* An international effort should be undertaken to diffuse best practices that minimize greenhouse gas emissions. For croplands, this can be considering the mix and rotation of crops to minimize topsoil erosion and the need for fertilizers. For cattle and other livestock, this may include manure management practices and the use of methane capture technologies. Technology such as drones and information systems that allow for precision agriculture should be developed and deployed. Efforts to create efficiency in the supply chain, such as minimizing spoilage by investing in cold storage, should be encouraged. Capital investments could be subsidized by national governments and by international aid organizations and NGOs. Innovative debt-financing instruments such as those pioneered by green banks could be promoted.

In some regions, incentives will likely be necessary to *encourage farmers to switch from unsustainable practices.* For several reasons, local farmers may be dissuaded from adopting sustainable practices. As a matter of policy, various carrots and sticks could be used to persuade farmers to switch, such as restrictions and regulations on undesirable practices and subsidies for switching. Downstream companies in the supply chain could prove particularly effective in driving change by requiring their suppliers to adopt decarbonized approaches. Such pressure could operate at the global level by large multinational food companies and retailers and at the local level by small restaurants and groceries.

When decarbonization proves particularly challenging, consideration should be given to *encouraging consumers to switch to climate-friendly alternatives*. One way to do so is to raise the cost of nonsustainable foods. Placing a tax on cattle or regulating practices that ultimately raise the cost of production will have the downstream effect of raising prices and lowering demand. Such efforts are certainly not without controversy. More palpable may be more subtle, behavioral nudges that try to get consumers to favor less-carbon-intensive foods: labeling products to clearly communicate their climate impact, public advertising campaigns to encourage consumers to substitute meat with plant-based proteins, grassroots efforts to highlight the benefits of climate-friendly foods. All options should be on the table.

Last, a concerted effort to *create carbon sinks* should be pursued. The creation of a cap-and-trade emissions system could be one potential mechanism to incentivize the growth of forests on former cropland by placing a price on carbon and creating a mechanism by which carbon sinks are monetized. Public-private partnerships in which government and/or nonprofits subsidize farmers who grow forests could be another. International collaboration will be important, as developed economies are best positioned to subsidize forest growth in less-developed countries.

A COORDINATED EFFORT

The plan proposed here requires numerous initiatives across the many regions and countries of the world. A partial solution will not address our climate challenge. Globally electrifying vehicles and decarbonizing electricity generation don't even get us half-way to net-zero emissions by 2050. If Europe successfully decarbonizes its economy, but the United States and China continue to be major emitters, global climate change will continue unabated. Similarly, if developed economies can rise to the decarbonization challenge, but developing nations increase their greenhouse gas footprint as they grow, global warming and climate change will continue.

The extent of change requires a coordinated effort across regions and stakeholders. East and west. North and south. Public and private. Organizations and individuals. Fortunately, the groundwork for such a coordinated effort has been laid over the past thirty years. Starting with Rio in 1992 when the UN Framework Convention on Climate Change was signed, and then to the Kyoto Protocol in 1997, to the 2010 Copenhagen Accord, to the 2016 Paris Agreement, the world has gathered to negotiate a response to climate change. Unfortunately, the negotiations have focused largely on individual national emissions targets that few countries have been able to successfully meet.

A technology innovation prospective suggests another approach. Rather than focus on emissions targets, focus on technology shifts. We envision a coordinated effort to track and market technologies. A smaller set of countries and private stakeholders could target technology goals in line with our broader "moon-shot" concept. Consider automobiles. The top ten auto companies capture over 50 percent of global market share.[11] They come from four countries: the United States, Japan, Germany, and South Korea. Imagine a coalition between these four countries and ten companies to accelerate the production of electric vehicles, to drive down the cost of batteries, and to retire fossil-fuel-burning vehicles.

Even better, consider commercial airplanes. Boeing and Airbus are effectively a duopoly, producing 91 percent of new airplanes. A handful of other players, such as Canada's Bombardier, Brazil's Embraer, and Japan's Mitsubishi, make up the remaining market share. Each of these companies struggled during the pandemic of 2020 and received significant subsidies from their national governments. Imagine, once again, a coalition of nations and airplane manufacturing pushing to decarbonize air travel.

The highest-emitting industrials subsectors have fairly high levels of concentration. In 2018, the top ten steel companies made up roughly a quarter of all global production, led by ArcelorMittal out of Luxembourg and including Chinese companies China Baowu, HBIS, Shagang, Ansteel, Jianlong, and Shougang Groups.[12] The top ten cement companies command a little over a third of all global production, led by LafargeHolcim in Switzerland, HeidelbergCement in Germany, and Cemex in Mexico.[13] In both cases, a relatively small coalition of nations and companies could partner to develop net-zero-emission options.

Other sectors will require a different type of approach. Electrical generation is dispersed. In the United States alone, there are over three thousand electric utilities. While a small group of leading generators could band together to support research to lower the costs of renewables, a much broader coordinated effort among nation-states would likely be necessary. Perhaps rather than overall emissions targets in the next UN negotiations on climate change, nations could focus on timetables for the retirement of coal plants and eventually gas-fired power plants.

As we've discussed, diffuse sectors such as buildings and agriculture are particularly vexing. There are millions of farmers, construction companies, and building operators throughout the world. There is not an obvious coalition of large producers that have significant share of global production. One possibility would be to build networks of downstream companies, for example, for agriculture, large international food and beverage companies such as Pepsi and Nestle and retail grocers like Walmart and Amazon. At the end of the day, agriculture and buildings will likely require a global forum such as the United Nations to help coordinate efforts.

WE CHOOSE OPTIMISM

The challenge before the world is overwhelming, requiring a profound shift in so many large economic sectors over the course of a few decades. But try we must. The impacts associated with continuing to emit greenhouse gases are likely to grow exponentially as concentrations in the atmosphere increase. Even the forecasted difference between a 2.0 degrees Celsius raise and a 1.5 degrees Celsius raise is significant. At 2.0 degrees Celsius, 37 percent versus 17 percent of humanity is likely to be exposed to severe heat waves. Sixty-one million more people in Earth's urban areas will experience drought conditions. The risks from forest fires, extreme weather events and invasive species will grow. Now imagine what a 3- to 4-degree change in average global temperatures may bring.[14]

We choose to end on an optimistic note. While overwhelming in the abstract, if we breakdown the climate change challenge to the specific sectors and technologies that need to change, a path forward becomes evident:

First, accelerate current trends toward net-zero-emission technologies in electrical generation, most prominently wind and solar. In the short run, adopt policies that lower the cost of renewables relative to fossil fuels. Invest in modernizing the grid infrastructure to a smart grid with significant storage capabilities. And all the while, invest in research "moonshots" to develop breakthrough clean technology.

Second, encourage a fast turnover to electric vehicles, powered either by batteries or hydrogen fuel-cells, that are already disrupting the auto industry. Invest in charging infrastructure while energizing research in next-generation technologies, especially in challenging sectors such as air travel and shipping.

Third, accelerate the electrification of industrial production through various carrots and sticks. For the most challenging sectors, such as cement and petrochemicals, pursue targeted public-private partnerships to research and develop clean alternatives. Finally, encourage substitution in downstream markets and incentivize carbon capture utilization and storage when necessary.

Fourth, encourage building electrification through an incentive portfolio approach. Adopt behavioral nudges to further incentivize electrification from the demand side. Last, encourage international private-public partnerships to push for opportunities to make buildings carbon sinks that have net-negative emissions.

Fifth, invest in education and infrastructure and adopt incentives to encourage farmers to switch to more sustainable practices. Work the demand side, encouraging downstream companies and consumers to switch to climate-friendly alternatives. Finally, and most important, coordinate a global effort to create carbon sinks through the growing of forests and the like.

None of this will be easy. There is no single silver bullet. Decarbonization will require a comprehensive effort across nations and markets. Now is the time to band together as global citizens to solve this problem. The global pandemic of 2020 has increased awareness of our connected humanity. Perhaps this will be the catalyst needed to motivate global coordination and action. We put our faith in the human capacity for innovation and change to lead us to a brighter and more sustainable future.

NOTES

CHAPTER 1: THE PATH TO 2050

1. Rebecca Lindsey and LuAnn Dahlman, "Climate Change: Global Temperature," NOAA Report, January 16, 2020, https://www.climate.gov/news-features/understanding -climate/climate-change-global-temperature.

2. Ibid.

3. The Ocean Portal Team, "Sea Level Rise," *Smithsonian*, April 2018, https://ocean. si.edu/through-time/ancient-seas/sea-level-rise.

4. "Global Climate Change," NASA, accessed October 2020, https://climate.nasa. gov/climate_resources/24/graphic-the-relentless-rise-of-carbon-dioxide/.

5. "Response to Congressional Inquiry on National Security Implications of Climate-Related Risks and a Changing Climate," US Department of Defense, RefID: 8–6475571, May 22, 2015, https://archive.defense.gov/pubs/150724-congressional-report -on-national-implications-of-climate-change.pdf?source=govdelivery.

6. "Global Carbon Emissions," CO2-earth, accessed October 2020, https://www.co2. earth/global-co2-emissions.

7. Global Carbon Project, accessed October 2020, https://www.globalcarbonproject. org/.

8. P. Friedlingstein, M. W. Jones, M. O'Sullivan, R. M. Andrew, J. Hauck, G. P. Peters, W. Peters, et al., "Global Carbon Budget 2019," *Earth System Science Data* 11, no. 4 (2019): 1783–1838, https://doi.org/10.5194/essd-11-1783-2019.

9. Fred Pearce, "What Would a Global Warming Increase of 1.5 Degrees Be Like?" *Yale Environment 360* June 16, 2016, https://e360.yale.edu/features/what_would_a_ global_warming_increase_15_degree_be_like.

10. "Analysis: How Much 'Carbon Budget' Is Left to Limit Global Warming to 1.5C?," *Carbon Brief*, April 19, 2018, https://www.carbonbrief.org/analysis-how-much-carbon -budget-is-left-to-limit-global-warming-to-1-5c.

11. Some sectors may be able to offset others if they are able to achieve negative emissions by creating carbon sinks. More on that in subsequent chapters.

12. See Gautam Ahuja, Laurence Capron, Michael Lenox, and Dennis Yao, "Strategy and the Institutional Envelope," *Strategy Science* 3, no. 2 (2018): 2–10.

CHAPTER 2: THE ENERGY SECTOR

1. O. Edenhofer, R. Pichs-Madruga, Y. Sokona, E. Farahani, S. Kadner, K. Seyboth, A. Adler, et al., eds., "Intergovernmental Panel on Climate Change (IPCC): Summary for Policymakers," in *Climate Change 2014, Mitigation of Climate Change*, contribution of Working Group III to the Fifth Assessment Report of the Intergovernmental Panel on Climate Change,(Cambridge, UK, and New York: Cambridge University Press, 2014).

2. "Global Emissions from Economic Sector, Greenhouse Gas Emission Sources," US Environmental Protection Agency, accessed March 7, 2021, https://www.epa.gov/ghgemissions/global-greenhouse-gas-emissions-data.

3. "Electricity Production by Source, World," Our World in Data, accessed October 2020, https://ourworldindata.org/grapher/world-electricity-by-source.

4. "Coal and Electricity," World Coal Association, accessed April 2021, https://www.worldcoal.org/coal-facts/coal-electricity/.

5. Bureau of Reclamation, Hydropower Program, US Department if the Interior, updated February 3, 2016, https://www.usbr.gov/power/edu/history.html.

6. "Discover Hydropower," National Hydropower Association, accessed December 2017, https://www.hydro.org/waterpower/hydropower/.

7. Office of Energy Efficiency & Renewable Energy, "Hydropower Technology Development," US Department of Energy, accessed December 2017, https://energy.gov/eere/water/hydropower-technology-development.

8. This is equivalent to powering nearly eighteen million American homes in the Northwest United States. "Megawatt," Northwest Power and Conversation Council, accessed March 2, 2020, https://www.nwcouncil.org/history/Megawatt.

9. "Country Profile: China" (from the 2020 Hydropower Status Report), International Hydropower Association, https://www.hydropower.org/country-profiles/china.

10. Rocio Uria-Martinez, Megan Johnson, and Patrick O'Connor, Oak Ridge National Laboratory, "U.S. Department of Energy Hydropower Market Report: 2017 Update," April 2017, https://energy.gov/sites/prod/files/2017/04/f34/US-Hydropower-Market-Report-2017-Update_20170403.pdf.

11. Ibid.

12. "Monthly Energy Review," US Energy Information Administration, September 2017, https://www.eia.gov/electricity/data.php#generation.

13. "Monthly Energy Review, Table 8.1: Nuclear Energy Overview," US Energy Information Administration, February 2018, https://www.eia.gov/totalenergy/data/monthly/pdf/sec8_3.pdf.

14. Ibid, 24, 27.

15. "Nuclear Power in World Today," World Nuclear Association, updated November 2020, https://www.world-nuclear.org/information-library/current-and-future-generation/nuclear-power-in-the-world-today.aspx.

16. Ibid.

17. "Plans for Nuclear Reactors Worldwide," World Nuclear Association, updated November 2020, https://www.world-nuclear.org/information-library/current-and-future-generation/plans-for-new-reactors-worldwide.aspx.

18. Ibid.,

19. Ibid, 121.

20. "Renewable Energy Now Accounts for a Third of Global Power Capacity," International Renewable Energy Agency Press Release, April 2, 2019, https://www.irena.org/newsroom/pressreleases/2019/Apr/Renewable-Energy-Now-Accounts-for-a-Third-of-Global-Power-Capacity.

21. "EIA Expects U.S. Electricity Generation from Renewables to Soon Surpass Nuclear and Coal," US Energy Information Administration, January 30, 2020, https://www.eia.gov/todayinenergy/detail.php?id=42655.

22. Zachary Shahan, "History of Wind Turbines," *Renewable Energy World*, November 21, 2014, http://www.renewableenergyworld.com/ugc/articles/2014/11/history-of-wind-turbines.html.

23. Ibid.

24. An investment tax credit is the amount of money that can be deducted from the investor's income taxes.

25. Ilya Chernyakhovskiy, Tian Tian, Joyce McLaren, Mackay Miller, and Nina Geller, "U.S. Laws and Regulations for Renewable Energy Grid Interconnections," National Renewable Energy Laboratory, September 2016, https://www.nrel.gov/docs/fy16osti/66724.pdf.

26. "Turbine Timeline: 1980s," American Wind Energy Association, accessed January 2018, https://www.awea.org/turbine-timeline-1980s.

27. Office of Energy Efficiency & Renewable Energy, "History of Wind Energy," US Department of Energy, accessed January 2018, https://energy.gov/eere/wind/history-us-wind-energy.

28. "Turbine Timeline: 1990s," American Wind Energy Association, accessed January 2018, https://www.awea.org/turbine-timeline-1990s.

29. Ibid.

30. Office of Energy Efficiency and Renewable Energy, "WINDExchange," US Department of Energy, accessed September 2020, https://windexchange.energy.gov/maps-data/321.

31. "Wind Has Surpassed Hydro as Most-Used Renewable Electricity Generation Source in U.S.," US Energy Information Agency, February 26, 2020, https://www.eia.gov/todayinenergy/detail.php?id=42955.

32. "Levelized Cost of Energy Analysis—Version 13.0," Lazard, November 2019, https://www.lazard.com/perspective/lcoe2019.

33. Ibid.

34. Ryan Wiser, Mark Bolinger, Ben Hoen, Dev Millstein, Joe Rand, Galen Barbose, Naïm Darghouth, et al., "2016 Wind Energy Technology Data Update: 2020 Edition," Lawrence Berkeley National Laboratory, August 2020, https://emp.lbl.gov/sites/default/files/2020_wind_energy_technology_data_update.pdf.

35. Philip Gordon, "2019 a Record Year for Corporate Clean Energy PPA's Says BNEF," Smart Energy International, January 29, 2020, https://www.smart-energy.com/renewable-energy/2019-a-record-year-for-corporate-clean-energy-ppas-says-bnef/.

36. Wiser, Bolinger, et al., "2016 Wind Energy Technology Data Update: 2020 Edition."

37. Ibid.

38. Ibid.

39. Ibid.

40. Joyce Lee and Feng Zhao, "Global Wind Report 2019," Global Wind Energy Council, March 25, 2020, https://gwec.net/docs/global-wind-report-2019/.

41. "World Wind Capacity at 650.8 GW, Corona Crisis Will Slow Down Markets in 2020, Renewables to be Core of Economic Stimulus Programmes," World Wind Energy Association Press Release, April 16, 2020, https://wwindea.org/blog/2020/04/16/world-wind-capacity-at-650-gw/.

42. Lee and Zhao, "Global Wind Report 2019."

43. Ibid.

44. "World Energy Resources: Wind 2016," World Energy Council, https://www.worldenergy.org/wp-content/uploads/2017/03/WEResources_Wind_2016.pdf.

45. Wiser, Bolinger, et al., "2016 Wind Energy Technology Data Update: 2020 Edition."

46. Ibid.

47. Edis Osmanbasic, "The Future of Wind Turbines: Comparing Direct Drive and Gearbox," engineering.com, April 7, 2020, https://www.engineering.com/AdvancedManufacturing/ArticleID/20149/The-Future-of-Wind-Turbines-Comparing-Direct-Drive-and-Gearbox.aspx.

48. Ibid.

49. Jason Deign, "Future of Airborne Wind Energy in Doubt as Google Parent Drops Makani," Greentech Media, February 19, 2020, https://www.greentechmedia.com/articles/read/airborne-wind-energy-in-doubt-as-alphabet-drops-makani.

50. Alice Orrell, Danielle Preziuso, Nik Foster, Scott Morris, and Juliet Homer, Pacific Northwest National Laboratory, "2018 Distributed Wind Market Report," US Department of Energy, https://www.energy.gov/eere/wind/downloads/2018-distributed-wind-market-report#:~:text=Key%20Findings%3A,representing%20%24226%20million%20in%20investment.

51. Ibid.

52. Office of Energy Efficiency and Renewable Energy, "US Distributed Wind Manufacturers Selected to Advance Wind Technologies and Grid Support Capabilities Through DOE Competitiveness Improvement Project," August 11, 2020, https://www.energy.gov/eere/articles/us-distributed-wind-manufacturers-selected-advance-wind-technologies-and-grid-support .

53. Justin Gerdes, "Struggling Distributed Wind Sector Eyes Role in Microgrids Market," Greentech Media, April 28, 2020, https://www.greentechmedia.com/articles/read/distributed-wind.

54. Nordex acquired Acciona in 2016 and Siemens Wind Power consolidated with Gamesa in 2017.

55. Wiser, Bolinger, et al., "2016 Wind Energy Technology Data Update: 2020 Edition."

56. Craig Richard, "Vestas Leads the Pack with Squeezed Market Share," *Wind Power Monthly*, February 18, 2020, https://www.windpowermonthly.com/article/1674420 /vestas-leads-pack-squeezed-market-share.

57. Ryan Wiser and Mark Bolinger, Lawrence Berkeley National Laboratory, "2016 Wind Technologies Market Report," US Department of Energy, https://www.energy. gov/sites/prod/files/2017/10/f37/2016_Wind_Technologies_Market_Report_101317.pdf.

58. Ryan Wiser and Mark Bolinger, Lawrence Berkeley National Laboratory, "2018 Wind Technologies Report," US Department of Energy, https://emp.lbl.gov/sites /default/files/wtmr_final_for_posting_8-9-19.pdf.

59. Wiser, Bolinger, et al., "2016 Wind Energy Technology Data Update: 2020 Edition" (Wind Energy Capital Expenditures (Capex)).

60. Jacques Beaudry-Losique, Ted Boling, Jocelyn Brown-Saracino, Patrick Gilman, Michael Hahn, Chris Hart, Jesse Johnson, et al., "A National Offshore Wind Strategy: Creating an Offshore Wind Energy Industry in the United States," US Department of Energy, February 7, 2011, https://www.energy.gov/sites/prod/files/2013/12/f5/national_ offshore_wind_strategy.pdf.

61. Ibid.

62. "Wind Energy Technologies Office Project Map," US Department of Energy, accessed October 2020, https://www.energy.gov/eere/wind/wind-energy-technologies-office-projects-map.

63. National Offshore Wind R&D Consortium, US Department of Energy, accessed October 2020, https://www.energy.gov/eere/wind/national-offshore-wind-rd -consortium.

64. Ibid.

65. Walter Musial, Philipp Beiter, Paul Spitsen, Jake Nunemaker, Vahan Gevorgian, Aubryn Cooperman, Rob Hammond, and Matt Shields, "2019 Offshore Wind Technology Data Update," National Renewable Energy Laboratory, US Department of Energy, October 2020, https://www.nrel.gov/docs/fy21osti/77411.pdf.

66. Ibid.

67. Vineyard Wind webpage, www.vineyardwind.com.

68. Liz Prevost, Energy News Network, "Study: Offshore Wind Farms Won't Keep Most People from Enjoying the Beach," *Renewable Energy World*, July 24, 2020, https:// www.renewableenergyworld.com/2020/07/24/study-offshore-wind-farms-wont-keep -most-people-from-enjoying-the-beach/#gref.

69. Walter Musial, Philipp Beiter, Paul Schwabe, Tian Tian, Tyler Stehly, and Paul Spitsen, "2016 Offshore Wind Technologies Market Report," US Department of Energy, August 2017, https://energy.gov/eere/wind/downloads/2016-offshore-wind-technologies -market-report.

70. Ibid.

71. Walter Musial, Philipp Beiter, Paul Spitsen, Jake Nunemaker, Vahan Gevorgian, Aubryn Cooperman, Rob Hammond, and Matt Shields, "2019 Offshore Wind Technology Update," National Renewable Energy Laboratory, US Department of Energy, October 2020, https://www.nrel.gov/docs/fy21osti/77411.pdf.

72. Office of Energy Efficiency and Renewable Energy, "Computing America's Offshore Wind Energy Potential," September 9, 2016, US Department of Energy, https://energy.gov/eere/articles/computing-america-s-offshore-wind-energy-potential.

73. The Business Network for Offshore Wind, "Leadership 100 Work Plan," 2019, https://www.offshorewindus.org/wp-content/uploads/2019/06/L100WhitePaperJun.3.2019.pdf.

74. Ibid.

75. Offshore Wind Outlook 2019, "World Energy Outlook Special Report," US Energy Information Administration, November 2019, https://www.iea.org/reports/offshore-wind-outlook-2019.

76. "Offshore Wind Will Surge to Over 234 GW by 2030, Led by Asia-Pacific," Global Wind Energy Council, August 5, 2020, https://gwec.net/gwec-offshore-wind-will-surge-to-over-234-gw-by-2030-led-by-asia-pacific/.

77. Musial, Beiter, Spitsen, et al., "2019 Offshore Wind Technology Update."

78. Ibid.

79. "Offshore Wind Will Surge to Over 234 GW by 2030, Led by Asia-Pacific."

80. "Future of Wind: Deployment, Investment, Technology, Grid Integration and Socio-Economic Aspects" (A Global Energy Transformation paper), International Renewable Energy Agency, Abu Dhabi, 2019, https://www.irena.org/-/media/Files/IRENA/Agency/Publication/2019/Oct/IRENA_Future_of_wind_2019.pdf.

81. "Research: DOE Wind Vision," American Wind Energy Association, accessed February 2018, https://www.awea.org/doe-wind-vision.

82. Office of Energy Efficiency & Renewable Energy, "The History of Solar," US Department of Energy, accessed October 2020, https://www1.eere.energy.gov/solar/pdfs/solar_timeline.pdf.

83. Ibid.

84. Under a feed-in tariff policy, governments set a price for renewable energy sources compensating generators directly and require utilities to purchase the green power at this price.

85. Loan Programs Office, "LPO Financial Performance," US Department of Energy, November 2014, https://energy.gov/sites/prod/files/2014/11/f19/DOE-LPO-MiniReport_Final%2011%2013%2014_0.pdf.

86. "The Recovery Act and Clean Energy," US Department of Energy, February 26, 2016, https://energy.gov/articles/recovery-act-and-clean-energy.

87. Office of Energy Efficiency and Renewable Energy, "SunShot 2030," US Department of Energy, accessed October 2020, https://www.energy.gov/eere/solar/sunshot-2030.

88. Ibid.

89. "Solar Industry Research Data," Solar Energy Industries Association, accessed October 2020, https://www.seia.org/solar-industry-research-data.

90. Ibid.

91. Ibid.

92. "World Energy Resources 2016, Chapter 8: Solar," World Energy Council, https://www.worldenergy.org/data/resources/resource/solar/.

93. "Renewable Capacity Statistics 2020," International Renewable Energy Agency, March 2020, https://www.irena.org/publications/2020/Mar/Renewable-Capacity -Statistics-2020.

94. "Levelized Cost of Energy Analysis—Version 13.0."

95. Ibid.

96. Ibid.

97. Mark Bollinger, Joachim Seel, and Kristina Homachi LaCommare, "Utility-Scale Solar 2016: An Empirical Analysis of Project Cost, Performance, and Pricing Trends in the United States," report number 2001005, Lawrence Berkeley National Laboratory, September 2017, https://emp.lbl.gov/publications/utility-scale-solar -2016-empirical.

98. David Feldman, Eric O'Shaughnessy, and Robert Margolis, "Q3/Q4 2019 Solar Industry Update," National Renewable Energy Laboratory, February 18, 2020, https:// www.nrel.gov/docs/fy20osti/76158.pdf.

99. Bollinger, Seel, and Homachi LaCommare, "Utility-Scale Solar 2016."

100. John Fialka, "Why China Is Dominating the Solar Industry," *Scientific American*, December 19, 2016, https://www.scientificamerican.com/article/why-china-is -dominating-the-solar-industry/.

101. Paula Mints, "2015 Top Ten PV Cell Manufacturers," *Renewable Energy World*, April 8, 2016, http://www.renewableenergyworld.com/articles/2016/04/2015-top-ten -pv-cell-manufacturers.html.

102. Colville Finlay, "Top 10 Module Suppliers in 2017," PVTech, January 15, 2018, https://www.pv-tech.org/editors-blog/top-10-module-suppliers-in-2017 and Solar Edition Top 10 Module Manufacturers Market Share in the Global Solar Panel Module Market, January 28, 2020, https://solaredition.com/top-10-module-manufacturers -market-share-in-the-global-solar-panel-module-market/.

103. Lin Corin, "2020 Market Module Forecast," *PV Magazine*, February 18, 2020, https://www.pv-magazine.com/2020/02/18/2020-module-market-forecast/.

104. Ibid.

105. Stephen Lacey, "BP Jumps Back into Solar with a $200 Million Investment in Europe's Biggest Project Developer," Greentech Media, December 15, 2017, https://www. greentechmedia.com/articles/read/bp-jumps-back-into-solar#gs.xqIXb8w.

106. BP Press Release, December 5, 2019, https://www.bp.com/en/global/corporate/ news-and-insights/press-releases/lightsource-bp-to-accelerate-global-solar-growth -with-further-investment-from-bp.html.

107. Ibid.

108. James Murray, "How the Six Major Oil Companies Have Invested in Renewable Energy Projects," NS Energy, January 16, 2020, https://www.nsenergybusiness.com/ features/oil-companies-renewable-energy/.

109. "The Oil and Gas Industry in Energy Transitions," IEA World Energy Outlook Special Report, January 2020, https://www.iea.org/reports/the-oil-and-gas-industry-in -energy-transitions.

110. "Photovoltaics Report," Fraunhofer Institute for Solar Energy Systems, with

support of PSE Projects GmbH, September 16, 2020, https://www.ise.fraunhofer.de/content/dam/ise/de/documents/publications/studies/Photovoltaics-Report.pdf.

111. Ibid.

112. "PV Cells 101: A Primer on the Solar Photovoltaic Cell," US Department of Energy, December 3, 2019, https://www.energy.gov/eere/solar/articles/pv-cells-101-primer-solar-photovoltaic-cell.

113. Ibid.

114. "Photovoltaics Report."

115. Ibid.

116. "PV Cells 101: Part 2, Solar Photovoltaic Cell Research Directions," US Department of Energy, December 3, 2019, https://www.energy.gov/eere/solar/articles/pv-cells-101-part-2-solar-photovoltaic-cell-research-directions.

117. "Blocking Vibrations That Remove Heat Could Boost Efficiency of Next-Gen Solar Cells," Oak Ridge National Laboratory, October 5, 2020, https://www.ornl.gov/news/blocking-vibrations-remove-heat-could-boost-efficiency-next-gen-solar-cells.

118. Kelly Pickerell, "How Does a New Single-Axis Tracking Process Increase Solar Plant Efficiency?" *Solar Power World*, June 15, 2016, https://www.solarpowerworldonline.com/2015/06/how-dpes-a-new-single-axis-tracking-process-increase-solar-plant-efficiency/.

119. Ravi Manghani and Chloe Holden, "How Tracker Technology Is Expanding the Footprint for Solar," Greentech Media, September 28, 2020, https://www.greentechmedia.com/articles/read/how-tracker-technology-is-expandingthefootprint-for-solar.

120. Ran Fu, David Feldman, and Robert Margolis, "US Solar Photovoltaic System Cost Benchmark: Q1 2018," National Renewable Energy Laboratory, https://www.nrel.gov/docs/fy19osti/72399.pdf.

121. "Solar Industry Research Data."

122. "Solar Market Insight Report 2020 Q3," SEIA/Wood Mackenzie Power & Renewables, September 10, 2020, https://www.seia.org/research-resources/solar-market-insight-report-2020-q3.

123. "Annual Energy Outlook 2020 (Electricity)," International Energy Agency, January 29, 2020, https://www.eia.gov/outlooks/aeo/.

124. "Renewables 2019: Market Analysis and Forecast from 2019 to 2024," International Energy Agency, October 2019, https://www.iea.org/reports/renewables-2019.

125. "EIA Projects That Renewables Will Provide Nearly Half of World Electricity by 2050," Today in Energy, US Energy Information Administration, October 2, 2019, https://www.eia.gov/todayinenergy/detail.php?id=41533.

126. "Non-Powered Dam Resource Assessment," Oak Ridge National Laboratory, accessed October 2017, http://nhaap.ornl.gov/content/non-powered-dam-potential.

127. Energy BC, "Run of River Projects," accessed December 2017, http://www.energybc.ca/runofriver.html.

128. Bloomberg, "Beginning of the End for Megadam Projects in China as Solar and Wind Power Rise," *The Japan Times*, July 4, 2020, https://www.japantimes.co.jp/news/2020/07/04/business/megadam-projects-china-solar-wind-power/.

129. Reuters, "China to Impose New Restrictions on Small Hydro Plants," November 13, 2019, https://www.reuters.com/article/us-china-hydropower/china-to-impose -new-restrictions-on-small-hydro-plants-idUSKBN1XN0ES.

130. Ibid.

131. "Small Nuclear Power Reactors," World Nuclear Association, updated March 2018, http://www.world-nuclear.org/information-library/nuclear-fuel-cycle/nuclear-power -reactors/small-nuclear-power-reactors.aspx.

132. T. Bruckner, I. A. Bashmakov, Y. Mulugetta, H. Chum, A. de la Vega Navarro, J. Edmonds, A. Faaij, et al. "Chapter 7, Energy Systems," in *Climate Change 2014: Mitigation of Climate Change*, contribution of Working Group III to the Fifth Assessment Report of the Intergovernmental Panel on Climate Change, 2014, http://www.ipcc.ch/ pdf/assessment-report/ar5/wg3/ipcc_wg3_ar5_chapter7.pdf.

133. "Small Nuclear Power Reactors," World Nuclear Association, updated October 2020, https://www.world-nuclear.org/information-library/nuclear-fuel-cycle/nuclear -power-reactors/small-nuclear-power-reactors.aspx.

134. "Nuclear Fusion Power," World Nuclear Association, updated November 2017, http://www.world-nuclear.org/information-library/current-and-future-generation/ nuclear-fusion-power.aspx.

135. Fracking is the injection of fluids into the shale bed to facilitate the extraction of oil and gas.

136. Foster's Technology S-Curve shows technology improvement with greater effort to improve and innovate the technology. It's important to note that it is effort, not time, that drives the S-curve. The marginal return to effort is often low at first as innovators experiment with the technology, trying different designs. As the knowledge base increases, progress accelerates rapidly and efforts yield big gains (the steepest part of the S-curve). As the technology nears maturity, additional investment will no longer result in significant improvements in performance.

137. "Coal and Electricity," World Coal Association.

138. G. Seetharaman, "Coal Is Here to Stay Despite India's Ambitious Goals for Renewable Energy," *The Economic Times*, October 15, 2020, https://economictimes .indiatimes.com/industry/energy/power/india-will-not-be-able-to-achieve-its-renew able-energy-targets-anytime-soon/articleshow/69286279.cms?from=mdr.

139. Christine Shearer, Aiqun Yu, and Ted Nace, "Out of Step: China Is Driving the Continued Growth of the Global Coal Fleet," *Global Energy Monitor*, November 2019, https://endcoal.org/wp-content/uploads/2019/11/Out-of-Step-English-final. pdf.

140. Saurabh, "Coal Makes a Comeback in India, New Capacity Up 73% in 2019," CleanTechnica, January 20, 2020, https://cleantechnica.com/2020/01/20/coal-makes-a -comeback-in-india-new-capacity-up-73-in-2019/.

141. "International Energy Outlook 2019," US Energy Information Administration, September 24, 2019, https://www.eia.gov/outlooks/archive/ieo19/.

142. "Sustainable Data Centers," Facebook, accessed May 22, 2020, https://sustain ability.fb.com/innovation-for-our-world/sustainable-data-centers/.

143. "Renewables 2019: Market Analysis and Forecast from 2019 to 2024," IEA Fuel Report, October 2019, https://www.iea.org/reports/renewables-2019.

144. "Renewable Energy Market Update: Outlook for 2020 and 2021," IEA Fuel Report, May 2020, https://www.iea.org/reports/renewable-energy-market-update/2020 -and-2021-forecast-overview.

145. Seth Kerschner, "United States: Greenhouse Gas Trade Schemes, White & Case LLP," September 20, 2017, https://www.lexology.com/library/detail.aspx?g=0f6bf054 -27dd-4cc0-b856-107b1ad0854e.

146. "The Regional Greenhouse Gas Initiative: 10 Years in Review," Acadia Center, 2019, https://acadiacenter.org/wp-content/uploads/2019/09/Acadia-Center_RGGI_10 -Years-in-Review_2019-09-17.pdf.

147. Ibid.

148. Rachel Becker, "California Re-Evaluating Its Landmark Climate Strategy," *Cal Matters*, June 24, 2020, https://calmatters.org/environment/2020/06/california-climate -strategy-cap-trade/.

149. Ibid.

150. "Market Stability Reserve, Energy, Climate Change, Environment, Climate Action, EU Action, EU Emissions Trading System (EU ETS)," European Union, accessed October 2020, https://ec.europa.eu/clima/policies/ets/reform_en.

151. EMBER Carbon Price Viewer, accessed March 8, 2021, https://ember-climate. org/data/carbon-price-viewer/.

152. "Most CO2 Prices Are Insufficient Says the World Bank," *Bloomberg Weekly Brief*, Sustainable Finance, January 3, 2018, https://newsletters.briefs.bloomberg.com/ document/TxrTRyZlQqupLKg4W7J22w—_9ez2hhvxnqgzbspk5q/year-ahead.

153. "State and Trends of Carbon Pricing 2020," World Bank Group, May 2020, https://openknowledge.worldbank.org/bitstream/handle/10986/33809/9781464815867. pdf?sequence=4&isAllowed=y.

154. Ibid.

155. Chad Qian, "Three Carbon Tax Bills Introduced in Congress," Tax Foundation, August 1, 2019, https://taxfoundation.org/carbon-tax-bills-introduced-congress/.

156. Ibid.

157. "100 Years with Coal Age," Coal Age, *Coal Age News*, September 14, 2012, https:// www.coalage.com/features/100-years-with-coal-age/.

158. "Most Coal-Fired Electric Capacity Was Built Before 1980," Today in Energy, US Energy Information Agency, June 28, 2011, https://www.eia.gov/todayinenergy/detail. php?id=1990.

159. "Annual Energy Review, Table 7.9: Coal Prices, 1949–2011," US Energy Information Agency, September 27, 2012, https://www.eia.gov/totalenergy/data/annual/show text.php?t=ptb0709.

160. "Natural Gas Shale of the Century," *The Economist*, June 2, 2012, https://www. economist.com/node/21556242.

161. "Electricity in the United States," US Energy Information Agency, accessed May 22, 2020, https://www.eia.gov/energyexplained/electricity/electricity-in-the-us.php.

162. "Coal Made Up More Than 80% of Retired Electricity Generating Capacity in 2015," Today in Energy, US Energy Information Agency, March 8, 2016, https://www.eia.gov/todayinenergy/detail.php?id=25272.

163. "Analysis of the Impacts of the Clean Power Plan," US Energy Information Agency, May 22, 2015, https://www.eia.gov/analysis/requests/powerplants/cleanplan/.

164. "Renewable Portfolio Standards," Clean Energy States Alliance, accessed October 2020, https://www.cesa.org/projects/renewable-portfolio-standards/.

165. "U.S. Renewables Portfolio Standards 2021 Status Update: Early Release," Lawrence Berkeley National Laboratory, February 2021, https://emp.lbl.gov/publications/us-renewables-portfolio-standards-3.

166. Ibid.

167. Brad Plumer and Nadja Popovich, "How Will the Clean Power Plan Repeal Change Carbon Emissions for Your State?" *New York Times*, October 10, 2017, https://www.nytimes.com/interactive/2017/10/10/climate/clean-power-plan-emissions-your-state.html.

168. "Deregulated Energy States & Markets," Electric Choice, updated 2020, https://www.electricchoice.com/map-deregulated-energy-markets/.

169. Ibid.

170. Management Information Services, Inc., "60 Years of Energy Incentives: Analysis of Federal Expenditures for Energy Development," prepared for the Nuclear Energy Institute, October 2011, http://www.misi-net.com/publications/NEI-1011.pdf.

171. Ibid.

172. The White House Office of the Press Secretary, Fact Sheet, "The Recovery Act Made the Largest Single Investment in Clean Energy in History, Driving the Deployment of Clean Energy, Promoting Energy Efficiency, and Supporting Manufacturing," February 25, 2016, https://obamawhitehouse.archives.gov/the-press-office/2016/02/25/fact-sheet-recovery-act-made-largest-single-investment-clean-energy.

173. Ibid.

174. Ibid.

175. Congressional Research Service, "The Value of Energy Tax Incentives for Different Types of Energy Resources," updated March 2019, https://fas.org/sgp/crs/misc/R44852.pdf.

176. "In front of the meter" refers to grid facing while "behind the meter" refers to distributed sources (e.g., electric vehicle batteries).

177. Julia Spector, "The Five Most Promising Long-Duration Storage Technologies Left Standing," Greentech Media, March 31, 2020, https://www.greentechmedia.com/articles/read/most-promising-long-duration-storage-technologies-left-standing.

178. "Levelized Cost of Storage Analysis—Version 6.0," Lazard, https://www.lazard.com/media/451418/lazards-levelized-cost-of-storage-version-60.pdf.

179. Ibid.

180. "Levelized Cost of Energy Analysis—Version 14.0."

181. Ibid.

182. William Driscoll, "NREL Study Backs Hydrogen for Long-Duration Storage,"

PV Magazine, July 3, 2020, https://pv-magazine-usa.com/2020/07/03/nrel-study-backs -hydrogen-for-long-duration-storage/.

183. "Top 5 Energy Storage Trends of 2019," *POWER* magazine, October 27, 2019, https://www.powermag.com/top-5-energy-storage-trends-of-the-year/.

184. Wood Mackenzie Power & Renewables and US Energy Storage Association, "US Energy Storage Monitor: Q3 2020 Executive Summary," September 2020, https://www.woodmac.com/research/products/power-and-renewables/us-energy-storage-monitor/.

185. M. M. Hand, S. Baldwin, E. DeMeo, J. M. Reilly, T. Mai, D. Arent, G. Porro, et al., eds. "Renewable Electricity Futures Study," 4 vols., 2012, National Renewable Energy Laboratory, http://www.nrel.gov/analysis/re_futures/.

186. Alex King and Rod Eggert. "Rare Earths and Other Critical Materials: Status Update," May 2017, Critical Materials Institute, May 2017, https://cmi.ameslab.gov/materials/rare-earths-and-critical-materials-status-update.

187. "The Critical Materials Institute (About)," accessed January 2018, https://cmi.ameslab.gov/about.

188. "Critical Materials Institute Names Four Projects to Support Innovation in the Nation's Materials Supply Chain," DOE Ames Laboratory, October 15, 2020, https://www.ameslab.gov/news/critical-materials-institute-names-four-projects-to-support -innovation-in-the-nation-s.

189. Claudiu C. Pavel, Roberto Lacal-Arántegui, Alain Marmier, Doris Schüler, Evangelos Tzimas, Matthias Buchert, Wolfgang Jenseit, and Darina Blagoeva, "Substitution Strategies for Reducing the Use of Rare Earths in Wind Turbines," *Resources Policy* 52 (June 2017): 349–357, https://www.sciencedirect.com/science/article/pii/S0301420717300077.

190. "Copper: An Outlook on Global Supply and Demand," JLT Specialty, November 8, 2017, https://www.jltspecialty.com/our-insights/thought-leadership/mining/copper -an-outlook-on-global-supply-and-demand.

191. Shuhei Ochiai, "Japanese Cobalt Traders Find There Is None Left to Buy," *Nikkei Asian Review*, January 17, 2018, https://asia.nikkei.com/Markets/Commodities/Japanese -cobalt-traders-find-there-is-none-left-to-buy.

CHAPTER 3: THE TRANSPORTATION SECTOR

1. O. Edenhofer, R. Pichs-Madruga, Y. Sokona, E. Farahani, S. Kadner, K. Seyboth, A. Adler, et al., eds., "Intergovernmental Panel on Climate Change (IPCC), 2014: Summary for Policymakers," in *Climate Change 2014, Mitigation of Climate Change*, contribution of Working Group III to the Fifth Assessment Report of the Intergovernmental Panel on Climate Change (Cambridge, UK, and New York: Cambridge University Press, 2014).

2. "Sources of Greenhouse Gas Emissions (2018)," US Environmental Protection Agency, accessed July 9, 2020, https://www.epa.gov/ghgemissions/sources-greenhouse -gas-emissions.

3. "Fast Facts on Transportation Greenhouse Gas Emissions (2018)," US Environmental Protection Agency, accessed March 3, 2021, https://www.epa.gov/greenvehicles/fast-facts-transportation-greenhouse-gas-emissions.

4. "Greenhouse Gas Emissions from Transport in Europe," European Environment Agency, December 17, 2019, https://www.eea.europa.eu/data-and-maps/indicators/transport-emissions-of-greenhouse-gases/transport-emissions-of-greenhouse-gases-12.

5. "The Clean Energy Ministerial and Electric Vehicles Initiative, Government Fleet Declaration," November 16, 2016, https://iea.blob.core.windows.net/assets/e7dc869b-ca7b-4659-a7c4-1b8360189a5b/EVI_Government_Fleet_Declaration.pdf.

6. Sandra Wappelhorst, "The End of the Road? An Overview of Combustion Engine Car Phase-Out Announcements Across Europe," International Council on Clean Transportation Briefing, May 2020, https://theicct.org/sites/default/files/publications/Combustion-engine-phase-out-briefing-may11.2020.pdf.

7. "China Fossil Fuel Deadline Shifts Focus to Electric Car Race," *Bloomberg News*, September 10, 2017, https://www.bloomberg.com/news/articles/2017-09-10/china-s-fossil-fuel-deadline-shifts-focus-to-electric-car-race-j7fktx9z.

8. "History of the Electric Car," US Department of Energy, September 15, 2014, https://www.energy.gov/articles/history-electric-car.

9. US Congress, H.R. 8800—Electric Vehicle Research, Development, and Demonstration Act, September 17, 1976, https://www.congress.gov/bill/94th-congress/house-bill/8800.

10. "History of the Electric Car," US Department of Energy, September 15, 2014, https://www.energy.gov/articles/history-electric-car.

11. "Bureau of Transportation Statistics, National Transportation Statistics: Table 4-23: Average Fuel Efficiency of U.S. Light Duty Vehicles," US Department of Transportation, April 2017, https://www.rita.dot.gov/bts/sites/rita.dot.gov.bts/files/publications/national_transportation_statistics/2011/html/table_04_23.html.

12. "New Concept Cars Demonstrate Clean, Efficient Transportation Technologies," US Department of Energy, March 23, 2001, https://www1.eere.energy.gov/vehiclesandfuels/pdfs/success/pngv3_23_01.pdf.

13. "Zero-Emission Vehicle Legal and Regulatory Activities and Background," California Air Resources Board, accessed September 14, 2017, https://www.arb.ca.gov/msprog/zevprog/zevregs/zevregs.htm.

14. Stephen Edelstein, "How Does GM's Fabled EV1 Stack Up Against the Current Crop of Electrics?" Digital Trends, February 28, 2013, https://www.digitaltrends.com/cars/how-does-gms-fabled-ev1-stack-up-against-the-current-crop-of-electrics/.

15. PNS NOW, "Who Killed the Electric Car?" PBS, June 9, 2006, http://www.pbs.org/now/shows/223/.

16. "Zero-Emission Vehicle Legal and Regulatory Activities and Background."

17. PNS NOW, "Who Killed the Electric Car?"

18. Don Sherman, "What Came Before: The Real History of the Toyota Prius," *Car and Driver* (accessed September 13, 2017), http://www.caranddriver.com/flipbook/what-came-before-the-real-history-of-the-toyota-prius#10.

19. "Hybrid Vehicle Sales by Model," Alternative Fuels Data Center, US Department of Energy, updated January 2016, https://www.afdc.energy.gov/data/?q=Sales.

20. Sami Haj-Assaad, "How the Toyota Prius Killed the Honda Insight in the Hybrid

Wars," Auto.com, December 4, 2015, http://www.autoguide.com/auto-news/2015/12/how-the-toyota-prius-killed-the-honda-insight-in-the-hybrid-wars.html.

21. "Patent Counts by Class by Year, CY 1977–2015 (class 930 HEVs)," US Patent Trademark Office, https://www.uspto.gov/web/offices/ac/ido/oeip/taf/cbcby.pdf.

22. "Hybrid Vehicle Sales by Model."

23. Bureau of Transportation Statistics, "Table 1-15: Annual U.S. Motor Vehicle Production and Factory Sales," US Department of Transportation, https://www.rita.dot.gov/bts/sites/rita.dot.gov.bts/files/publications/national_transportation_statistics/html/table_01_15.html_mfd.

24. "U.S. All Grades All Formulations Retail Gasoline Prices Dollars per Gallon," US Energy Information Agency, accessed May 2017, https://www.eia.gov/dnav/pet/hist/LeafHandler.ashx?n=PET&s=EMM_EPM0_PTE_NUS_DPG&f=M.

25. Ibid.

26. Bureau of Transportation Statistics, "Table 1-15."

27. "Hybrid Vehicle Sales by Model."

28. "All Hybrid Car Models & Efficient Vehicles," HybridCars.com, accessed August 2017, http://www.hybridcars.com/hybrid-cars-list.

29. Bureau of Transportation Statistics, "Table 1-15"; and "Hybrid Vehicle Sales by Model."

30. Zak Mustapha, "Are Hybrid Cars Still a Worthy Investment In 2016?" *Huffington Post* (blog), August 16, 2016, http://www.huffingtonpost.com/zak-mustapha/are-hybrid-cars-still-a-w_b_11533264.html.

31. Will Sierzchula, "Explaining Stagnation in the Hybrid-Electric Vehicle Market," *Scientific American* (blog), February 6, 2015, https://blogs.scientificamerican.com/plugged-in/explaining-stagnation-in-the-hybrid-electric-vehicle-market/.

32. Ibid.

33. Bureau of Transportation Statistics, "Table 1-19: Hybrid-Electric, Plug-In Electric, and Electric Vehicles Sales," US Department of Transportation, https://www.bts.gov/content/gasoline-hybrid-and-electric-vehicle-sales.

34. "China Eases Green Rules for Petrol-Electric Hybrids, Giving Makers Space to Manoeuvre," Reuters, June 21, 2020, https://www.reuters.com/article/us-china-autos-hybrid/china-eases-green-rules-for-petrol-electric-hybrids-giving-makers-space-to-manoeuvre-idUSKBN23T09O.

35. "Driving into 2025: The Future of Electric Vehicles," JP Morgan, October 10, 2018, https://www.jpmorgan.com/global/research/electric-vehicles.

36. International Council on Clean Transportation Technical Brief No. 1, July 2015. The Toyota power-split design is distinguished by the use of two large electric motors and a planetary gear system in place of conventional transmission.

37. Greg Kumparak, Matt Burns, and Anna Escher. "A Brief History of Tesla," July 28, 2015, TechCrunch, https://techcrunch.com/gallery/a-brief-history-of-tesla/.

38. "Fisker Automotive's Road to Ruin: How a Billion-Dollar Startup Became a Billion-Dollar Disaster," April 17, 2013, PrivCo, http://www.privco.com/fisker-automotives-road-to-ruin/.

39. John Voelcker, "Fisker Assets Sold for $149 Million to Wanxiang, Chinese Parts Maker," Green Car Reports, February 15, 2014, http://www.greencarreports.com/news/1090379_fisker-assets-sold-for-149-million-to-wanxiang-chinese-parts-maker; "Karma Owner Plans $375 Million China Electric Car Factory," Bloomberg.com, August 8, 2016, https://www.bloomberg.com/news/articles/2016-08-08/wanxiang-plans-50-000-unit-year-electric-car-plant-in-china.

40. Karma Automotive, "Karma Automotive Plant Launches Revero," PR Newswire, May 15, 2017, http://www.prnewswire.com/news-releases/karma-automotive-plant-launches-revero-300457639.html.

41. Stephen Ewing, "2020 Karma Revero GT First Drive Review: Third Time's the Charm," Road Show by CNET, October 7, 2019, https://www.cnet.com/roadshow/news/2020-karma-revero-gt-first-drive-review/.

42. Murray Slovick, "Fisker Aims to Launch Emotion EV with Solid State Battery in 2020," Electronic Design, May 29, 2018, https://www.electronicdesign.com/markets/automotive/article/21806566/fisker-aims-to-launch-emotion-ev-with-solidstate-battery-in-2020.

43. Jeff Cobb, "The List: Chevrolet Volt Awards and Accolades Earned Through 2011," GM Volt, http://gm-volt.com/2011/11/21/volt-accolades-and-awards-from-inception-through-2011/.

44. Nissan Leaf News, Nissan Motor Corporation, accessed March 10, 2021, http://www.nissan-global.com/EN/NISSAN/LEAF/.

45. David Gluckman, "2011 Nissan Leaf SL: Nissan's First Try at an EV Might Make a Good Second Car," Car and Driver, August 2011, http://www.caranddriver.com/reviews/2011-nissan-leaf-sl-long-term-road-test-review.

46. "President Obama Announces $2.4 Billion in Grants to Accelerate the Manufacturing and Deployment of the Next Generation of U.S. Batteries and Electric Vehicles," US Department of Energy, August 5, 2009, https://energy.gov/articles/president-obama-announces-24-billion-grants-accelerate-manufacturing-and-deployment-next.

47. ZEV Program Implementation Task Force, "Multi-State ZEV Action Plan," Northeast States for Coordinated Air Use Management, May 2014, http://www.nescaum.org/topics/zero-emission-vehicles.

48. David Scutt, "2016 Was a Record-Breaking Year for Global Car Sales, and It Was Almost Entirely Driven by China," Business Insider, January 19, 2017, http://www.businessinsider.com/2016-was-a-record-breaking-year-for-global-car-sales-and-it-was-almost-entirely-driven-by-china-2017-1. China sales: http://www.scmp.com/business/china-business/article/2061642/china-2016-car-sales-surge-fastest-rate-three-years, U.S. Sales: Annual U.S. Motor Vehicle Production and Factory Sales, Europe Sales: http://www.acea.be/statistics/tag/category/key-figures.

49. Bloomberg, "Tesla Pays Back Balance of DOE Loan," Automotive News, May 23, 2013, http://www.autonews.com/article/20130522/OEM05/130529956/tesla-pays-back-balance-of-doe-loan.

50. "U.S. Plug-In Electric Vehicle Sales by Model," US Department of Energy, Alternative Fuels Data Center, updated January 2016, https://www.afdc.energy.gov/data/?q=Sales.

51. Ibid.

52. Kumparak, Burns, and Escher, "A Brief History of Tesla."

53. "U.S. Plug-In Electric Vehicle Sales by Model."

54. "USA Plug-In Vehicle Sales for 2016," EV Volumes.com, http://www.ev-volumes.com/news/usa-plug-in-vehicle-sales-for-2016/.

55. "Tesla Q4 2019 Vehicle Production & Deliverables," Tesla, January 3, 2020, https://ir.tesla.com/news-releases/news-release-details/tesla-q4-2019-vehicle-production-deliveries.

56. Chris Woodyard, "Elon Musk Says Rivals Are Now Using Tesla Patents," *USA Today*, October 14, 2014, https://www.usatoday.com/story/money/cars/2014/10/14/tesla-musk-patents/17247723/.

57. Fred Lambert, "Tesla's Battery Strategy Is Inspiring New Electric Vehicle Startups, But Not Legacy Automakers," Electrek, December 8, 2016, https://electrek.co/2016/12/08/tesla-battery-strategy-inspiring-electric-vehicle-startups/.

58. "Electric Vehicles Outlook 2019," Bloomberg New Energy Finance, https://bnef.turtl.co/story/evo2019.

59. "Global Li-Ion Batteries Market, Forecast to 2025 (Description)," Research and Markets, October 2019, https://www.researchandmarkets.com/reports/4850636/global-li-ion-batteries-market-forecast-to-2025?utm_source=dynamic&utm_medium=GNOM&utm_code=p3vffw&utm_campaign=1314714+-+Analysis+on+the+Global+Li-ion+Batteries+Market%2c+2019-2025+-+Installed+Production+Capacity+of+the+Top+10+Suppliers+Will+Increase+from+150+GWh+in+2018+to+About+740+GWh+by+2025&utm_exec=joca22ognomd.

60. Mark Kane, "Tesla Gigafactory 3 Already Produced About 50,000 Model 3," INSIDEEVs, July 11, 2020, https://insideevs.com/news/433483/tesla-gigafactory-3-produced-50000-model-3/.

61. "Who Is Winning the Global Lithium Ion Battery Arms Race?" Benchmark Mineral Intelligence, January 26, 2019, https://www.benchmarkminerals.com/who-is-winning-the-global-lithium-ion-battery-arms-race/.

62. George Crabtree, Elizabeth Kocs, and Lynn Trahey, "The Energy-Storage Frontier: Lithium-Ion Batteries and Beyond," *Materials Research Society Bulletin* 40 (December 2015), https://www.ny-best.org/sites/default/files/resources/CrabtreeKocsTrahey_TheEnergyStorageFrontierLithiumIonBatteriesAndBeyond_MRSBulletin40106715.pdf.

63. "How Much Is a Tesla? All Tesla Models and Prices in 2020," Solar Reviews, December 9, 2020, https://www.solarreviews.com/blog/how-much-do-teslas-electric-vehicles-cost.

64. Damian Carrington, "Dyson Could Become Next Tesla with Its Electric Car, Says Expert," *The Guardian*, May 11, 2016, https://www.theguardian.com/environment/2016/may/11/dysons-electric-car-development-could-become-the-next-tesla.

65. "Tesla's Musk Hints at Battery Capacity Jump Ahead of Industry Event," Reuters, August 25, 2020, https://www.reuters.com/article/us-tesla-batteries/teslas-musk-hints-of-battery-capacity-jump-ahead-of-industry-event-idUSKBN25L0MC.

66. "Compare Electric Cars and Plug-in Hybrids by Features, Price, Range," Plug-In

Cars.com, accessed September 2017, http://www.plugincars.com/cars?field_isphev_value_many_to_one=pure+electric.

67. Fred Lambert, "Tesla Model 3 vs BMW 3 Series: How Pricing and Options Compare," Electrek, July 21, 2017, https://electrek.co/2017/07/31/tesla-model-3-vs-bmw-3-series/.

68. Fred Lambert, "Electric Vehicle Battery Cost Dropped 80% in 6 Years Down to $227/kWh—Tesla Claims to Be Below $190/kWh," Electrek, January 30, 2017, https://electrek.co/2017/01/30/electric-vehicle-battery-cost-dropped-80–6-years-227kwh-tesla-190kwh/.

69. Rob Day, "Low-Cost Batteries Are About to Transform Multiple Industries," Forbes, December 3, 2019, https://www.forbes.com/sites/robday/2019/12/03/low-cost-batteries-are-about-to-transform-multiple-industries/#14cdacc41054.

70. Tom Randall, "The Electric Car Revolution Now Faces Its Biggest Test," Bloomberg, April 24, 2017, https://www.bloomberg.com/news/articles/2017-04-24/the-electric-car-revolution-tesla-began-faces-its-biggest-test.

71. Cecilia Jamasmie, "Lithium Prices to Remain Low as "Hype" Meets Reality—CRU," Mining.com, August 21, 2019, https://www.mining.com/lithium-prices-to-remain-low-as-hype-has-met-reality-cru/.

72. Emmanuel Latham, Ben Kilbey, and Abdulrhman Ehtaiba, "Lithium Supply Is Set to Triple by 2025. Will It Be Enough?" S&P Global, October 24, 2019, https://www.spglobal.com/en/research-insights/articles/lithium-supply-is-set-to-triple-by-2025-will-it-be-enough.

73. Ibid.

74. "Cobalt Outlook to 2030, 16th Ed.," Roskill Market Reports (Overview), https://roskill.com/market-report/cobalt/.

75. Oilprice.com, "Cobalt Squeeze Threatens the Electric Vehicle Boom," Safehaven, August 9, 2020, https://safehaven.com/commodities/industrial-metals/Cobalt-Squeeze-Threatens-The-Electric-Vehicle-Boom.html.

76. "Study Finds Cobalt Supply Can Meet Demand for EVs and Electronic Batteries Through 2030," Green Car Congress, February 20, 2020, https://www.greencarcongress.com/2020/02/20200220-co.html.

77. Makiko Yamazaki, "Exclusive: Panasonic Aims to Boost Energy Density in Tesla Batteries by 20%," Reuters, July 30, 2020, https://www.reuters.com/article/us-panasonic-tesla-exclusive/exclusive-panasonic-aims-to-boost-energy-density-in-tesla-batteries-by-20-executive-idUSKCN24V1GB; Reuters, "CATL Is Developing a New EV Battery with No Nickel or Cobalt," Autoblog, August 16, 2020, https://www.autoblog.com/2020/08/16/china-catl-ev-battery-nickel-cobalt/.

78. Donna Lu, "Can We Quit Cobalt Batteries Fast Enough to Make Electric Cars Viable?" NewScientist, February 20, 2020, https://www.newscientist.com/article/2234567-can-we-quit-cobalt-batteries-fast-enough-to-make-electric-cars-viable/.

79. Roberto Baldwin, "China's CATL Has a Million-Mile EV Battery Pack Ready to Go," Car and Driver, June 8, 2020, https://www.caranddriver.com/news/a32801823/million-mile-ev-battery-pack-revealed/#:~:text=CATL%20chairman%20Zeng%20Yuqun%20told,much%20as%201.2%20million%20miles.

80. "New Cobalt-Free Lithium Ion Battery Reduces Cost Without Sacrificing Performance," Futuretimeline.net, July 17, 2020, https://www.futuretimeline.net/blog/2020/07/17-cobalt-free-batteries-future.htm.

81. Lu, "Can We Quit Cobalt Batteries Fast Enough to Make Electric Cars Viable?"

82. Roberto Baldwin, "Toyota's Quick Charging Solid-State Battery Coming in 2025," *Car and Driver*, July 27, 2020, https://www.caranddriver.com/news/a33435923/toyota-solid-state-battery-2025/.

83. "Electric Vehicle Charging Stations," US DOE Alternative Fuels Data Center, accessed August 2020, https://www.afdc.energy.gov/fuels/electricity_locations.html.

84. "Charging Is Our Priority," Tesla (blog), August 24, 2017, https://www.tesla.com/blog/charging-our-priority.

85. "Supercharger," Tesla.com, accessed March 4, 2021, https://www.tesla.com/supercharger.

86. "Global EV Outlook 2020," International Energy Agency, June 2020, https://www.iea.org/reports/global-ev-outlook-2020.

87. Ibid.

88. Ibid.

89. Neil Roland, "Obama Kills Development of Hydrogen Fuel Cell Vehicles," *Automotive News*, May 8, 2009, http://www.autonews.com/article/20090508/OEM05/305089880/&template=print.

90. "Fuel Cell Technologies Office: 2016 Recap and the Year Ahead," US Department of Energy, January 18, 2017, https://energy.gov/eere/fuelcells/articles/fuel-cell-technologies-office-2016-recap-and-year-ahead.

91. Danielle Muoio, "Automakers Are Betting on Hydrogen-Powered Cars—Here Are 12 in the works," *Business Insider*, May 17, 2017, http://nordic.businessinsider.com/12-hydrogen-car-projects-2017-5/.

92. Charles Morris, "Daimler Becomes the Latest Automaker to Abandon Hydrogen-Powered Passenger Cars," *Charged Electric Vehicle Magazine*, April 27, 2020, https://chargedevs.com/newswire/daimler-becomes-the-latest-automaker-to-abandon-hydrogen-powered-passenger-cars/.

93. Charles Morris, "BMW Reveals Details of Hydrogen Fuel Cell Powertrain System," *Charged Electric Vehicle Magazine*, April 7, 2020, https://chargedevs.com/newswire/bmw-reveals-details-of-hydrogen-fuel-cell-powertrain-system/.

94. Richard Truett and Hans Greimel, "GM, Honda Partner to Build Hydrogen Fuel Cells in 2020," *Autoweek*, January 31, 2017, http://autoweek.com/article/technology/gm-honda-partner-build-hydrogen-fuel-cells-2020.

95. John Voelcker, "Toyota, Honda, Nissan, Other Japan Firms to Fund Hydrogen Fueling," *Green Car Reports*, May 26, 2017, http://www.greencarreports.com/news/1110668_toyota-honda-nissan-other-japan-firms-to-fund-hydrogen-fueling.

96. James Ayre, "Toyota Making 5,600 Hydrogen Fuel Cell Patents Free to Use," CleanTechnica, January 8, 2015, https://cleantechnica.com/2015/01/08/toyota-making-5600-hydrogen-fuel-cell-patents-free-use-industry-companies/.

97. "US Renewable Energy Patents: What GM, GE, IBM, and Other Top Corporates Are Working On," CB Insights Research Briefs, February 14, 2017, https://www.cb insights.com/blog/renewable-energy-patents-trends-corporates/.

98. Ibid.

99. Ibid.

100. Tim Pohlmann, "The Patent Race for Fuel Cell Vehicles," *IAM Magazine*, August 6, 2019, https://www.iam-media.com/patent-race-fuel-cell-vehicles.

101. Ibid.

102. "Progress and Accomplishments in Hydrogen and Fuel Cells," US DOE Fuel Cell Technologies Office, April 2016, https://energy.gov/sites/prod/files/2017/02/f34/fcto -progress-accomplishments-april-2016.pdf; and "Fuel Cell Vehicle Challenges," US Department of Energy, accessed July 2017, http://www.fueleconomy.gov/feg/fcv_challenges .shtml.

103. Jean Baronas, Gerhard Achtelik, et al., "Joint Agency Staff Report on Assembly Bill 8: 2019 Annual Assessment of Time and Cost Needed to Attain 100 Hydrogen Refueling Stations in California," California Energy Commission and California Air Resources Board, 2019, Publication Number CEC-600-2019-039, https://ww2.energy. ca.gov/2019publications/CEC-600-2019-039/CEC-600-2019-039.pdf.

104. "Refueling the Future of Mobility: Hydrogen and Fuel Cell Solutions for Transportation (Volume 1)," Deloitte China, 2020, https://www2.deloitte.com/content/dam /Deloitte/cn/Documents/finance/deloitte-cn-fueling-the-future-of-mobility-en-200101.pdf.

105. "The Future of Hydrogen," International Energy Agency, June 2019, https:// www.iea.org/reports/the-future-of-hydrogen.

106. Ibid.

107. "Path to Hydrogen Competitiveness: A Cost Perspective," Hydrogen Council, January 2020, https://hydrogencouncil.com/wp-content/uploads/2020/01/Path-to -Hydrogen-Competitiveness_Full-Study-1.pdf.

108. "Hydrogen Initiative Overview," The Clean Energy Ministerial, accessed September 2020, https://www.cleanenergyministerial.org/initiative-clean-energy-ministerial /hydrogen-initiative.

109. "Hydrogen," International Energy Agency, June 2020, https://www.iea.org/reports /hydrogen.

110. Ibid.

111. "Alternative Fueling Station Counts by State," US DOE Alternative Fuels Data Center, accessed August 2020, www.afdc.energy.gov/afdc/fuels/stations_counts.html.

112. "Global EV Outlook 2020," International Energy Agency, June 2020, https:// www.iea.org/reports/global-ev-outlook-2020.

113. Mark Kane, "Global EV Sales for 2019 Now In: Tesla Model 3 Totally Dominated," INSIDEEVs, February 2, 2020, https://insideevs.com/news/396177/global-ev-sales -december-2019/.

114. Colin McKerracher, Ali Izadi-Najafabadi, Aleksandra O'Donovan, Nick Albanese, Nikolas Soulopolous, David Doherty, Milo Boers, et al., "Electric Vehicle Outlook

2020," accessed March 4, 2021, Bloomberg New Energy Finance, https://about.bnef.com/electric-vehicle-outlook/.

115. Ibid.

116. Ibid.

117. Kane, "Global EV Sales for 2019 Now In: Tesla Model 3 Totally Dominated."

118. "Global Market for Hydrogen Fuel Cell Vehicles 2017—Research and Markets," *Business Wire*, April 18, 2017, http://www.businesswire.com/news/home/20170418006120/en/Global-Market-Hydrogen-Fuel-Cell-Vehicles-2017.

119. "On the Road," Waymo, accessed August 2017, https://waymo.com/ontheroad/.

120. "Partnering with Volvo Car Group to Scale the Waymo Driver," Waymo (blog), June 25, 2020, https://blog.waymo.com/2020/06/partnering-with-volvo-car-group-to.html.

121. "Top 30 Self-Driving Technology and Car Companies," GreyB, April 26, 2020, https://www.greyb.com/autonomous-vehicle-companies/#:~:text=There%20are%20over%20250%20autonomous,or%20driverless%20cars%20a%20reality.

122. Ibid.

123. Daniel Faggella, "Self-Driving Car Timeline for 11 Top Automakers," Venture-Beat, June 4, 2017, https://venturebeat.com/2017/06/04/self-driving-car-timeline-for-11-top-automakers/.

124. Aaron Aupperlee, "Uber's Self-Driving Fleet Logs More Than 1 Million Miles in First Year," *Tribune Review*, September 14, 2017, http://triblive.com/local/allegheny/12734361-74/ubers-self-driving-fleet-logs-more-than-1-million-autonomous-miles-in-first.

125. Andrew Hawkins, "Riding in Waymo One, the Google Spinoff's First Self-Driving Taxi Service," *The Verge*, December 5, 2018, https://www.theverge.com/2018/12/5/18126103/waymo-one-self-driving-taxi-service-ride-safety-alphabet-cost-app.

126. SAFE Press Release, "SAFE Analysis Shows 80 Percent of Light-Duty Autonomous Vehicles Use Alternative Fuel Powertrains," February 14, 2017, http://secureenergy.org/press/safe-analysis-shows-80-percent-light-duty-autonomous-vehicles-use-alternative-fuel-powertrains/.

127. Aarian Marshall, "The Intersection Between Self-Driving Cars and Electric Cars," *WIRED*, July 13, 2020, https://www.wired.com/story/intersection-self-driving-cars-electric/.

128. Ibid.

129. "Quick Facts (2020 Public Transportation Fact Book)," American Public Transportation Association, https://www.apta.com/wp-content/uploads/APTA-2020-Fact-Book.pdf.

130. "Autonomous Vehicle Sales to Surpass 33 Million Annually in 2040, Enabling New Autonomous Mobility in More Than 26% of New Car Sales," IHS Markit, January 2, 2018, https://ihsmarkit.com/research-analysis/autonomous-vehicle-sales-to-surpass-33-million-annually-in-2040-enabling-new-autonomous-mobility-in-more

-than-26-percent-of-new-car-sales.html#:~:text=More%20than%2033%20million%20
autonomous,business%20information%20provider%20HIS%20Markit.

131. Michael Sivak and Brandon Schoettle, "Relative Costs of Driving Electric and Gasoline Vehicles in the Individual U.S. States," University of Michigan's Transportation Research Institute, 2018.

132. Sarwant Singh, "Over 1,700 Start-Ups Are Disrupting the Automotive Industry," *Forbes*, May 17, 2017, https://www.forbes.com/sites/sarwantsingh/2017/05/17/over-1700-start-ups-are-disrupting-the-automotive-industry/#2648e8b45145.

133. Zal Dastur, "Automotive Technology Incubators and Accelerators by Big Auto," Lucep, April 2, 2018, https://lucep.com/automotive-technology-incubators-and-accelerators-by-big-auto/.

134. "The Future of Rail," International Energy Agency, January 2019, https://www.iea.org/reports/the-future-of-rail.

135. Ibid.

136. Vaclav Smil, "Electric Container Ships Are Stuck on the Horizon," IEEE Spectrum, February 27, 2019, https://spectrum.ieee.org/transportation/marine/electric-container-ships-are-stuck-on-the-horizon.

137. "Tracking Transport 2019 (Shipping)," International Energy Agency, accessed April 2020, https://www.iea.org/reports/tracking-transport-2019/international-shipping#abstract (link is updated annually and has been replaced with more recent 2020 report summary).

138. "Our Work: Environment," International Maritime Organization, accessed August 2020, http://www.imo.org/en/OurWork/Environment/PollutionPrevention/Air-Pollution/Pages/GHG-Emissions.aspx.

139. "Tracking Transport 2020 (Shipping)," accessed May 2020, https://www.iea.org/reports/international-shipping. Link for 2020 data (which is similar to what we provide here) is https://www.iea.org/reports/international-shipping.

140. Tracking Transport 2019 (Aviation), accessed April 2020, https://www.iea.org/reports/aviation (link is updated annually and has been replaced with more recent 2020 report summary).

141. Ibid.

142. Ibid.

143. "Electric Flight: Laying the Groundwork for Zero-Emission Aviation," Airbus, accessed June 2020, https://www.airbus.com/innovation/future-technology/electric-flight.html#objective.

144. Scott Hardmana, Amrit Chandanb, Gil Tala, and Tom Turrentinea, "The Effectiveness of Financial Purchase Incentives for Battery Electric Vehicles—A Review of the Evidence," Renewable and Sustainable Energy Reviews, Plug-in Hybrid and Electric Vehicle Research Center, Institute of Transportation Studies, University of California, Davis, 2017.

145. Neil Winton, "Diesel Sales Stumble in Europe, Undermined by VW Scandal, Health Worries," *Forbes*, September 15, 2016, https://www.forbes.com/sites/

neilwinton/2016/09/15/diesel-sales-stumble-in-europe-undermined-by-vw-scandal
-health-worries/#3e7d3bb37ee0.

146. "Global EV Outlook 2017," International Energy Agency, June 6, 2017, https://
webstore.iea.org/global-ev-outlook-2017.

147. "Global EV Outlook 2020," International Energy Agency, June 2020, https://
www.iea.org/reports/global-ev-outlook-2020.

148. Jim Matavalli, "China to Subsidize Electric Cars and Hybrids," June 2, 2010,
https://wheels.blogs.nytimes.com/2010/06/02/china-to-start-pilot-program-providing
-subsidies-for-electric-cars-and-hybrids.

149. Jose Pontes, "China Electric Car Sales Demolish US & European Electric Car
Sales," CleanTechnica, January 25, 2017, https://cleantechnica.com/2017/01/25/china
-electric-car-sales-demolish-us-european-sales.

150. "Global EV Outlook 2020."

151. White House Press Release, "Obama Administration Announces New Actions
to Accelerate the Deployment of Electrical Vehicles and Charging Infrastructure," November 3, 2016, https://obamawhitehouse.archives.gov/the-press-office/2016/11/03/
obama-administration-announces-new-actions-accelerate-deployment.

152. "Alternative Fuel Corridors," US Department of Transportation, updated
June 25, 2020, https://www.fhwa.dot.gov/environment/alternative_fuel_corridors/.

153. Rob Stumpf, "Ford Wants a Repeat of 'Cash for Clunkers' as New Car Sales
Tank," The Drive, April 3, 2020, https://www.thedrive.com/news/32877/ford-wants-a
-repeat-of-cash-for-clunkers-as-new-car-sales-tank.

154. Ibid.

155. Jim Gorzelany, "Could a New 'Cash for Clunkers' Program Jump-Start Electric Car Sales?" Forbes, October 29, 2019, https://www.forbes.com/sites/jimgor
zelany/2019/10/29/could-a-new-cash-for-clunkers-program-jump-start-electric-car
-sales/#7f7a8f4f3484.

156. Ibid.

157. Chelsea Mes and Ryan Beene, "Schumer Floats Plan to Take Gas-Powered
Vehicles Off U.S. Roads By 2040," Bloomberg, October 24, 2019, https://www.bloom
berg.com/news/articles/2019-10-25/schumer-floats-454-billion-clunkers-plan-to-boost
-clean-cars.

CHAPTER 4: THE INDUSTRIALS SECTOR

1. "Trends in Atmospheric Carbon Dioxide, Carbon Cycle Greenhouse Gases,"
NOAA Global Monitoring Laboratory, accessed November 2020, https://www.esrl.noaa.
gov/gmd/ccgg/trends/global.html.

2. "Global Greenhouse Gas Emissions Data," US Environmental Protection Agency,
accessed August 2018, https://www.epa.gov/ghgemissions/global-greenhouse-gas
-emissions-data.

3. "Tracking Industry Report," International Energy Agency, May 2019, https://www.
iea.org/reports/tracking-industry.

4. "Decoupling of Global Emissions and Economic Growth Confirmed," International

Energy Agency, March 16, 2016, https://www.iea.org/news/decoupling-of-global-emissions-and-economic-growth-confirmed.

5. "Global Emissions in 2019," International Energy Agency, February 11, 2020, https://www.iea.org/articles/global-co2-emissions-in-2019.

6. Ibid.

7. "Greenhouse Gas Emissions for Major Economies 1990–2020," Center for Climate and Energy Solutions, Climate Basics: Energy/Emissions Data, Global Emissions, accessed October 2018, https://www.c2es.org/content/international-emissions/.

8. "US Energy-Related Carbon Dioxide Emissions, 2017," US Energy Information Administration, "Environment: Analysis and Projections," September 25, 2018, https://www.eia.gov/environment/emissions/carbon/.

9. "World Steel in Figures 2020," World Steel Association, https://www.worldsteel.org/steel-by-topic/statistics/World-Steel-in-Figures.html.

10. Frank Zhong, "The Chinese Steel Industry at a Crossroads," presentation at the China Iron Ore 2018 conference (Beijing), accessed September 2018, https://www.worldsteel.org/en/dam/jcr:295ce643-fff1–4a23–8db8-d24bf3b154f2/PPT%2520fo%2520MB%2520iron%2520ore%2520conference%25202018_EN_final.pdf.

11. "World Steel in Figures 2020."

12. The US iron and steel manufacturing industry has operated at a trade deficit, with imports exceeding exports by a factor of three. Jonathan Hadad, "Iron & Steel Manufacturing Industry in the US," IBISWorld Industry Report 33111, October 2018. (The 2020 update is available at https://www.ibisworld.com/united-states/market-research-reports/iron-steel-manufacturing-industry/.)

13. "Steel Facts," World Steel Association, accessed October 2020, https://www.worldsteel.org/about-steel/steel-facts.html.

14. "World Steel in Figures 2020."

15. Ibid.

16. Ibid.

17. Ibid.

18. "Coal: Uses of Coal, How Is Steel Produced?" World Coal Association, accessed July 2018, https://www.worldcoal.org/coal/uses-coal/how-steel-produced.

19. "Steel Facts."

20. "Coal: Uses of Coal, How Is Steel Produced?"

21. "Available and Emerging Technologies for Reducing Greenhouse Gas Emissions from the Iron and Steel Industry," US EPA Office of Air and Radiation, September 2012, https://www.epa.gov/sites/production/files/2015–12/documents/ironsteel.pdf.

22. "Steel Facts."

23. "Steel's Contribution to a Low Carbon Future," World Steel Association, accessed July 2018, https://www.worldsteel.org/publications/position-papers/steel-s-contribution-to-a-low-carbon-future.html.

24. "CCS for Iron and Steel Production," Global CCS Institute Insights, August 23, 2013, https://www.globalccsinstitute.com/insights/authors/dennisvanpuyvelde/2013/08/23/ccs-iron-and-steel-production.

25. "Available and Emerging Technologies for Reducing Greenhouse Gas Emissions from the Iron and Steel Industry."

26. "CCS for Iron and Steel Production."

27. "Available and Emerging Technologies for Reducing Greenhouse Gas Emissions from the Iron and Steel Industry."

28. Industrial Efficiency Technology Database, "Electric Arc Furnace," The Institute for Industrial Productivity, accessed July 2018, http://ietd.iipnetwork.org/content/electric-arc-furnace.

29. "Steel Statistical Yearbook 2019" (concise version), World Steel Association, https://www.worldsteel.org/steel-by-topic/statistics/steel-statistical-yearbook.html.

30. Luke Hickman, "The Rise of EAFs Provides Flexibility to Steel Producers," *Freedonia Focus Reports*, April 3, 2017, https://www.freedoniafocusreports.com/Content/Blog/2017/04/03/The-Rise-of-EAFs-Provides-Flexibility-to-Steel-Producers.

31. "Electric Arc Furnace Steelmaking Costs 2018," Steelonthenet.com, https://www.steelonthenet.com/cost-eaf.html; and "Basic Oxygen Furnace Route Steelmaking Costs 2018," Steelonthenet.com, both accessed September 2018, https://www.steelonthenet.com/cost-bof.html.

32. "Steel Statistical Yearbook 2019."

33. Zhong, "The Chinese Steel Industry at a Crossroads."

34. Frank Zhong, "Is It Time for China to Switch to Electric Arc Furnace Steelmaking?" World Steel Association (blog), February 13, 2018, https://www.worldsteel.org/media-centre/blog/2018/Is-it-time-for-China-to-switch-to-EAF-steelmaking.html.

35. Muyu Xu and Tom Daly, "China to Cut More Coal, Steel Output to Defend 'Blue Skies,'" Reuters, March 4, 2018, https://www.reuters.com/article/us-china-parliament-steel-coal/china-to-cut-more-coal-steel-output-to-defend-blue-skies-idUSKBN1GH034.

36. Avetik Chalabyan, Yuanpeng Li, Richard Tang, Steven Vercammen, Vivi Zhao, and Jane Zhou, "How Should Steelmakers Adapt at the Dawn of the EAF Mini-Mill Era in China?" McKinsey & Company Report, June 25, 2019, https://www.mckinsey.com/industries/metals-and-mining/our-insights/how-should-steelmakers-adapt-at-the-dawn-of-the-eaf-mini-mill-era-in-china.

37. "Steel Facts."

38. Ibid. Note that GJ = gigajoule, which is equivalent to 1 billion joules or 277 kWh of energy.

39. "Fact Sheet: Climate Change Mitigation by Technology, Innovation and Best Practice Transfer," World Steel Association, February 2018, https://www.worldsteel.org/en/dam/jcr:0191b72f-987c-4057-a104-6c06af8fbc2b/fact_technology%2520transfer_2018.pdf.

40. Simone Landolina and Araceli Fernandez, "Global Iron & Steel Technology Roadmap," presentation at the IEA Kick-Off Workshop, November 20, 2017, https://www.iea.org/media/workshops/2017/ieaglobalironsteeltechnologyroadmap/ISTRM_Session0_IEA_201117.pdf.

41. Based on information provided by the US Department of Energy, Energy Efficiency and Renewable Energy Office, July 2018.

42. "Charcoal from Renewable Forests for Carbon-Neutral Steel," ArcelorMittal, News and Media: Our Stories, accessed October 2018, https://corporate.arcelormittal. com/news-and-media/our-stories/charcoal-from-renewable.

43. Cédric Philibert, "Renewable Energy for Industry: From Green Energy to Green Materials and Fuels," IEA Insights Series 2017, https://www.iea.org/publications/insights /insightpublications/Renewable_Energy_for_Industry.pdf.

44. Sinistering is the compacting of iron ore and added minerals, using a combination of high heat and pressure, to prepare iron ore fines for the blast furnace stage.

45. Philibert,"Renewable Energy for Industry."

46. "Hydrogen-Based Steelmaking to Begin in Hamburg," ArcelorMittal, https:// corporate.arcelormittal.com/media/case-studies/hydrogen-based-steelmaking-to-be gin-in-hamburg.

47. Thomas Graedel, A. Dubreuil, Michael Gerst, Seiji Hashimoto, Yuichi Mori-guchi, Daniel Müller, Claudia Pena, et al., "Recycling Rates of Metals: A Status Report," World Resources Forum, 2011, https://www.wrforum.org/uneppublicationspdf /recycling-rates-of-metals.

48. "Iron and Steel Technology Roadmap," International Energy Agency, October 2020, https://www.iea.org/reports/iron-and-steel-technology-roadmap.

49. "Bandwidth Study on Energy Use and Potential Energy Saving Opportunities in US Iron and Steel Manufacturing," US Department of Energy, Energy Efficiency & Renewable Energy Office, June 2015, https://www.energy.gov/sites/prod/files/2015/08/f26/ iron_and_steel_bandwidth_report_0.pdf.

50. Avetik Chalabyan et al., "Tsunami, Spring Tide, or High Tide? The Growing Importance of Steel Scrap in China, McKinsey & Company, March 2017, https://www.mck insey.com/~/media/mckinsey/industries/metals%20and%20mining/our%20insights/ the%20growing%20importance%20of%20steel%20scrap%20in%20china/the-growing -importance-of-steel-scrap-in-china.ashx#:~:text=Obsolete%20scrap%20consumption %20in%20China,world%2C%20accounting%20for%20about%2047.

51. "Cement History," Understanding Cement, accessed June 2018, https://www. understanding-cement.com/history.html#.

52. "Joseph Aspdin's Portland Cement," Today in Science History, accessed June 2018, https://todayinsci.com/A/Aspdin_Joseph/AspdinJoseph-Cement.htm.

53. Cement and concrete often are used interchangeably. Concrete is a mixture of aggregates and paste. The aggregates are sand and gravel or crushed stone; the paste is water and Portland cement (the binder for the concrete).

54. Kishan Mudavath, "Difference Between Wet and Dry Process of Cement," We Civil Engineers (blog), March 28, 2018, https://wecivilengineers.wordpress. com/2018/03/28/difference-between-wet-and-dry-process-of-cement/.

55. Ibid.

56. "Manufacturing—The Cement Kiln," Understanding Cement, accessed June 2018, https://www.understanding-cement.com/kiln.html#.

57. Ernst Worrell and Christina Galitsky,. "Energy Efficiency Improvement and Cost Saving Opportunities for Cement Making: An ENERGY STAR Guide for Energy and

Plant Managers," US Environmental Protection Agency, March 2008, https://escholar
ship.org/uc/item/8wm6q3v3.

58. Lisa J. Hanle, Kamala R. Jayaraman, and Joshua S. Smith, "CO$_2$ Emissions Profile
of the US Cement Industry," US Environmental Protection Agency, accessed October
2018, https://www3.epa.gov/ttnchie1/conference/ei13/ghg/hanle.pdf.

59. "Economics of the US Cement Industry," Portland Cement Association, accessed
July 2018, http://www.cement.org/structures/manufacturing/Cement-Industry-Over
view.

60. "2013 Technology Map of the European Strategic Energy Technology Plan (SET-
Plan): Technology Descriptions, Chapter 20:1 The Cement Industry," Joint Research
Centre of the European Commission, April 9, 2014, http://hub.globalccsinstitute.com/
publications/2013-technology-map-european-strategic-energy-technology-plan-set
-plan-technology-descriptions/201-cement-industry.

61. "Mineral Commodity Summaries," US Geological Survey, January 2020, https://
pubs.usgs.gov/periodicals/mcs2020/mcs2020-cement.pdf.

62. "China: First in Cement," Global Cement, July 23, 2013, http://www.globalcement
.com/magazine/articles/796-china-first-in-cement.

63. L. Burange and Shruti Yamini, "Performance of Indian Cement Industry: The
Competitive Landscape," Working Paper (Table 3), Department of Economics, University of Mumbai, WP No.UDE(CAS)25/(9)/3/2008, September 2008, https://www.
researchgate.net/publication/280727328_Performance_of_Indian_Cement_Industry_
The_Competitive_Landscape.

64. "Vietnam Cement Report 2015," PR Newswire, April 20, 2016, https://www.
prnewswire.com/news-releases/vietnam-cement-report-2015-300254887.html.

65. "Cement Tracking Report," International Energy Agency, June 2020, https://
www.iea.org/reports/cement.

66. Dylan Miller, "Cement Manufacturing in the US," IBISWorld Industry Report
32731, June 2018, www.ibisworld.com.

67. Ibid.

68. Ibid.

69. Ibid.

70. "Mineral Commodity Summaries, 1998–2020 reports," US Geological Survey,
https://www.usgs.gov/centers/nmic/mineral-commodity-summaries.

71. "PCA: US Cement Demand to See Modest Decline in 2020–21," ICR Newsroom,
October 16, 2020, https://www.cemnet.com/News/story/169702/pca-us-cement-demand
-to-see-modest-decline-in-2020–21.html.

72. "Cement Production in the United States and Worldwide from 2010 to 2020,"
Statista, accessed May 5, 2021, https://www.statista.com/statistics/219343/cement
-production-worldwide/.

73. Ana Swanson, "How China Used More Cement in 3 Years than the U.S. Did
in the Entire 20th Century," *Washington Post*, March 24, 2015, https://www.washington
post.com/news/wonk/wp/2015/03/24/how-china-used-more-cement-in-3-years-than
-the-u-s-did-in-the-entire-20th-century/?utm_term=.8e38808da6b6.

74. Mineral Commodity Summaries, January 2020.

75. Zhou Cheng, "Interview with CUCC Chairman Cui Xingtai: The Chinese Cement Industry in 2020 and CUCC's COVID-19 Response," China Cement Net, World Cement Association, https://www.worldcementassociation.org/blog/news/interview-with-cucc-chairman-cui-xingtai-the-chinese-cement-industry-in-2020-and-cucc-s-covid-19-response.

76. "Global Cement Market to Reach 6.08 Billion Tons by 2026 (summary)," Expert Market Research, accessed March 4, 2021, https://www.expertmarketresearch.com/pressrelease/global-cement-market.

77. Cement Industry Overview, Portland Cement Association, https://www.cement.org/structures/manufacturing/Cement-Industry-Overview.

78. "Ranking of Selected Cement Manufacturers in FY 2017, Based on North American Revenue," Statista, accessed September 2018, https://www.statista.com/statistics/235293/leading-us-cement-manufacturers/.

79. Janet Mutegi, "World's 10 Largest Cement Companies," Construction Kenya, September 2, 2019, https://www.constructionkenya.com/5390/largest-cement-companies-world/.

80. Ibid.

81. Araceli Fernandez and Yvonne Leung, "Technology Roadmap: Low-Carbon Transition in the Cement Industry," International Energy Agency and the Cement Sustainability Initiative of the World Business Council for Sustainable Development, April 6, 2018, https://webstore.iea.org/technology-roadmap-low-carbon-transition-in-the-cement-industry.

82. N. A. Madlool, R. Saidur, M. S. Hossain, and N. A. Rahim, "A Critical Review on Energy Use and Savings in the Cement Industries," *Renewable and Sustainable Energy Reviews* 15, no. 4 (May 2011): 2042–2060, https://www.sciencedirect.com/science/article/pii/S1364032111000207.

83. Jos G. J. Olivier, Greet Janssens-Maenhout, Marilena Muntean, and Jeroen A. H. W. Peters, "Trends in Global CO_2 Emissions: 2016 Report," PBL Netherlands Environmental Assessment Agency and EU Joint Research Centre, 2016, http://edgar.jrc.ec.europa.eu/news_docs/jrc-2016-trends-in-global-co2-emissions-2016-report-103425.pdf.

84. Ibid.

85. "2016 U.S. Cement Industry Annual Yearbook, Table 50: Plant Fuel Mix," Portland Cement Association, http://www2.cement.org/econ/pdf/Yearbook2016_2sided.pdf.

86. "Cement: Tracking Clean Energy Progress," International Energy Agency, updated May 23, 2018, https://www.iea.org/tcep/industry/cement/.

87. Fernandez and Leung, "Technology Roadmap," p. 14, Fig. 2.

88. Worrell, Kermeli, and Galitsky, "Energy Efficiency Improvement and Cost Saving Opportunities for Cement Making," August 2013, US Environmental Protection Agency, https://www.energystar.gov/sites/default/files/buildings/tools/ENERGY%20STAR%20Guide%20for%20the%20Cement%20Industry%2028_08_2013%20Final.pdf.

89. Ibid.

90. "Available and Emerging Technologies for Reducing Greenhouse Gas Emissions from the Portland Cement Industry," US EPA Office of Air and Radiation, October 2010, https://www.epa.gov/sites/production/files/2015-12/documents/cement.pdf.

91. Ibid., p. 39.

92. "Increasing the Use of Alternative Fuels at Cement Plants: International Best Practice," International Finance Corporation (World Bank Group), 2017, https://www.ifc.org/wps/wcm/connect/cb361035-1872-4566-a7e7-d3d1441ad3ac/Alternative_Fuels_08+04.pdf?MOD=AJPERES.

93. Ibid.

94. "EREF Releases Analysis on National Landfill Tipping Fees," *Waste Today*, October 29, 2019, https://www.wastetodaymagazine.com/article/eref-releases-analysis-national-msw-landfill-tipping-fees/.

95. Ibid.; and Rob Watson, "The Cost to Landfill MSW in the US Continues to Rise Despite Soft Demand," July 10, 2017, https://nrra.net/sweep/the-cost-to-landfill-msw-in-the-us-continues-to-rise-despite-soft-demand/.

96. Fernandez and Leung, "Technology Roadmap."

97. "Cement Tracking Report, June 2020."

98. "Clinker Substitution: Five Parallel Routes: Resource Efficiency," Cembureau, accessed July 2018, http://lowcarboneconomy.cembureau.eu/index.php?page=clinker-substitution.

99. NRMCA Research Engineering and Standards Committee, "SIP 1—Limits on Quantity of Supplementary Cementitious Materials," Specification in Practice, National Ready Mixed Concrete Association, 2015, https://www.nrmca.org/aboutconcrete/downloads/SIP1.pdf.

100. Based on industry discussions.

101. Claude Goguen, "Portland-Limestone Cement," *Precast Inc. Magazine*, National Precast Concrete Association, June 2, 2014, https://precast.org/2014/06/portland-limestone-cement/.

102. "Global Green Cement Market 2017–2018," Allied Market Research, www.alliedmarketresearch.com; and "Cement Production Globally and in the U.S. from 2010 to 2017," Statista, accessed March 4, 2021, https://www.statista.com/statistics/219343/cement-production-worldwide/. Note that cementitious material made from industrial waste includes fly ash, steel slag, recycled aggregates, and others.

103. Ibid.

104. "Green Cement Market Size by Product, by Application, Industry Analysis Report, Regional Outlook, Growth Potential, Price Trend, Competitive Market Share & Forecast 2020–2026 (Summary)," Global Market Insights, October 2020, https://www.gminsights.com/industry-analysis/green-cement-market.

105. "Global Green Cement Market to Cross USD 678.2 Mn by 2026 (Summary)," Global Market Insights, October 27, 2020, https://www.globenewswire.com/news-release/2020/10/27/2114904/0/en/Global-Green-Cement-Market-to-cross-USD-678-2-Mn-by-2026-Global-Market-Insights-Inc.html.

106. "Solutions," Solidia, accessed September 2020, https://www.solidiatech.com/solutions.html.

107. Sean Monkman and Mark MacDonald, "Making Concrete with Carbon Dioxide," Concrete Construction, May 15, 2017, https://www.concreteconstruction.net/concrete-production-precast/making-concrete-with-carbon-dioxide_o.

108. "Technology," CarbonCure, accessed July 2018, https://www.carboncure.com/technology/.

109. "Technology," Carbicrete, accessed July 2018, http://carbicrete.com/technology/.

110. "About Us," Carbon Capture Machine, https://ccmuk.com/ and Carbon Upcycling UCLA, http://www.co2upcycling.com/ (both accessed September 2018).

111. "E-Crete," The Zeobond Group, http://www.zeobond.com/products-e-crete.html; and "Earth Friendly Concrete," Wagners, https://www.wagner.com.au/main/what-we-do/ earth-friendly-concrete/efc-home (both accessed September 2018).

112. "World's First Public Building with Structural Geopolymer Concrete," Geopolymer Instutute, October 18, 2013, https://www.geopolymer.org/news/worlds-first-public-building-with-structural-geopolymer-concrete/.

113. "Petrochemicals and EPCA: A Passionate Journey," European Petrochemical Association, accessed August 2018, https://epca.eu/ebooks/history/index.html#1/z.

114. Ibid.

115. Ibid.

116. Eren Cetinkaya, Nathan Liu, Theo Jan Simons, and Jeremy Wallach, "Petrochemicals 2030: Reinventing the Way to Win in a Changing Industry," McKinsey & Company Chemicals, February 2018, https://www.mckinsey.com/industries/chemicals/our-insights/petrochemicals-2030-reinventing-the-way-to-win-in-a-changing-industry.

117. Tayeb Benchaita, "Greenhouse Gas Emissions from New Petrochemical Plants," Inter-American Development Bank, Environmental Safeguards Unit,Technical Note No. IDB-TN-562, July 2013, https://publications.iadb.org/bitstream/handle/11319/5962/Greenhouse%20Gas%20Emissions%20from%20New%20Petrochemical%20Plants%20.pdf;sequence=1.

118. Scott Carpenter, "Why the Oil Industry's $400 Billion Bet on Plastics Could Backfire," Forbes, September 5, 2020, https://www.forbes.com/sites/scottcarpenter/2020/09/05/why-the-oil-industrys-400-billion-bet-on-plastics-could-backfire/?sh=23d8834c43fe.

119. Darshan Kalyani, "Petrochemical Manufacturing in the US," IBISWorld Industry Report 32511, December 2017, www.ibisworld.com.

120. Heather Doyle, "US Chemical Capacity to Increase by More Than 50 Million Tonnes," Petrochemical Update, May 18, 2018, http://analysis.petchem-update.com/engineering-and-construction/us-chemical-capacity-increase-more-50-million-tonnes.

121. "Petrochemicals and EPCA: A Passionate Journey."

122. "2020 Facts and Figures of the European Chemical Industry," European Chemical Industry Council, https://cefic.org/app/uploads/2019/01/The-European-Chemical-Industry-Facts-And-Figures-2020.pdf.

123. Florian Budde, Obi Ezekoye, Thomas Hundertmark, Manuel Prieto, and Theo Jan Simons, "Chemicals 2025: Will the Industry Be Dancing to a Very Different Tune?" McKinsey & Company, March 14, 2017, https://www.mckinsey.com/industries /chemicals/our-insights/chemicals-2025-will-the-industry-be-dancing-to-a-very -different-tune.

124. "Technology Roadmap: Energy and GHG Reductions in the Chemical Industry via Catalyic Processes," International Energy Agency, International Council of Chemical Associations, and DECHEMA, May 2013, https://webstore.iea.org/technology-road map-energy-and-ghg-reductions-in-the-chemical-industry-via-catalytic-processes.

125. "Inventory of US Greenhouse Gas Emissions and Sinks: 1990–2016," US Environmental Protection Agency, April 12, 2018, https://www.epa.gov/sites/production/ files/2018–01/documents/2018_complete_report.pdf.

126. Zachary J. Schiffer and Karthish Manthiram, "Electrification and Decarbonization of the Chemical Industry," *Joule* 1, nos. 10–14 (September 6, 2017), https://www.cell. com/joule/pdf/S2542–4351(17)30015–6.pdf.

127. Benchaita, "Greenhouse Gas Emissions from New Petrochemical Plants."

128. Schiffer and Manthiram, "Electrification and Decarbonization of the Chemical Industry."

129. "Technology Roadmap: Energy and GHG Reductions in the Chemical Industry via Catalyic Processes."

130. Greenhouse Gas Reporting Program, "GHGRP Chemicals, Trend of Annual Reported GHG Emissions from Chemicals," US Environmental Protection Agency, September 26, 2020, https://www.epa.gov/ghgreporting/ghgrp-chemicals#trends -subsector.

131. Benchaita, "Greenhouse Gas Emissions from New Petrochemical Plants."

132. Ibid.

133. Ibid.

134. "Tracking Industry 2020," International Energy Agency, June 2020, https:// www.iea.org/reports/tracking-industry-2020.

135. Ibid.

136. Ibid.

137. "Technology Roadmap: Energy and GHG Reductions in the Chemical Industry via Catalytic Processes."

138. Daniel Posen, Paulina Jaramillo, Amy E. Landis, and W. Michael Griffin, "Greenhouse Gas Mitigation for U.S. Plastics Production: Energy First, Feedstocks Later," IOP Science, *Environmental Research Letters* 12, no. 3 (March 16, 2017), http:// iopscience.iop.org/article/10.1088/1748–9326/aa60a7.

139. Renee Cho, "The Truth About Bioplastics," *State of the Planet: Sustainability* (blog), Earth Institute, Columbia University, December 13, 2017, https://blogs. ei.columbia.edu/2017/12/13/the-truth-about-bioplastics/.

140. Bernard Marr, "The 4th Industrial Revolution Is Here—Are You Ready?" *Forbes*, August 13, 2018, https://www.forbes.com/sites/bernardmarr/2018/08/13/the-4th -industrial-revolution-is-here-are-you-ready/#22297bc9628b.

141. Binny Samuel, "What Does a Manufacturing Plant of the Future Look Like? (Part 1)," *Internet of Things* (blog), IBM, November 21, 2017, https://www.ibm.com/blogs/internet-of-things/iot-plant-future-part-1/.

142. "Impact of the Fourth Industrial Revolution on Supply Chains," World Economic Forum, October 2017, http://www3.weforum.org/docs/WEF_Impact_of_the_Fourth_Industrial_Revolution_on_Supply_Chains_.pdf.

143. Avetik Chalabyan, Elena Jänsch, Tom Niemann, Tobias Otto, Benedikt Zeumer, and Ksenia Zhuravleva, "How 3-D Printing Will Transform the Metals Industry," McKinsey & Company Metals and Mining, August 2017, https://www.mckinsey.com/industries/metals-and-mining/our-insights/how-3d-printing-will-transform-the-metals-industry; Jason Bordoff, "How 3-D Printing Could Decrease Carbon Emissions. Or Maybe Increase Them," *Leadership* (blog), *Wall Street Journal*, June 8, 2016, https://blogs.wsj.com/experts/2016/06/08/how-3-d-printing-could-decrease-carbon-emissions-or-maybe-increase-them/.

144. "Technology Roadmap: Low-Carbon Transition in the Cement Industry."

145. Compound annual growth rate (CAGR) is defined as the mean annual growth rate of an investment over a specified period of time longer than one year.

146. "Technology Roadmap: Low-Carbon Transition in the Cement Industry."

147. "Iron and Steel Technology Roadmap," International Energy Agency, October 2020, https://www.iea.org/reports/iron-and-steel-technology-roadmap.

148. Becky E. Hites, "The Growth of EAF Steelmaking," *Recycling Today*, April 2020, http://magazine.recyclingtoday.com/article/april-2020/the-growth-of-eaf-steelmaking.aspx.

149. "The Future of Petrochemicals: Toward a More Sustainable Chemical Industry," International Energy Agency, October 2018, https://www.iea.org/reports/the-future-of-petrochemicals.

150. "Technology Roadmap Energy and GHG Reductions in the Chemical Industry via Catalytic Processes."

151. "Manufacturing a Brighter Tomorrow," Breakthrough Energy, accessed August 2018, http://www.b-t.energy/.

152. "Federal Science Budget Tracker, Fiscal Year 2018," American Institute of Physics, https://www.aip.org/fyi/federal-science-budget-tracker/FY2018#tabs-section-doe-applied-energy.

153. "Final FY18 Appropriations: DOE Applied Energy R&D," American Institute of Physics, April 10, 2018, https://www.aip.org/fyi/2018/final-fy18-appropriations-doe-applied-energy-rd.

154. "Federal Science Budget Tracker, Fiscal Year 2019."

155. Philibert, "Renewable Energy for Industry."

156. "Harnessing the Sun to Clean up Industrial Processes," SOLPART, February 2020, https://www.solpart-project.eu/wp-content/uploads/2020/02/SOLPART-final-brochure.pdf.

157. Ibid.

158. Heliogen, accessed November 2020, https://heliogen.com/.

159. Jonathan Shieber, "Heliogen's New Tech Could Unlock Renewable Energy for Industrial Manufacturing," TechCrunch, November 19, 2019, https://techcrunch.com/2019/11/19/heliogens-new-technology-could-unlock-renewable-energy-for-industrial-manufacturing/.

160. Elie Bellevrat and Kira West, "Clean and Efficient Heat for Industry," International Energy Agency, January 23, 2018, https://www.iea.org/newsroom/news/2018/january/commentary-clean-and-efficient-heat-for-industry.html.

161. Linda Hardesty, "It Takes 2.8 Acres of Land to Generate 1GWh of Solar Energy Per Year, Says NREL," Energy Manager Today, August 1, 2013, https://www.energymanagertoday.com/it-takes-2-8-acres-of-land-to-generate-1gwh-of-solar-energy-per-year-says-nrel-094185/.

162. Eric Wesoff, "US Steel Mill to Get Powered by 300 MW of Solar," PV Magazine, October 5, 2020, https://www.pv-magazine.com/2020/10/05/us-steel-mill-to-get-powered-by-300-mw-of-solar/.

163. Ibid.

164. Amel Ahmed, "California Cap-and-Trade Is Working—For Other States," PBS News Hour, July 15, 2018, https://www.pbs.org/newshour/science/california-cap-and-trade-is-working-for-other-states.

165. Olivier, Janssens-Maenhout, Muntean, and Peters, "Trends in Global CO_2 Emissions: 2016 Report."

166. Emma Foehringer Merchant, "Can Updated Tax Credits Bring Carbon Capture into the Mainstream?" Greentech Media, February 22, 2018, https://www.greentechmedia.com/articles/read/can-updated-tax-credits-make-carbon-capture-mainstream#gs.wljfACQ.

167. James Temple, "The Carbon-Capture Era May Finally Be Starting," MIT Technology Review, February 20, 2018, https://www.technologyreview.com/s/610296/the-carbon-capture-era-may-finally-be-starting/.

168. Ibid.

169. Ibid.

170. Jan Theulen, "From CO2 to Fish Feed," HeidelbergCement, October 23, 2019, https://blog.heidelbergcement.com/en/from-co2-to-fish-feed.

171. Hadad, "Iron & Steel Manufacturing in the US."

172. Miller, "Cement Manufacturing in the US."

173. LEED Certification, Slag Cement Association, accessed October 2018, https://www.slagcement.org/sustainability/leedcertification.aspx.

174. Stephen Nellis, "Apple Buys First-Ever Carbon-Free Aluminum from Alcoa-Rio Tinto Venture," Reuters, December 5, 2019, https://www.reuters.com/article/us-apple-aluminum/apple-buys-first-ever-carbon-free-aluminum-from-alcoa-rio-tinto-venture-idUSKBN1Y91RQ.

175. Ibid.

176. "2019 U.S. Consumer Sustainability Survey," CGS, accessed March 4, 2021, https://www.cgsinc.com/en/infographics/CGS-Survey-Reveals-Sustainability-Is-Driving-Demand-and-Customer-Loyalty.

177. "More Than Half of Consumers Would Pay More for Sustainable Products Designed to Be Reused or Recycled, Accenture Survey Finds," Accenture News Room, June 4, 2019, https://newsroom.accenture.com/news/more-than-half-of-consumers-would-pay-more-for-sustainable-products-designed-to-be-reused-or-recycled-accenture-survey-finds.htm.

178. "2019 Retail Sustainability Infographic," CGS, accessed March 4, 2021, https://www.cgsinc.com/sites/default/files/media/resources/pdf/CGS_2019_Retail_Sustainability_infographic.pdf.

CHAPTER 5: THE BUILDINGS SECTOR

1. "68% of the World Population Projected to Live in Urban Areas by 2050, says UN," UN Department of Economic and Social Affairs, May 6, 2018, https://www.un.org/development/desa/en/news/population/2018-revision-of-world-urbanization-prospects.html.

2. Ibid.

3. Vanessa Bertollini, "Here's What Building the Future Looks Like for a 10-Billion-Person Planet," Autodesk, August 24, 2018, https://www.autodesk.com/redshift/building-the-future/.

4. "About MaterialsCAN," Interface, accessed September 2020, https://www.interface.com/US/en-US/campaign/transparency/materialsCAN-en_US.

5. "2019 Global Status Report for Buildings and Construction: Towards a Zero-Emission, Efficient and Resilient Buildings and Construction Sector," Global Alliance for Buildings and Contruction, UN Environment and IEA, https://www.worldgbc.org/sites/default/files/2019%20Global%20Status%20Repor%20ofor%20Buildings%20and%20Construction.pdf.

6. Ibid.

7. Ibid.

8. "Global Status Report 2017 for Buildings and Construction: Towards a Zero-Emission, Efficient, and Resilient Buildings and Construction Sector," Global Alliance for Buildings and Construction, UN Environment and IEA, https://www.worldgbc.org/sites/default/files/UNEP%20188_GABC_en%20%28web%29.pdf.

9. "Global Energy Consumption Driven More by Electricity in Residential, Commercial Buildings," Today in Energy, US Energy Information Administration, October 21, 2019, https://www.eia.gov/todayinenergy/detail.php?id=41753.

10. O. Lucon, D. Ürge-Vorsatz, A. Zain Ahmed, H. Akbari, P. Bertoldi, L.F. Cabeza, N. Eyre, et al., "Buildings," in: *Climate Change 2014: Mitigation of Climate Change.*, contribution of Working Group III to the Fifth Assessment Report of the Intergovernmental Panel on Climate Change, ed. O. Edenhofer,et al. (Cambridge, UK, and New York: Cambridge University Press, 2014), https://www.ipcc.ch/site/assets/uploads/2018/02/ipcc_wg3_ar5_chapter9.pdf.

11. "EIA Updates Its U.S. Energy Consumption by Source and Sector Chart," Today in Energy, US Energy Information Administration, August 28, 2019, https://www.eia.gov/todayinenergy/detail.php?id=41093.

12. "Data and Statistics, World Industry Balances 2019," International Energy Agency, www.iea.org/data-and-statistics.

13. "2019 Global Status Report for Buildings and Construction."

14. Adela Muresan, "Who Lives Largest? The Growth of Urban American Homes in the Last 100 Years," Property Shark, September 8, 2016, https://www.propertyshark.com/Real-Estate-Reports/2016/09/08/the-growth-of-urban-american-homes-in-the-last-100-years/.

15. "Characteristics of New Housing, Highlights of 2019," United States Census Bureau, https://www.census.gov/construction/chars/highlights.html.

16. Ibid.

17. "Carbon Dioxide Emissions Grow in the Residential Sector," Today in Energy, US Energy Information Administration, June 27, 2011, https://www.eia.gov/todayinenergy/detail.php?id=1970.

18. "EIA Updates Its U.S. Energy Consumption by Source and Sector Chart."

19. "Residential Consumption Survey," US Energy Information Administration, 2015, https://www.eia.gov/consumption/residential/data/2015/.

20. "Tracking Buildings: Appliances and Equipment," International Energy Agency, June 2020, https://www.iea.org/reports/tracking-buildings/appliances-and-equipment.

21. "The Future of Cooling," International Energy Agency, May 2018, https://www.iea.org/reports/the-future-of-cooling.

22. International Energy Agency data and statistics website, https://www.iea.org.

23. "Electrification of Buildings and Industry in the United States, Lawrence Berkeley National Laboratory, March 2018.

24. "2015 Residential Energy Consumption Survey (RECS)," US Energy Information Administration, revised May 31, 2018, https://www.eia.gov/consumption/residential/reports/2015/overview/index.php?src=%E2%80%B9%20Consumption%20%20%20%20%20Residential%20Energy%20Consumption%20Survey%20(RECS)-f3.

25. Ibid.

26. "Heating Oil Explained (2018 data)," US Energy Information Administration, https://www.eia.gov/energyexplained/heating-oil/use-of-heating-oil.php.

27. "Use of Energy Explained: Energy Use in Homes (2015 data)," US Energy Information Administration, https://www.eia.gov/energyexplained/index.php?page=us_energy_homes.

28. "2015 Residential Energy Consumption Survey (RECS)."

29. A degree day, as defined by EIA, "compares the mean (the average of the high and low) outdoor temperatures recorded for a location to a standard temperature, usually 65° Fahrenheit in the United States." Heating degree day is "a measure of how cold the temperature was on a given day or during a period of days."

30. "Monthly Energy Review," US Energy Information Administration, March 2020, https://www.eia.gov/totalenergy/data/monthly/archive/00352003.pdf.

31. "International Energy Outlook 2019 with Projections to 2050," US Energy Information Administration, September 24, 2019, https://www.eia.gov/ieo.

32. Ibid.

33. "Energy Efficiency Indicators 2019, Statistics Report—December 2019," International Energy Agency, https://www.iea.org/reports/energy-efficiency-indicators-2019.

34. "International Energy Outlook 2019."

35. "EIA Updates Its U.S. Energy Consumption by Source and Sector Chart."

36. "Data and Statistics, World Industry Balances 2019," International Energy Agency, www.iea.org/data-and-statistics.

37. "Why the Buildings Sector?" Architecture 2030, accessed June 2020, https://architecture2030.org/buildings_problem_why/.

38. "Use of Energy Explained: Energy Use in Commercial Buildings (2012 data)," US Energy Information Administration, https://www.eia.gov/energyexplained/use-of-energy/commercial-buildings-in-depth.php.

39. Jessica Leung, "Decarbonizing U.S. Buildings," Center for Climate and Energy Solutions, July 2018, https://www.c2es.org/document/decarbonizing-u-s-buildings/.

40. "US Energy Facts Explained," US Energy Information Administration, updated May 2020, https://www.eia.gov/energyexplained/us-energy-facts/.

41. "Uncovering the US Natural Gas Commercial Sector," American Gas Association, January 2017, https://www.aga.org/contentassets/70b4444e883f479ba0efa91a901 40f33/uncovering_the_us_natural_gas_commercial_sector_final.pdf.

42. Ibid.

43. Ibid.

44. "EIA Updates Its U.S. Energy Consumption by Source and Sector Charts."

45. "Global Status Report 2017 for Buildings and Construction."

46. Parag Rastogi, Sönke Frederik Horn, Marilyne Andersen, and Werner Lang, "Towards Assessing the Sensitivity of Buildings to Changes in Climate," PLEA 2013: 29th Passive and Low Energy Architecture Conference, Munich, Germany, September 10–12, 2013, https://infoscience.epfl.ch/record/187507.

47. "Choosing and Installing Geothermal Heat Pumps," US Department of Energy, accessed June 2020, https://www.energy.gov/energysaver/choosing-and-installing -geothermal-heat-pumps.

48. Mark Schultz, "How Much Does a Geothermal Heat System Cost? Earth River Geothermal (blog), https://earthrivergeothermal.com/how-much-does-a-geothermal -heat-pump-system-cost/.

49. "Water Heater Buying Guide," *Consumer Reports*, February 12, 2020, https://www.consumerreports.org/cro/water-heaters/buying-guide/index.htm.

50. "Cost Savings Comparison," Washington Gas, accessed April 2020, https://www.washingtongas.com/home-owners/savings/cost-savings.

51. "Electricity Rates by State," Choose Energy, accessed May 2020, https://www.chooseenergy.com/electricity-rates-by-state/.

52. "Natural Gas and Electricity," CenterPoint Energy, accessed May 2020, https://www.centerpointenergy.com/en-us/Services/Pages/natural-gas-electricity-cost-com parison.aspx?sa=mn&au=bus.

53. Paul Hope, "Gas or Electric Range: Which One Is Better? *Consumer Reports*, November 22, 2019, https://www.consumerreports.org/ranges/gas-or-electric-range -which-is-better/.

54. "How Much Does It Cost to Install a Heat Pump?" Improvenet, July 26, 2018, https://www.improvenet.com/r/costs-and-prices/heat-pump-installation-cost-estimator.

55. Paige Jadun, Colin McMillan, Daniel Steinberg, Matteo Muratori, Laura Vimmer-stedt, and Trieu Mai, *Electrification Futures Study: End-Use Electric Technology Cost and Performance Projections Through 2050* (Golden, CO: National Renewable Energy Labora-tory, 2017), NREL/TP-6A20–70485, https://www.nrel.gov/docs/fy18osti/70485.pdf.

56. Ibid.

57. Sherri Billimoria, Leia Guccione, Mike Henchen, and Leah Louis-Prescott, "The Economics of Electrifying Buildings," Rocky Mountain Institute, 2018, https://rmi.org/ insight/the-economics-of-electrifying-buildings/.

58. Ibid.

59. Ibid.

60. "Residential Heat Pump Market Size, Share & Trends Analysis Report by Tech-nology (Air to Air, Water Source), by Power Source (Electric Powered, Gas Powered), by Region, and Segment Forecasts, 2019–2025 (summary)," Grandview Research, Sep-tember 2019, https://www.grandviewresearch.com/industry-analysis/residential-heat -pump-market.

61. Christopher Curtland, "VRF Systems in the US Market," *Buildings Industry News*, April 27, 2012, https://www.buildings.com/article-details/articleid/13997/title/vrf -systems-emerging-in-us-market.

62. "A Complete Guide to VRF Systems," Del-Air Mechanical Contractors Inc., De-cember 2, 2019, https://www.delairmechanical.com/blog/2019/december/a-complete -guide-to-vrf-systems/.

63. Chris Badger, "Variable Refrigerant Flow (VRF) Market Strategies Report," Northeast Energy Efficiency Partnerships, September 2019, https://neep.org/variable -refrigerant-flow-vrf-market-strategies-report.

64. Ibid.

65. Jadun et al., *Electrification Futures Study*.

66. "Reducing Costs and Achieving Value with VRF Systems," 2019 White Paper, Mitsubishi Electric Trane HVAC US, https://cms.mitsubishipro.com/files/documents/ Reducing%20Costs%20and%20Achieving%20Value%20with%20VRF%20Systems.pdf.

67. "What Is the Average Utility Cost Per Square Foot of Commercial Property? Iota Communications, July 23, 2020, https://www.iotacommunications.com/blog/average -utility-cost-per-square-foot-commercial-property/.

68. "2018 Sustainability Report," Kilroy Realty Corporation, https://kilroyrealty. com/sites/default/files/kilroy-realty-corporation-sustainability-report-2018.pdf.

69. "Infographic: Net Zero or Zero Carbon? Green Buildings Explained," Proud Green Building, accessed May 2020, https://www.proudgreenbuilding.com/news/info graphic-net-zero-or-zero-carbon-green-buildings-explained/.

70. Global Status Report 2019 for Buildings and Construction.

71. "Embodied Carbon in Building Materials for Real Estate," Urban Land Institute Greenprint, November 2019, https://americas.uli.org/191119embodiedcarbon/.

72. Rima Sabrina Aouf, "Embodied Carbon in Construction Calculator Launches to Tackle Industry Emissions," dezeen, February 21, 2020, https://www.dezeen.com/2020/02/21/embodied-carbon-in-construction-calculator/.

73. "Embodied Carbon in Construction Calculator," Building Transparency, accessed June 2020, https://www.buildingtransparency.org/en/.

74. Jean Lotus, "Hemp Used for Construction Gains Popularity in U.S.," UPI, July 18, 2019, https://www.upi.com/Top_News/US/2019/07/18/Hemp-used-for-construction-gains-popularity-in-US/6831563287029/.

75. Ibid.

76. Ibid.

77. Swinerton Builders, "Critical Mass: Why Builders Are Increasingly Opting for Engineered Timber Products," *Pudget Sound Business Journal*, April 1, 2019, https://www.bizjournals.com/seattle/feature/table-of-experts/critical-mass-why-builders-are-increasingly-opting.html.

78. Potsdam Institute for Climate Impact Research, "Buildings Can Become a Global CO_2 Sink If Made Out of Wood Instead of Cement and Steel," *Science Daily*, https://www.sciencedaily.com/releases/2020/01/200127134828.htm.

79. Ibid.

80. "About Green Roofs," Green Roofs for Healthy Cities, accessed May 2020, https://greenroofs.org/about-green-roofs.

81. Takanori Kuronuma, Hitoshi Watanabe, Tatsuaki Ishihara, Daitoku Kou, Kazunari Toushima, Masaya Ando, and Satoshi Shindo, "CO_2 Payoff of Extensive Green Roofs with Different Vegetation Species," *Sustainability* 10, no. 7 (2018): 2256, 10.3390/su10072256, https://www.researchgate.net/publication/326134431_CO2_Payoff_of_Extensive_Green_Roofs_with_Different_Vegetation_Species.

82. Muhammad Shafique, Xiaolong Xue, and Xiaowei Luo, "An Overview of Carbon Sequestration of Green Roofs in Urban Areas, *Urban Forestry & Urban Greening* 47 (2020): 126515, ISSN 1618–8667, https://doi.org/10.1016/j.ufug.2019.126515, http://www.sciencedirect.com/science/article/pii/S1618866719303668.

83. "Levelized Cost of Energy Analysis—Version 13.0," Lazard, November 2019, https://www.lazard.com/media/451086/lazards-levelized-cost-of-energy-version-130-vf.pdf.

84. Ibid.

85. Sarah Mikhitarian, "Homes with Solar Panels Sell for 4.1% More," Zillow, April 16, 2017, https://www.zillow.com/research/solar-panels-house-sell-more-23798/.

86. "Cumulative U.S. Solar Additions," SEIA Solar Industry Research Data, accessed December 9, 2020, https://www.seia.org/solar-industry-research-data.

87. Mikhitarian, "Homes with Solar Panels Sell for 4.1% More."

88. "Zero Carbon Buildings for All," World Resources Institute, accessed June 2020, https://wrirosscities.org/ZeroCarbonBuildings.

89. "The 2030 Challenge," Architecture 2030, accessed June 2020, https://architecture2030.org/2030_challenges/2030-challenge/.

90. Bridget Cogley, "AIA Makes Climate Crisis Top Priority," dezeen, September 19, 2019, https://www.dezeen.com/2019/09/19/aia-climate-change-action-statement/.

91. "San Francisco International Airport," Blue Planet, accessed May 2020, http://www.blueplanet-ltd.com/#services.

92. Justin Gerdes, "A Boom Is Coming for All-Electric Homes Despite Lagging Consumer Awareness," Greentech Media, March 25, 2020, https://www.greentechmedia.com/articles/read/a-boom-is-coming-for-all-electric-homes-despite-lag-in-consumer-awareness.

93. Erik J. Martin, "Top Green Features Home Buyers Want in 2019," HSH, June 13, 2019, https://www.hsh.com/first-time-homebuyer/top-green-home-features-buyers-want.html.

94. "Quick Start Guide MLS Green Fields, Edition 1," Council of Multiple Listings Services, 2018, https://cdn.ymaws.com/members.councilofmls.org/resource/resmgr/files/CMLSQuickGreenFields.pdf.

95. "Study Finds Green Home Building Continues to Gain Traction," National Association of Home Builders, September 27, 2017, https://www.nahb.org/News-and-Economics/Industry-News/Press-Releases/2017/09/study-finds-green-home-building-continues-to-gain-traction.

96. "World Green Building Trends 2018 Smartmarket Report," Dodge Data and Analytics, https://www.worldgbc.org/sites/default/files/World%20Green%20Building%20Trends%202018%20SMR%20FINAL%2010–11.pdf.

97. WELL Building Standard (V2), https://www.wellcertified.com/certification/v2/.

98. Daniel Overbey, "Why the 2018 IgCC Is Critical to the Future of Green Building," Building Enclosure, January 23, 2019, https://www.buildingenclosureonline.com/blogs/14-the-be-blog/post/88027-why-the-2018-igcc-is-critical-to-the-future-of-green-building.

99. "Overview of the International Green Construction Code," International Code Council, accessed June 2020, https://www.iccsafe.org/products-and-services/i-codes/2018-i-codes/igcc/.

100. Leung, "Decarbonizing U.S. Buildings."

101. "Why LEED?" US Green Buildings Council, https://www.usgbc.org/leed/why-leed; and "ENERGY STAR Certification for Your Buildings," US EPA ENERGY STAR, both accessed May 2020, https://www.energystar.gov/buildings/facility-owners-and-managers/existing-buildings/earn-recognition/energy-star-certification.

102. "Green Building Certifications at All Time High in Nation's Largest Metros," CBRE, August 23, 2018, https://www.cbre.us/about/media-center/2018-us-green-building-adoption-index.

103. "LEED Zero," US Green Buildings Council, accessed May 2020, https://www.usgbc.org/programs/leed-zero.

104. "Embodied Carbon in Building Materials for Real Estate," Urban Land Institute Americas, accessed May 5, 2021, https://americas.uli.org/research/centers-initiatives/greenprint-center/greenprint-resources-2/best-practices-in-sustainable-real-estate/embodied-carbon-in-building-materials-for-real-estate/.

105. Paul Melton, "The Urgency of Embodied Carbon and What You Can Do About It," Building Green, September 10, 2018, https://www.buildinggreen.com/feature/urgency-embodied-carbon-and-what-you-can-do-about-it.

106. "Advancing Net Zero," World Green Building Council, accessed June 2020, https://www.worldgbc.org/advancing-net-zero.

107. "WorldGBC's Net Zero Carbon Building Commitment Surpasses 80 Signatories," World Green Building Council, accessed June 2020, https://www.worldgbc.org/news-media/worldgbc%E2%80%99s-net-zero-carbon-building-commitment-surpasses-80-signatories.

108. "Bringing Embodied Carbon Upfront," World Green Building Council, accessed June 2020, https://www.worldgbc.org/embodied-carbon.

109. "Zero Carbon Certification," International Living Future Institute, accessed June 2020, https://living-future.org/zero-carbon-certification/.

110. Ibid.

111. "Zero Energy Home Certification," Zero Energy Project, accessed June 2020, https://zeroenergyproject.org/build/certifying-zero-energy-home-performance/.

112. Niina Leskinen, Jussi Vimpari, and Seppo Junnila, "A Review of the Impact of Green Building Certification on the Cash Flows and Values of Commercial Properties," *Sustainability* 12 (March 31, 2020): 2729, doi:10.3390/su12072729, file:///C:/Users/DuffR/Downloads/sustainability-12–02729-v2%20(1).pdf.

113. Jonathan Mingle, "To Cut Carbon Emissions, a Movement Grows to 'Electrify Everything,'" *Yale Environment 360*, April 14, 2020, https://e360.yale.edu/features/to-cut-carbon-emissions-a-movement-grows-to-electrify-everything.

114. Ibid.

115. Ibid.

116. "C40 Cities Annual Report 2019," C40 Cities Climate Leadership Group, Inc., https://c40-production-images.s3.amazonaws.com/other_uploads/images/2574_C40_2019_Annual_Report.original.pdf?1587634742.

117. Ibid.

118. Brad Smith, "Microsoft Will Be Carbon Negative by 2030," Microsoft (blog), January 16, 2020, https://blogs.microsoft.com/blog/2020/01/16/microsoft-will-be-carbon-negative-by-2030/.

119. Heather Clancy, Microsoft's Quest to Go 'Carbon Negative' Inspires $1B Fund," Greenbiz, January 16, 2020, https://www.greenbiz.com/article/microsofts-quest-go-carbon-negative-inspires-1b-fund.

120. "The Net Zero Carbon Buildings Commitment," World Green Building Council, accessed June 2020, https://www.worldgbc.org/thecommitment.

121. "Commitment Signatories," World Green Building Council, accessed June 2020, https://www.worldgbc.org/commitment-signatories?cat=business.

122. "Zero Carbon Buildings for All," World Resources Institute and Global Alliance for Buildings and Construction, accessed May 2020, https://globalabc.org/about/about-globalabc.

123. Urban Land Institute Greenprint Embodied Carbon Report.

124. Amber Mahone, Charles Li, Zack Subin, Michael Sontag, Gabe Mantegna, Alexis Karolides, Alea German, and Peter Morris, "Residential Building Electrification in California April 2019: Consumer Economics, Greenhouse Gases and Grid Impacts," Energy and Environmental Economics Inc., April 2019, https://www.ethree.com/wp-content/uploads/2019/04/E3_Residential_Building_Electrification_in_California_April_2019.pdf; and Alisa Petersen, Michael Gartman, and Jacob Corvidae, "The Economics of Zero Energy Homes: Single Family Insights," Rocky Mountain Institute, updated 2019, https://rmi.org/wp-content/uploads/2018/10/RMI_Economics_of_Zero_Energy_Homes_2018.pdf.

125. Amanda Voss, "Do Energy Retrofits Pay?" *ProRemodeler*, November 12, 2015, https://www.proremodeler.com/do-energy-retrofits-pay.

126. Conversations with industry experts.

127. Conversations with industry experts.

128. Conversations with industry experts.

129. "A Whole House Approach to Energy Efficiency," Sacramento Municipal Utility District, accessed May 2020, https://www.smud.org/en/Rebates-and-Savings-Tips/Improve-Home-Efficiency.

130. Robert Walton, "Massachusetts Approves 3-Year Efficiency Plan with First Fuel-Switching Incentives," Utility Dive, January 20, 2019, https://www.utilitydive.com/news/massachusetts-approves-3-year-efficiency-plan-with-first-fuel-switching-inc/547237/.

131. "Decision Modifying the Energy Efficiency Three-Prong Test Related to Fuel Substitution," Public Utilities Proposed Decision, Agenda ID #17555 (REV. 1), Ratesetting, Item 24, Commission of the State of California, August 1, 2019, https://docs.cpuc.ca.gov/PublishedDocs/Published/G000/M310/K053/310053527.PDF.

132. "Property Assessed Clean Energy Programs," US Department of Energy, accessed June 2020, https://www.energy.gov/eere/slsc/property-assessed-clean-energy-programs.

133. Ibid.

134. Kathryn Cleary and Karen Palmer, "Energy-as-a-Service: A Business Model for Expanding Deployment of Low-Carbon Technologies," Resources for the Future, December 2019, https://media.rff.org/documents/IB_19-09_EaaS.pdf.

135. Metrus, https://www.metrusenergy.com/: and SparkFund, https://www.sparkfund.com/.

136. "2015 Green Bond Market Roundup," The Climate Bonds Initiative, https://www.climatebonds.net/files/files/2015%20GB%20Market%20Roundup%2003A.pdf.

137. James Langton, "Green Bonds to Bounce Back in 2021: Moody's," *Investment Executive*, March 11, 2021, https://www.investmentexecutive.com/news/research-and-markets/green-bonds-to-bounce-back-in-2021-moodys/#:~:text=In%20a%20new%20report%2C%20the,year's%20total%20of%20%24225%20billion.

138. Esther Whieldon, "Moody's Predicts Green, Sustainable Bond Market Will Hit Record $400B in 2020," S&P Global, February 3, 2020, https://www.spglobal.com/marketintelligence/en/news-insights/latest-news-headlines/moody-s-predicts-green-sustainable-bond-market-will-hit-record-400b-in-2020-56919081.

139. "The Growth of Green Bonds," Goldman Sachs, April 22, 2019, https://www. goldmansachs.com/insights/pages/from_briefings_22-apr-2019.html.

140. "2019 Green Bond Market Summary," The Climate Bonds Initiative, February 2020, https://www.climatebonds.net/files/reports/2019_annual_highlights-final.pdf.

141. "The Growth of Green Bonds."

142. Ibid.

143. Ibid.

144. "2019 Green Bond Market Summary."

145. Sean Kidney, "Just Released: State of the Market 2016 Report: $694bn in Climate-Aligned Bonds: Up $94bn from 2015," The Climate Bond Initiative, July 1, 2016, https://www.climatebonds.net/2016/07/just-released-state-market-2016-report-694bn -climate-aligned-bonds-94bn-2015.

146. "2019 Green Bond Market Summary."

147. "Green Bonds," Fannie Mae, accessed June 2020, https://multifamily.fanniemae. com/financing-options/specialty-financing/green-financing/green-bonds.

148. "Multifamily Green Bond Impact Report 2012–2018," Fannie Mae, https://multi family.fanniemae.com/sites/g/files/koqyhd161/files/migrated-files/content/tool/mf -green-bond-impact-report.pdf.

149. "Green Bonds."

150. Shanny Basar, "Demand for Green Bonds Exceeds Vanilla Equivalents," Markets Media, April 22, 2020, https://www.marketsmedia.com/demand-for-green-bonds -exceeds-vanilla-equivalents/.

CHAPTER 6: THE AGRICULTURE SECTOR

1. Joshua Berlinger, "Queensland Floods: 500,000 Cattle Survived Years-Long Drought Only to Die in the Rain," February 13, 2019, https://www.cnn.com/2019/02/13/ australia/cattle-crisis-australia-intl/index.html.

2. "Livestock and Poultry: World Markets and Trade," USDA Foreign Agricultural Service, October 2020, https://apps.fas.usda.gov/psdonline/circulars/livestock_poultry. pdf.

3. P. J. Huffstutter and Humerya Pamuk, "Exclusive: More Than 1 Million Acres of U.S. Cropland Ravaged by Floods," Reuters, March 29, 2019, https://www.reuters.com/ article/us-usa-weather-floods-exclusive/exclusive-more-than-1-million-acres-of-u-s -cropland-ravaged-by-floods-idUSKCN1RA2AW.

4. "Report: Farmers Prevented from Planting Crops on More Than 19 Million Acres," US Department of Agriculture News Release, August 12, 2019, https://www. fsa.usda.gov/news-room/news-releases/2019/report-farmers-prevented-from-planting -crops-on-more-than-19-million-acres.

5. Chuang Zhao et al., "Temperature Increase Reduces Global Yields of Major Crops in Four Independent Estimates," Procedings of the National Academy of Sciences of the United States of America, July 10, 2017, https://www.pnas.org/ content/114/35/9326#F2.

6. Ibid.

7. "Global Greenhouse Emissions Data, Global Emissions by Sector," US Environmental Protection Agency, accessed March 2019, https://www.epa.gov/ghgemissions/global-greenhouse-gas-emissions-data.

8. Ibid.

9. "Greenhouse Gas Emissions for Major Economies 1990–2020," Center for Climate and Energy Solutions, accessed October 2018, https://www.c2es.org/content/international-emissions/.

10. "Global Warming Potential Values," Greenhouse Gas Protocol , accessed April 2019, https://www.ghgprotocol.org/sites/default/files/ghgp/Global-Warming-Potential-Values%20%28Feb%2016%202016%29_1.pdf.

11. "Global Greenhouse Emissions Data, Global Emissions by Gas."

12. "World Population Prospects, File POP 1.1: Total Population by Region, Subregion and Country, Annually for 1950–2100, Estimates 1950–2020," UN Department of Economic and Social Affairs, August 2019, https://esa.un.org/unpd/wpp/publications/files/wpp2017_keyfindings.pdf.

13. "World Population Prospects, File PPP, POPTOT: Probablistic Projection of Total Population by Region, Subregion, Country or Area, 2020–2100," UN Department of Economic and Social Affairs, August 2019, https://population.un.org/wpp/Download/Probabilistic/Population/.

14. "FAO's Work on Climate Change," UN Climate Change Conference, 2017, http://www.fao.org/3/a-i8037e.pdf.

15. "Water in Agriculture," World Bank, accessed November 2020, https://www.worldbank.org/en/topic/water-in-agriculture#:~:text=In%20most%20cases%2C%20such%20reallocation,to%20the%20evapotranspiration%20of%20crops.

16. "Agricultural Outlook 2018–2027, Chapter 1: Overview," Organisation for Economic Co-operation and Development / UN Food and Agriculture Organization, 2018, http://www.fao.org/docrep/i9166e/i9166e_Chapter1.pdf.

17. S. Smith, M. Bustamante, H. Ahammad, H. Clark, H. Dong, E.A. Elsiddig, H. Haberl, et al., "Agriculture, Forestry and Other Land Use (AFOLU)," in *Climate Change 2014: Mitigation of Climate Change*, contribution of Working Group III to the Fifth Assessment Report of the Intergovernmental Panel on Climate Change, ed. O. Edenhofer, et al. (Cambridge, UK, and New York: Cambridge University Press, 2014).

18. P. Smith, D. Martino, Z. Cai, D. Gwary, H. Janzen, P. Kumar, B. McCarl, et al., "Agriculture," in *Climate Change 2007: Mitigation*, contribution of Working Group III to the Fourth Assessment Report of the IPCC, ed. B. Metz, et al. (Cambridge, UK, and New York: Cambridge University Press, 2007), https://www.ipcc.ch/site/assets/uploads/2018/02/ar4-wg3-chapter8-1.pdf.

19. "Water in Agriculture."

20. "FAO's Work on Climate Change."

21. "REDD+ Reducing Emissions from Deforestation and Forest Degradation," UN Food and Agriculture Organization, accessed October 2020, http://www.fao.org/redd/en/.

22. "Emission Data for Enteric Fermentation, Manure Management, and Synthetic Nitrogen Fertilizers," UN Food and Agriculture Organization Corporate Statistical Database, accessed October 2020, http://www.fao.org/faostat/en/#data/GT/visualize.

23. "FAO's Role in Animal Production," UN Food and Agriculture Organization, accessed March 2019, http://www.fao.org/animal-production/en/.

24. Richard Waite, "2018 Will See High Meat Consumption in the U.S., but the American Diet Is Shifting," World Resources Institute (blog), January 24, 2018, https://www.wri.org/blog/2018/01/2018-will-see-high-meat-consumption-us-american-diet-shifting.

25. Ibid.

26. "Global Livestock Environmental Assessment Model (GLEAM), Emissions by Commodity and Emission Intensities," UN Food and Agriculture Organization, accessed March 2019, http://www.fao.org/gleam/results/en/.

27. Ibid.

28. Ibid.

29. Ibid.

30. Nitrification is the oxidation of ammonia or ammonium to nitrate. Denitrification reduces NO_3 to molecular nitrogen NO_2 under anaerobic conditions.

31. Soren O. Peterson, "Greenhouse Gas Emissions from Liquid Dairy Manure: Prediction and Mitigation," *Journal of Dairy Science* 101, no. 7 (July 2018): 6642–6654, https://www.sciencedirect.com/science/article/pii/S0022030217311165.

32. Horacio A. Aguirre-Villegas and Rebecca A. Larson, "Evaluating Greenhouse Gas Emissions from Dairy Manure Management Practices Using Survey Data and Life-cycle Tools," *Journal of Cleaner Production* 143, no. 1 (February 2017): 169–179, https://www.sciencedirect.com/science/article/pii/S0959652616321953.

33. Ibid.

34. R. Roehe, R. J. Dewhurst, C-A Duthie, J. A. Rooke, N.McKain, D. W. Ross, et al. "Bovine Host Genetic Variation Influences Rumen Microbial Methane Production with Best Selection Criterion for Low Methane Emitting and Efficiently Feed Converting Hosts Based on Metagenomic Gene Abundance," *PLoS Genetics* 12, no. 2 (2016): e1005846, https://doi.org/10.1371/journal.pgen.1005846.

35. Getachew Nigatu and Ralph Seeley, "Growth in Meat Consumption for Developing and Emerging Economies Surpasses That for Developed World," USDA Economic Research Service, July 5, 2016, https://www.ers.usda.gov/amber-waves/2015/july/growth-in-meat-consumption-for-developing-and-emerging-economies-surpasses-that-for-the-developed-world/#:~:text=Per%20capita%20meat%20consumption%20for,0.4%20percent%20for%20developed%20countries.

36. "Livestock and Poultry: World Markets and Trade," USDA Foreign Agricultural Service, October 11, 2018.

37. N. Alexandratos and J. Bruinsma, "World Agriculture Towards 2030/2050: The 2012 Revision," ESA working paper No. 12–03, UN Food and Agriculture Organization, http://www.fao.org/3/a-ap106e.pdf.

38. Ibid.

39. Ibid.

40. "Africa Sustainable Livestock 2050," FAO Animal Production and Health Report, no. 12, Technical Meeting and Regional Launch, Addis Ababa, Ethiopia, February 21–23, 2017, http://www.fao.org/3/a-i7222e.pdf.

41. Ibid.

42. Lutz Goedde, Amandla Ooko-Ombaka, and Gillian Pais, "Winning in Africa's Agricultural Market," McKinsey & Company, February 2019, https://www.mckinsey.com/industries/agriculture/our-insights/winning-in-africas-agricultural-market.

43. " Agri-Tech Can Turn African Savannah into Global Food Basket—African Development Bank," Africa News, October 25, 2018, https://www.africanews.com/2018/10/25/agri-tech -can-turn-african-savannah-into-global-food-basket-african-development-bank//.

44. Ibid.

45. "Learning About Biogas Recovery," US Environmental Protection Agency, accessed April 2019, https://www.epa.gov/agstar/learn-about-biogas-recovery.

46. "Market Opportunities for Biogas Recovery Systems at U.S. Livestock Facilities," US Environmental Protection Agency, June 2018, https://www.epa.gov/sites/production /files/2018–06/documents/epa430r18006agstarmarketreport2018.pdf.

47. "AgSTAR Data and Trends," US Environmental Protection Agency, accessed October 2020, https://www.epa.gov/agstar/agstar-data-and-trends.

48. Alan Yu, "Waste Not, Want Not: Why Aren't More Farms Putting Poop to Good Use?" April 23, 2017, https://www.npr.org/sections/thesalt/2017/04/23/524878531/waste -not-want-not-why-arent-more-farms-putting-poop-to-good-use.

49. Michael Martz, "What a Gas! Dominion, Smithfield Team to Turn Methane from Hog Waste into Fuel for Homes and Businesses," Richmond Times-Dispatch, November 27, 2018, https://www.richmond.com/news/virginia/government-politics/ general-assembly/what-a-gas-dominion-smithfield-team-to-turn-methane-from/ article_1a9e6299–5f03–5a09-b79d-01969c7b8a05.html.

50. "Dominion Energy and Smithfield Foods to Invest Half Billion Dollars to Become Largest Renewable Natural Gas Supplier in the US," Dominion Energy News Release, October 23, 2019, https://news.dominionenergy.com/2019-10-23-Dominion -Energy-and-Smithfield-Foods-Invest-Half-Billion-Dollars-to-Become-Largest -Renewable-Natural-Gas-Supplier-in-U-S.

51. "Study Demonstrates 80pc Reduction in Methane Emissions from Cattle," Beef Central, October 8, 2020, https://www.beefcentral.com/production/study-demo nstrates-80pc-reduction-in-methane-emissions-from-cattle/.

52. Judith Lewis Menit, "How Eating Seaweed Can Help Cows to Belch Less Methane," Yale Environment 360, July 2, 2018, https://e360.yale.edu/features/how-eating-se aweed-can-help-cows-to-belch-less-methane.

53. Jane Byrne, "Greening Cattle Diets, US Company Looks to the Ocean," Feednavigator.com, October 23, 2020, https://www.feednavigator.com/Article/2020/10/23/ Greening-cattle-diets-US-company-looks-to-the-ocean.

54. Ibid.

55. Bezoar Laboratories, accessed March 14, 2021, https://www.bezoarlaboratories.com/company.

56. Thin Lei Win, "Fighting Global Warming, One Cow Belch at a Time," Reuters, July 19, 2018, https://www.reuters.com/article/us-global-livestock-emissions/fighting -global-warming-one-cow-belch-at-a-time-idUSKBN1K91CU.

57. P. J. Gerber, H. Steinfeld, B. Henderson, A. Mottet, C. Opio, J. Dijkman, A. Falcucci, and G. Tempio, "Tackling Climate Change Through Livestock—A Global Assessment of Emissions and Mitigation Opportunities," UN Food and Agriculture Organization, 2013, http://www.fao.org/3/a-i3437e.pdf.

58. "USDA and NIH Funded International Science Consortium Publishes Analysis of Domestic Cattle Genome Sequence: Research Will Lead to Better Understanding of Genetic Basis of Disease," National Institute for Food and Agriculture Press Release, April 23, 2009, https://nifa.usda.gov/press-release/usda-and-nih-funded-international -science-consortium-publishes-analysis-domestic.

59. "The Efficient Dairy Genome Project," University of Alberta/University of Guelph, accessed October 2020, https://genomedairy.ualberta.ca/.

60. Ibid.

61. "Breeding to Reduce Methane Emissions from Beef Cattle, Scottish Environment," Scottish Environment, Food and Agriculture Research Institutes, accessed March 5, 2021, https://sefari.scot/research/breeding-to-reduce-methane-emissions -from-beef-cattle.

62. Ellen Airheart, "Canada Is Using Genetics to Make Cows Less Gassy," WIRED, June 9, 2017, https://www.wired.com/story/canada-is-using-genetics-to-make-cows -less-gassy/.

63. Ibid.

64. Carl Zimmer, "How the First Farmers Changed History," New York Times, October 17, 2016, https://www.nytimes.com/2016/10/18/science/ancient-farmers-archaeology -dna.html.

65. Replantable Magazine, "The Fourth Agricultural Revolution," Medium, July 18, 2016, https://medium.com/replantable-magazine/the-fourth-agricultural-revolution -492a6aebdf9f.

66. Ibid.

67. Ibid.

68. "Global Opportunity Report 2017," DNV GLAS, United Nations Global Compact, and Sustainia, 2017, https://www.unglobalcompact.org/docs/publications/Global_ Opportunity_Report_2017_SM.pdf.

69. "FAO's Work on Climate Change."

70. "Global Opportunity Report 2017."

71. Christina Procopiou,"Thirty Percent of CO2 Released into Atmosphere from Soil Originates from the Deep Subsurface," Lawrence Berkeley National Laboratory, Earth & Environmental Sciences, October 30, 2018, https://eesa.lbl.gov/study-finds -30-percent-of-co2-released-into-atmosphere-from-soil-originates-in-the-deep-sub surface/.

72. Flora Southey, "Our World Is Entering a Fourth Agricultural Revolution Says UK Environment Secretary," FoodNavigator.com, January 4, 2019, https://www.foodnavigator.

com/Article/2019/01/04/Our-world-is-entering-a-fourth-agricultural-revolution-says
-UK-environment-secretary.

73. Laura Sayre, "How Carbon Farming Could Halt Climate Change," The Counter, August 10, 2017, https://thecounter.org/how-carbon-farming-could-halt-climate
-change/.

74. Cornelius Oertel, Jorg Matschullet, Kamal Zurba, Frank Zimmerman, and Stefan Erasmi, "Greenhouse Gas Emissions from Soils—A Review," *Geochemistry* 76, no. 3 (October 2016): 327–352, https://www.sciencedirect.com/science/article/pii/S0009281916300551.

75. Ibid.

76. Ibid.

77. Neville Millar, "Management of Nitrogen Fertilizer to Reduce Nitrous Oxide Emissions from Field Crops (E3152)," Michigan State University Extension, October 19, 2015, https://www.canr.msu.edu/resources/management_of_nitrogen_fertilizer_to
_reduce_nitrous_oxide_emissions_from_fi.

78. Ibid.

79. "Fertilizers by Nutrient," UN Food and Agriculture Organization Corporate Statistical Database, accessed March 14, 2021, http://www.fao.org/faostat/en/#data/RFN; and Alexandratos and Bruinsma, "World Agriculture Towards 2030/2050."

80. Alexandratos and Bruinsma, "World Agriculture Towards 2030/2050."

81. Ibid.

82. Ibid.

83. "Global and Regional Food Consumption Patterns and Trends, Chapter 3, Table 1," World Health Organization, https://www.who.int/dietphysicalactivity/publications/trs916/en/gsfao_global.pdf.

84. Ibid.

85. Alexandratos and Bruinsma, "World Agriculture Towards 2030/2050."

86. Sayre, "How Carbon Farming Could Halt Climate Change."

87. "Conserving Energy with Conservation Tillage: Conservation Tillage Techniques in Modern Agriculture Helping Reduce Emissions," *Modern Agriculture*, February 11, 2017, https://modernag.org/energy-conservation/conserve-energy-with-conservation
-tillage/.

88. "Regenerative Organic Agriculture and Climate Change: A Down to Earth Solution to Climate Change," Rodale Institute, 2014, https://rodaleinstitute.org/wp-content/uploads/Regenerative-Organic-Agriculture-White-Paper.pdf.

89. "It All Starts with Soil: Importance of Healthy Soil in Agriculture," *Modern Agriculture*, February 1, 2017, https://modernag.org/soil-health/the-benefits-of-fertile-soil/.

90. Ibid.

91. Ibid.

92. Millar, "Management of Nitrogen Fertilizer to Reduce Nitrous Oxide Emissions from Field Crops."

93. AgroCares, accessed October 2020, https://www.agrocares.com/en.

94. Peter Kipkemoi, "The Pros and Cons of Drones in Agriculture," Drone

Guru, January 27, 2019, http://www.droneguru.net/the-pros-and-cons-of-drones-in -agriculture/.

95. Ibid.

96. Ma Zhiping, "Hybrid Rice Yields Hope for Farmers," *China Daily*, April 23, 2019, https://www.chinadailyhk.com/articles/177/117/54/1555993699396.html.

97. Ibid.

98. Robert Flynn and John Idowu, "Nitrogen Fixation by Legumes," New Mexico State University, College of Agricultural, Consumer and Environmental Sciences, Guide A-121, June 2015, https://aces.nmsu.edu/pubs/_a/A129/.

99. Megan Molteni, "Farmers Can Now Buy Designer Microbes to Replace Fertilizer," *WIRED*, October 2, 2018, https://www.wired.com/story/farmers-can-now-buy -designer-microbes-to-replace-fertilizer/.

100. "Pivot Bio Raises $100 Million to Transform Agriculture Economics," Pivot Bio News Release, April 30, 2020, https://blog.pivotbio.com/press-releases/pivot-bio-raises -additional-100-million-to-transform-agriculture-economics.

101. Ibid.

102. "Vertical Farming Market in the United States: Outlook and Forecast 2019–2024," Arizton, 2019, www.arizton.com.

103. Urban Vine, "What Is a Growing Medium?" https://www.urbanvine.co/blog/3 -basic-types-of-soil-less-growing-methods-beginner-urban-growers-should-know-about.

104. Chris Michael, "The Best Crops for Vertical Farming," Zipgrow, January 17, 2017, http://blog.zipgrow.com/best-crops-for-vertical-farming/.

105. "State of Indoor Farming 2017," Agrilyst, https://www.agrilyst.com/stateofind oorfarming2017/.

106. Conrad Zeidler, Daniel Schubert, and Vincent Vrakking, "Vertical Farm 2.0: Designing an Economically Feasible Vertical Farm—A Combined European Endeavor for Sustainable Urban Agriculture," ResearchGate, 2017, https://www.researchgate.net/pub lication/321427717_Vertical_Farm_20_Designing_an_Economically_Feasible_Vertical _Farm_-_A_combined_European_Endeavor_for_Sustainable_Urban_Agriculture.

107. "Global Opportunity Report 2017."

108. "Sustainability in Three Dimensions: Reaching New Heights with Vertical Farms and Robots," *Modern Agriculture*, December 20, 2018, https://modernag.org/in novation/benefits-vertical-farming-robotics/.

109. David Widmar, "Global Acreage: Is the Expansion Over?" *Agriculture Economic Insights*, April 20, 2018, https://ageconomists.com/2018/04/30/global-acreage-is-the -expansion-over/.

110. "Vertical Farming Market in the United States: Outlook and Forecast 2019–2024."

111. Andy Corbley, "This 2-Acre Vertical Farm Produces More Than 'Flat Farms' That Are Using 720 Acres," The Good News Network, November 24, 2020, https://www. goodnewsnetwork.org/2-acre-vertical-farm-plenty-grows-350x-more/.

112. Aero Farms, accessed November 2020, https://aerofarms.com/environmental -impact/.

113. Boaz Toledano, "The Second Generation of Vertical Farming Is Approaching. Here's Why It's Important," *AgFunder News*, November 4, 2019, https://agfundernews.com/the-second-generation-of-vertical-farming-is-approaching-heres-why-its-important.html.

114. "State of Indoor Farming 2017."

115. "Workers per Hectare: Countries Compared," NationMaster, accessed April 2019, https://www.nationmaster.com/country-info/stats/Agriculture/Workers-per-hectare.

116. Toledano, "The Second Generation of Vertical Farming Is Approaching."

117. "Yes, This Is Actual Meat but No Animal Died for It," PETA, March 30, 2017, https://www.peta.org/living/food/memphis-meats-debuts-lab-grown-chicken-clean-meat/.

118. Emily Byrd, "Clean Meat's Path to Your Dinner Plate," Good Foods Institute, December 7, 2016, https://www.gfi.org/clean-meats-path-to-commercialization.

119. "World's First Lab-Grown Burger Is Eaten in London," BBC News, August 5, 2013, https://www.bbc.com/news/science-environment-23576143.

120. Jo Anderson and Chris Bryant, "Messages to Overcome Naturalness Concerns in Clean Meat Acceptance: Primary Findings," Faunalytics, July 2018, https://faunalytics.org/wp-content/uploads/2018/11/Clean-Meat-Acceptance-Primary-Findings.pdf.

121. Elaine Watson, "Clean Meat: How Do US Consumers Feel About Cell Cultured Meat?" FoodNavigator-USA.com, Aug. 1, 2018, https://www.foodnavigator-usa.com/Article/2018/08/01/Clean-meat-How-do-US-consumers-feel-about-cell-cultured-meat.

122. Ibid.

123. "Tyson Foods Invests in Cultured Meat with Stake in Memphis Meats," Tyson Foods, January 29, 2018, https://www.tysonfoods.com/news/news-releases/2018/1/tyson-foods-invests-cultured-meat-stake-memphis-meats.

124. Aradhana Aravindan and John Geddie, "Singapore Approves Sale of Lab-Grown Meat in World's First," December 1, 2020, https://www.reuters.com/article/us-eat-just-singapore/singapore-approves-sale-of-lab-grown-meat-in-world-first-idUSKBN28C06Z.

125. "Industrial Agriculture and Small Scale Farming" (summary of topic in report Agriculture at a Crossroads), Global Agriculture, accessed May 2019, https://www.globalagriculture.org/report-topics/industrial-agriculture-and-small-scale-farming.html.

126. Laura Siler, "Smartphone Ownership Is Growing Rapidly Around the World but Not Always Equally," Pew Research Center, February 5, 2019, https://www.pewresearch.org/global/2019/02/05/smartphone-ownership-is-growing-rapidly-around-the-world-but-not-always-equally/.

127. "The State of Broadband 2019 Report Highlights," Broadband Commission, https://broadbandcommission.org/Documents/SOBB-REPORT%20HIGHTLIGHTS-v3.pdf.

128. "What's Hot: 2019 Culinary Forecast," National Restaurant Association, https://www.restaurant.org/Downloads/PDFs/Research/WhatsHot/WhatsHotFinal2019.pdf.

129. "What's Hot 2020 Culinary Forecast," National Restaurant Association, https://www.restaurant.org/downloads/pdfs/research/whats_hot_2020.pdf.

130. Ibid.

131. "The Shifting Global Dairy Market," Cargill, 2018, https://www.cargill.com/doc/1432126152938/dairy-white-paper-2018.pdf.

132. Ibid.

133. Brianna Cameron and Shannon O'Neil, "State of the Industry Report: Plant Based Meat, Eggs, and Dairy (Version 1.4)," The Good Food Institute, June 2019, https://www.gfi.org/non-cms-pages/splash-sites/soi-reports/files/SOI-Report-Plant-Based.pdf.

134. Ibid.

135. Lillianna Byington, "Tracking the Plant-Based Protein Movement," Food Dive, November 16, 2020, https://www.fooddive.com/news/plant-based-protein-tracker/564886/.

136. Ibid.

137. "SAVE FOOD: Global Initiative on Food Loss and Waste Reduction," UN Food and Agriculture Organization, accessed May 2019, http://www.fao.org/save-food/resources/keyfindings/en/. FAO defines "loss" as food that is lost throughout the supply chain between producer and market and "waste" as the discarding of food that is otherwise safe for human consumption.

138. "Food Wastage Footprint & Climate Change," UN Food and Agriculture Organization, accessed March 5, 2021, http://www.fao.org/3/a-bb144e.pdf.

139. Ibid.

140. Ibid.

141. Paula Rodriquez, "What's New: How Is the Cold Chain Growing in Developing Countries?" InpiraFarms, August 14, 2018, http://www.inspirafarms.com/whats-new-how-is-the-cold-chain-growing-in-developing-countries/.

142. John M. Mandyck and Eric B. Schultz, *Food Foolish: The Hidden Connection Between Food Waste, Hunger, and Climate Change* (Palm Beach Gardens, FL: Carrier Corporation, 2015).

143. "27 Solutions to Food Waste, Financial Benefit," ReFED, accessed May 2019, https://www.refed.com/?sort=economic-value-per-ton.

144. "27 Solutions to Food Waste, Emissions Reduced," ReFED, accessed May 2019, https://www.refed.com/?sort=emissions-reduced. Note: Analysis takes into account the producing, processing, and transporting of food, and methane emissions from food disposed of in landfills.

145. Ibid.

146. "Waste Tracking and Analytics," ReFED, accessed May 2019, https://www.refed.com/solutions/waste-tracking-and-analytics.

147. UN Environment Programme, "Food Waste Index Report 2021," file:///C:/Users/DuffR/Downloads/FoodWaste%20(1).pdf.

148. "Consumer Education Campaigns," ReFED, accessed May 2019, https://www.refed.com/solutions/consumer-education-campaigns.

149. Ibid.

150. Julie Kurtz and Farm Aid, "Farm Bill 101." Farm Aid Fact Sheet, May 22, 2018, https://www.farmaid.org/issues/farm-policy/farm-bill-101/.

151. Ibid.

152. Ibid.

153. "What's in the 2018 Farm Bill? The Good, the Bad and the Offal . . . ," Farm Aid, December 20, 2018, https://www.farmaid.org/issues/farm-policy/whats-in-the-2018-farm-bill-the-good-the-bad-and-the-offal/.

154. Ibid.

155. Matthew Clancy, Keith Fuglie, and Paul Heisey, "U.S. Agricultural R&D in an Era of Falling Public Funding," US Department of Agriculture, Economic Research Service, May 2019, https://www.ers.usda.gov/amber-waves/2016/november/us-agricultural-rd-in-an-era-of-falling-public-funding/.

156. Ibid.

157. Clancy, Fuglie, and Heisey, "U.S. Agricultural R&D in an Era of Falling Public Funding."

158. Ibid.

159. Amy R. Beaudreault, "China's Growing Power for a Food Secure World," Center for Strategic and International Studies, January 8, 2020, https://www.csis.org/analysis/chinas-growing-power-food-secure-world.

160. Ibid.

161. Ibid.

162. "China, Africa Join for Broader Agricultural Cooperation," *Xinhua*, December 10, 2019, http://www.xinhuanet.com/english/2019–12/10/c_138621136.htm.

163. "Sustainable Land Use (Greening)," European Commission, accessed May 2019, https://ec.europa.eu/info/food-farming-fisheries/key-policies/common-agricultural-policy/income-support/greening_en.

164. "Commissioner Hogan Announces Idea for 'Farm Carbon Forest' Initiative," European Commission, May 15, 2019, https://ec.europa.eu/info/news/commissioner-hogan-announces-idea-farm-carbon-forest-initiative-2019-may-15_en.

165. Katherine J. Wu, "Golden Rice Approved as Safe for Consumption in the Philippines," *Smithsonian Magazine*, January 3, 2020, https://www.smithsonianmag.com/smart-news/golden-rice-approved-safe-consumption-philippines-180973897/.

166. "Engage the Chain: Top US Food and Beverage Companies Scope 3 Emission Disclosure and Reductions," Ceres, accessed May 2019, https://engagethechain.org/top-us-food-and-beverage-companies-scope-3-emissions-disclosure-and-reductions?_ga=2.13663287.1631956570.1560268424–1905717389.1560268424.

167. Ibid.

168. "Measure the Chain: Tools for Assessing GHG Emissions in Agricultural Supply Chains," Ceres, accessed May 2019, https://engagethechain.org/resources/measure-chain-tools-assessing-ghg-emissions-agricultural-supply-chains?_ga=2.111061507.742632478.1560269041–178895896.1560269041 (accessed May 2019).

169. "Improving the Visibility of Our Supply Chain," Unilever, accessed November 2020, https://www.unilever.com/sustainable-living/reducing-environmental-impact/

sustainable-sourcing/transforming-the-palm-oil-industry/improving-the-visibility-of
-our-supply-chain/.

170. #goodbadpalmoil, RSPO, accessed June 2019, https://rspo.org/about/goodbad
palmoil.

171. "Indigo Agriculture and Anheuser-Busch Partner to Meet Sustainability
Goals for Rice Production," Indigo Agriculture, March 11, 2019, https://www.indigoag
.com/pages/news/indigo-partners-with-anheuser-busch-for-sustainable-rice
?hsCtaTracking=078c2374-fda0–44b0–83ca-df7c70ee008a%7Cb71849f9-3882-45ba
-9af6–485ef85c75a2.

172. "Palm Oil Buyers Scorecard," Manufacturers, WWF, 2016, http://palmoil
scorecard.panda.org/check-the-scores/manufacturers.

173. Roundtable on Sustainable Palm Oil, accessed November 2020, https://www.
rspo.org/about.

174. "Major Food Companies Join to Address Climate Change and Healthy Soils
by Creating a New Standard Focused on Regenerative Agriculture," Green America,
March 6, 2018, https://www.greenamerica.org/press-release/major-food-companies
-join-address-climate-change-and-healthy-soils-creating-new-standard-focused
-regenerative.

175. "A Natural Path for U.S. Climate Action," Nature Conservancy, November 14,
2018, https://www.nature.org/en-us/what-we-do/our-insights/perspectives/a-natural
-path-for-u-s-climate-action/.

176. Joseph E. Fargione, Steve Bassett, Timothy Boucher, et al., "Natural Climate
Solutions for the United States," Science Advances 4, no. 11 (November 14, 2018), http://
advances.sciencemag.org/content/4/11/eaat1869.

177. Bob Berwyn, "Warming Drives Unexpected Pulses of CO2 from Forest Soil,"
Inside News, October 5, 2017, https://insideclimatenews.org/NEWS/05102017/FOREST
-SOIL-CO2-CARBON-GLOBAL-WARMING-CLIMATE-CHANGE-STUDY.

178. A. Baccini1, W. Walker, L. Carvalho, M. Farina, D. Sulla-Menashe, and R. A.
Houghton, "Tropical Forests Are a Net Carbon Source Based on Aboveground Mea-
surements of Gain and Loss," Science 358, no. 6360 (October 13, 2017), http://science.
sciencemag.org/content/358/6360/230.

179. Morgan Erikson-Davis, "Why New Forests Are Better at Sequestering Carbon
Than Old Ones," Pacific Standard, February 27, 2019, https://psmag.com/environment/
young-trees-suck-up-more-carbon-than-old-ones.

180. Ibid.

181. Graham Hill, "Hemp, and Lots of It, Could Be One Climate Solution," Huffington Post, December 6, 2017, https://www.huffpost.com/entry/hemp-and-lots-of-it
-could_b_328275.

182. Jenni Avons and Dan Kopf, "The Number of US Acres Devoted to Hemp Is 100
Times Greater Than Five Years Ago," Quartz, December 31, 2019, https://qz.com/1777341/
how-much-hemp-is-grown-in-the-us-2/.

183. Ibid.

184. "A New Crop for Rice Farmers: Carbon Offsets," Environmental Defense Fund,

accessed May 2019, https://www.edf.org/ecosystems/new-crop-rice-farmers-carbon
-offsets.

185. Sayre, "How Farming Could Halt Climate Change."

186. "First-Ever Rice Farming Carbon Credits Sold to Microsoft," AgWeb, June 14,
2017, https://www.agweb.com/article/first-ever-rice-farming-carbon-credits-sold-to
-microsoft-NAA-ben-potter.

187. Lauren Stine, "Carbon Harvest: Indigo Ag, Nori Announce First Corporate
Carbon Credit Buyers," October 15, 2020, https://agfundernews.com/carbon-harvest
-indigo-ag-nori-announce-first-corporate-carbon-credit-buyers.html.

188. Robert Parkhurst, "The Market for Grassland Carbon Credits Is on the Rise.
Here's Why," Environmental Defense Fund, July 19, 2018, http://blogs.edf.org/growin
greturns/2018/07/19/market-grassland-carbon-credits-conservation-climate-resilience/.

189. Ibid.

190. "The Plowprint Report: 2020," World Wildlife Fund, https://www.worldwildlife.
org/projects/plowprint-report.

CHAPTER 7: THE PATH FORWARD

1. Jean-Daniel Collomb, "The Ideology of Climate Change Denial in the United
States," *European Journal of American Studies* 9, no. 1 (2014), https://journals.openedition
.org/ejas/10305.

2. *Jefferson Innovation Summit Policy Playbook*, UVA Darden School of Business, 2018, https://jeffersoninnovationsummit.org/wp-content/uploads/2018/09/2018
_Policy_Playbook.pdf.

3. H.R.763, 116th Congress (2019–2020), accessed May 2020, https://www.congress.
gov/bill/116th-congress/house-bill/763/text.

4. William Nordhaus, "The Climate Club," *Foreign Affairs*, May/June 2020, https://
www.foreignaffairs.com/articles/united-states/2020-04-10/climate-club.

5. Marianna Mazzucato, *The Entrepreneurial State* (New York: Hachettet Book
Group, 2014).

6. See ibid. for a particularly eloquent argument for the importance of the state in
driving innovation.

7. Thomas P. Lyon and John W. Maxwell, "Astroturf: Interest Group Lobbying and
Corporate Strategy," *Journal of Economics & Management Strategy* 13 no. 4 (2004):
561–597, https://drive.google.com/file/d/0B16dMVHRjL5dOWtXdGNWZnNJemM/
view.

8. "How Consumers Value Fuel Economy: A Literature Review," US Environmental Protection Agency, 2010, https://nepis.epa.gov/Exe/ZyNET.exe/P1006VoO.txt?ZyA
ctionD=ZyDocument&Client=EPA&Index=2006%20Thru%202010&Docs=&Query=
&Time=&EndTime=&SearchMethod=1&TocRestrict=n&Toc=&TocEntry=&QField=
&QFieldYear=&QFieldMonth=&QFieldDay=&UseQField=&IntQFieldOp=0&ExtQFi
eldOp=0&XmlQuery=&File=D%3A%5CZYFILES%5CINDEX%20DATA%5C06THRU
10%5CTXT%5C00000016%5CP1006VoO.txt&User=ANONYMOUS&Password=anon
ymous&SortMethod=h%7C-&MaximumDocuments=1&FuzzyDegree=0&ImageQual

ity=r75g8/r75g8/x150y150g16/i425&Display=hpfr&DefSeekPage=x&SearchBack=ZyAc
tionL&Back=ZyActionS&BackDesc=Results%20page&MaximumPages=1&ZyEntry=1.

9. Michael Nicholas, "Estimating Electric Vehicle Charging Infrastructure Costs Across Major U.S. Metropolitan Areas," working paper, The International Council on Clean Transportation, 2019, https://theicct.org/publications/charging-cost-US.

10. Daniel Oberhaus, "Amazon, Google, Microsoft: Here's Who Has the Greenest Cloud," *WIRED*, December 10, 2019, https://www.wired.com/story/amazon-google -microsoft-green-clouds-and-hyperscale-data-centers/.

11. "Global Automotive Market Share in 2019 by Brand," Statista, https://www. statista.com/statistics/316786/global-market-share-of-the-leading-automakers/.

12. "The World's Largest Crude Steel Producers in 2019, by Production Volume," Statista, https://www.statista.com/statistics/271979/the-largest-steel-producers-world wide-ranked-by-production-volume/.

13. "Global Cement Top 100 Report 2017–2018," Global Cement, December 4, 2017, https://www.globalcement.com/magazine/articles/1054-global-cement-top-100 -report-2017–2018.

14. Alan Buis, "A Degree of Concern: Why Global Temperatures Matter, Part 2: Se-lected Findings of the IPCC Special Report on Global Warming," NASA, June 19, 2019, https://climate.nasa.gov/news/2865/a-degree-of-concern-why-global-temperatures -matter/.

INDEX

Page numbers in *italics* refer to figures.